Teaching and Learning Entrepreneurship in Higher Education

Teaching and Learning Entrepreneurship in Higher Education

John Branch, Anne Hørsted
and Claus Nygaard

THE LEARNING IN HIGHER EDUCATION SERIES

First published in 2017 by Libri Publishing

Copyright © Libri Publishing

Authors retain copyright of individual chapters.

The right of John Branch, Anne Hørsted and Claus Nygaard to be identified as the editors of this work has been asserted in accordance with the Copyright, Designs and Patents Act, 1988.

ISBN 978-1-911450-12-2

All rights reserved. No part of this publication may be reproduced, stored in any retrieval system or transmitted in any form or by any means, electronic, mechanical, photocopying, recording or otherwise, without the prior written permission of the copyright holder for which application should be addressed in the first instance to the publishers. No liability shall be attached to the author, the copyright holder or the publishers for loss or damage of any nature suffered as a result of reliance on the reproduction of any of the contents of this publication or any errors or omissions in its contents.

A CIP catalogue record for this book is available from The British Library

Cover design by Helen Taylor

Design by Carnegie Publishing

Libri Publishing
Brunel House
Volunteer Way
Faringdon
Oxfordshire
SN7 7YR

Tel: +44 (0)845 873 3837

www.libripublishing.co.uk

Contents

Foreword		vii
Chapter 1	An introduction to Teaching and Learning Entrepreneurship *John Branch, Anne Hørsted & Claus Nygaard*	1
Chapter 2	Exploring the links between Policy Making and the Landscape for Entrepreneurship Education in Higher Education *Diana Pauna & Maija Kale*	17
Chapter 3	Developing Holistic and Comprehensive Entrepreneurship Education Approaches *Dirk Ludewig*	39
Chapter 4	A Global Approach to Teaching Entrepreneurship in Japan *Sarah Louisa Birchley & Philip McCasland*	57
Chapter 5	The Role of Universities as Catalysts within Entrepreneurial Ecosystems *Hani T. Fadel, Moaz Mojaddidi & Osama M. Ashri*	79
Chapter 6	Integrating Innovation and Entrepreneurship into All Undergraduate Courses: The Case of La Trobe University in Australia *Silvia McCormack & Chris Scanlon*	101
Chapter 7	Planning to Teach Entrepreneurship: Our Rough Guide to Research-Informed, Practice-Based Curriculum Design at Aston University, UK *Julian Lamb & Geoff Parkes*	127
Chapter 8	Developing Student-Practitioners: Two Localised Methods for Teaching and Learning Entrepreneurship *Nathan Rauh-Bieri*	157

Chapter 9   Promoting Entrepreneurship in Social Services and
            Healthcare   179
            Sirkka-Liisa Kolehmainen

Chapter 10 An Integrated Framework for Stimulating
            Entrepreneurial Behaviour: A South African
            Example   203
            Tshidi Mohapeloa

Chapter 11 The Five Capacities of Entrepreneurship Educators:
            from Domain Experts to Supporters of Inherently
            Evolving, Unpredictable and Individually Founded
            Learning Processes   229
            Mette Lindahl Thomassen

Chapter 12 Guiding Students Towards an Entrepreneurial
            Mindset by Using the Berkeley Method of
            Entrepreneurship   257
            Charlotta Johnsson, Ikhlaq Sidhu, Mari Suoranta & Ken Singer

Chapter 13 Teaching Unemployed University Graduates to
            Think Like Entrepreneurs   283
            Anne Hørsted & Claus Nygaard

Foreword

Teaching and learning entrepreneurship in higher education is a multifaceted activity that has gained substantial interest worldwide over the last two decades. Be it in developing or developed countries or from the educators or policymakers, entrepreneurship teaching and learning in the higher education sector is high on the policy agenda.

This development should be seen in the light of the growing interest in what is called the *entrepreneurial society*. In academia as well as in policymaking, the entrepreneurial society is, as discussed in, for example, Audretsch & Phillips (2007) and Audretsch (2014), a society characterised by economic development through knowledge-based entrepreneurship. As such, the entrepreneurial society is seen as a remedy for several of the challenges facing the developing and developed economies alike in terms of the environment, employment, competitiveness, economic growth, and, ultimately, individual and societal well-being. Furthermore, contributing to this development is the emerging discussion on the quality of the new ventures created to a large extent initiated by Shane (2009) on the quality of the new ventures created. Hence, paying less attention to the entrepreneurship or number of start-ups *per se* and instead focusing on the formation of high-quality and high-growth start-ups.

The focus on knowledge and high-quality entrepreneurship means that the higher education sector with its potential to realise discontinuous technological innovations is seen as an important factor in terms of promoting and sustaining economic growth at a national as well as regional level. This role of the university – the entrepreneurial university (Clark, 1998) – has been highlighted in a number of policy documents from organisations such as the World Bank, OECD, and EU (for example, see OECD and the European Commission (2012) and Olsen & Maassen (2007)). All of them emphasising the need for entrepreneurial universities in terms of boosting economic growth and meeting the challenges associated with the new economy.

Hence, in addition to producing knowledge, the entrepreneurial university should also disseminate and commercialise it. In doing so, entrepreneurial universities are also involved in partnerships and networks with other academic institutions as well as the public and private sectors. In other words, an entrepreneurial university plays a role considerably bigger than just promoting and supporting entrepreneurship and entrepreneurial activity. The transformation into an entrepreneurial university therefore affects all parts of the university as well as all its activities, be they academic or administrative. Consequently, universities aiming at developing into entrepreneurial universities should develop new processes, governance structures, and strategies.

Etkowitz (2004) and Erkowitz & Viale (2010) take the discussion of the entrepreneurial university further and identify what they call the third academic revolution. The first academic revolution occurred in the early 19th century, when research was integrated into the academic agenda and hence the mission of the universities. The second academic revolution occurred when economic and social development were integrated as academic missions. As for the third academic revolution, Ezkowitz & Viale (2010) put it the following way:

> "The third academic revolution integrates forward and reverse linear models in a programmatic and regulatory framework, synthesizing knowledge, organization and institutions: the endogenous, exogenous and mesogenous drivers of innovation. The university thus becomes an increasingly important platform for societal transformation." (Ezkowitz & Viale, 2010:595)

They continue, addressing the link between the entrepreneurial university and economic development:

> "In a 'third academic revolution', the entrepreneurial university becomes the centre of gravity for economic development, knowledge creation and diffusion in both advanced and developing societies." (Ezkowitz & Viale, 2010:596)

Consequently, this broader scope requires that the universities develop new processes, governance structures, and strategies. It also puts emphasis on partnerships with other universities as well as with the public and private sector. The transformation into an entrepreneurial university therefore affects all parts of the university as well as all its activities, be they academic or administrative.

Furthermore, the observation that the development towards an entrepreneurial university essentially involves all activities and processes within the university has, as discussed in, for instance, Clark (1998) and Pinheiro & Stensaker (2014), generated the idea that the entrepreneurial university, in addition to the macroeconomic aspects discussed above, can be seen as a means to address the problems and challenges facing contemporary higher education worldwide at the micro or organisational level.

However, in this discussion of the new role of higher education institutions, probably the most important question – how and to whom is entrepreneurship being taught – has almost been forgotten. Hence, it should be obvious that the scope of this book is much wider than "just" teaching and learning entrepreneurship. With teaching and learning entrepreneurship in higher education as the common point of departure, the different chapters provide a broad discussion of how entrepreneurship education reaches outside the traditional borders and could contribute to the development of the entrepreneurial university as such. Hence, the discussion is very much in line with the overall discussion of the entrepreneurial university that emphasises the need to reach out far beyond the walls of business schools and entrepreneurship programmes.

The different cases presented in this book show that entrepreneurship learning and education is highly context-specific and to a large extent depends on institutional factors at the national level as well as at the level of the individual higher education institution. In other words, there is no "one-size-fits-all" model. This should, however, not be interpreted as though there is nothing to be learnt from the experiences of other higher education institutions – quite the contrary. Even though very different, the various cases presented in this book essentially all have in common that they focus on what Welsh et al. (2016) call the change process in the student; that is, the process of becoming something they previously were not. This desire to create an entrepreneurial mindset or attitude is seen in all the case studies presented in this volume. Hence, the current book could serve as a deep source of inspiration for anyone with an interest in developing entrepreneurship teaching and learning.

Anders Paalzow
President and Rector
Stockholm School of Economics in Riga, Latvia

Bibliography

Audretsch, D. B. (2014). From the entrepreneurial university to the university for the entrepreneurial society. *Journal of Technology Transfer*, Vol. 39, pp. 313–321.

Audretsch, D. & R. J. Phillips (2007). Entrepreneurship, State Economic Development Policy and the Entrepreneurial University. *The Papers on Entrepreneurship, Growth and Public Policy*, No. 1107, Max Planck Institute, Jena.

Etzkowitz, H. (2004). The evolution of the entrepreneurial university. *International Journal of Technology and Globalisation*, Vol. 1, No. 1.

Etzkowitz, H. & R. Viale (2010). Polyvalent Knowledge and the Entrepreneurial University: A Third Academic Revolution. *Critical Sociology*, Vol. 36, No. 4, pp. 595–609.

OECD and the European Commission (2012). Online Resource: http://www.oecd.org/site/cfecpr/guiding-framework.htm. [Accessed 9 January 2017].

Olsen, J. P. & P. Maassen (2007). European Debates on the Knowledge Institution: The Modernization of the University at the European Level. J. P. Olsen & P. Maassen (Eds.), *University dynamics and European Integration*, Springer, pp. 3–22.

Pinheiro, R. & B. Stensaker (2014). Designing the entrepreneurial university: The interpretation of a global idea. *Public Organization Review*, Vol. 14, No. 4, pp. 497–516.

Shane, S. (2009). Why encouraging more people to become entrepreneurs is bad public policy. *Small business Economics*, Vol. 33, pp. 141–149.

Welsh, D. H. B.; W. T. Tullar & H. Nemati (2016). Entrepreneurship education: Process, method or both? *Journal of Innovation and Knowledge*, Vol. 1, pp. 125–132.

Chapter 1
An introduction to Teaching and Learning Entrepreneurship

John Branch, Anne Hørsted & Claus Nygaard

Queens of Pop

For the past decade or so, the radio-waves (Or is it the iTunes-waves these days?) have been dominated by strong female singer-songwriters, who have seemingly mastered an alchemical combination of infectious pop melodies, fashion leadership, and simple but meaningful lyrics. Take Rachel Platten's 2015 hit *Fight Song*, for example. More importantly, however, these singer-songwriters have also come to serve, to some extent, as this generation's feminist—no, humanist—voice, by celebrating and propagating individuality, body image, and inner strength. And consequently, they have garnered legions of fans who do not fit neatly into any of the traditional racial, sexual, or economic music-listener categories.

Consider Taylor Swift. She rejected advances from the big record company A&R agents, in favour of both a self-directed career and, more notably, a self-managed image. And it earned her many accolades...and huge success. Katy Perry's *Firework* is an unstoppable sonic and spiritual force—a 'dance-rock anthem of self-empowerment'. But it might be *Born This Way*, a song from the album of the same name by Lady Gaga, which captures the contemporary zeitgeist so elegantly:

> *I'm beautiful in my way*
> *'Cause God makes no mistakes*
> *I'm on the right track, baby*
> *I was born this way*

Chapter 1

Made, Not Born

And so went the logic in entrepreneurship. Indeed, for many years there was a claim that entrepreneurs were simply born that way, that entrepreneurship was innate and therefore could not be taught (or learned). Accordingly, entrepreneurship was considered to be a subject unworthy of—or at a minimum, unnecessary in—higher education. Viewed from the student perspective, the logic followed suit. An entrepreneur is just naturally an entrepreneur, and studying entrepreneurship, therefore, is a meaningless enterprise. Borrowing Nike's slogan, entrepreneurs just do it.

But in recent years, a complete reversal of thinking in higher education has occurred. Indeed, entrepreneurs, it is claimed, are made, not born. In other words, entrepreneurship can be learned. As such, entrepreneurship is a subject worthy of—and actually necessary in—higher education.

Subsequently, institutions of higher education, at all levels and apparently in most countries around the world, have embraced the teaching and learning of entrepreneurship with fervour. Witness, for example, the growth of entrepreneurship centres, new venture incubators, and business plan competitions on college and university campuses. Note the way in which entrepreneurship now figures in discussions about the role of higher education. And reflect on the causal link between entrepreneurship training and economic development which is often articulated.

This book, therefore, reflects this switch in higher education from *if* to *how*. That is to say, it veers away from debates about the *legitimacy* of entrepreneurship teaching and learning in higher education towards discussions about the *efficacy* of entrepreneurship teaching and learning in higher education. And indeed, for the book, we as editors sought chapters which explored the teaching and learning of entrepreneurship, within the domain of higher education and with an emphasis on learning. We welcomed chapters from all scientific disciplines, and which followed any methodological tradition.

In putting this book together, we were guided, however, by the two broad but interrelated perspectives of theory and practice:

1. Theory: Chapters which aimed to improve our understanding of teaching and learning entrepreneurship;

2. Practice: Chapters which aimed to improve the performance of teaching and learning of entrepreneurship

Any chapter, however, irrespective of the guiding perspective, was required to address *entrepreneurship, learning,* and *higher education* explicitly. The call for chapter proposals, plus the subsequent review and re-submission process, resulted in the 12 chapters which follow.

The symposium at which the book was assembled, was held in October 2016 in Riga, the capital of Latvia. In addition to the academic symposium activities, authors explored the famous art nouveau districts of Riga, walked on the Baltic beaches of Jurmela, and sampled Latvia's culinary delights.

LiHE

This anthology is the product of the *Institute for Learning in Higher Education* (LiHE), an academic association which, as intimated by its name, focuses entirely on learning at the post-secondary level. The focus of the association reflects the shift from a transmission-based philosophy to a student-centred, learning-based approach. And its scope is limited to colleges, universities, and others institutions of higher education.

The main activity of the association is a symposium. About 10 years ago, Claus noted that professors usually attend conferences at which they present their scientific research in a 10-20-minute session, receive a few comments, then very often 'head to the bar for a drink'. He proposed an alternative, therefore, which *au contraire* returns to that ancient Greek format—the symposium—at which co-creation is key.

So, about 6 months prior to a symposium, a call for chapter proposals which has a relatively tightly-focused theme is announced on the association's website and on various electronic mailing lists. The June 2015 symposium, for example, had the theme *Assessing Learning in Higher Education*; previous themes have revolved around games and simulations, classroom innovations, and learning spaces (in higher education).

Authors submit chapter proposals, which are then double-blind reviewed. If a proposal is accepted, its author is given 4 months to complete it. The whole chapter is then double-blind reviewed, and if it is accepted, the author is invited to attend the symposium. There, all authors revise their own chapters, work together to revise each other's chapters, and collaborate to assemble an anthology which, about a month later, goes off to the publisher.

The Editors and the Teaching and Learning of Entrepreneurship

As editors, of course, we bring our own perspectives to the role, which are based on our own experiences with teaching and learning entrepreneurship. We have our own disciplinary backgrounds, which come with their own specific approaches to teaching and learning. And we have our own philosophical assumptions about entrepreneurship which, in turn, influence our views about its role in higher education.

John

Okay, *mea culpa*. Yep, I'm guilty. I was indeed one of those sceptics, those naysayers who harboured the opinion that entrepreneurs were simply born that way…or at least my experience suggested to me that entrepreneurs were a different breed. They seemed to have a very specific and enviable motivational drive. They possessed a certain temperament, who brushed off risk like lumberjacks brush off mosquitoes. They never sat still, always working on the next big thing.

Clay, one of the best MBA students of my entire career, was a perfect embodiment of this vision of an entrepreneur. Plus, he was charming, charismatic, confident. Before returning to business school, he had founded and run three or four companies. And almost immediately after graduation, he wound up in Spain managing a tech start-up worth millions.

So, when he called me with the idea to launch a business school in Barcelona, I could not resist his 'gravitational pull'. I jumped in wholeheartedly (and with 20 000 USD), designing a curriculum from scratch, and then recruiting a professorial corps for the first cohort of students. The excitement was contagious, and I day-dreamed of the global domination of the *Barcelona Management Institute*. But like so many start-ups, we failed fast, and we failed hard. After graduating our second cohort of students, we closed up shop, both literally and figuratively.

This experience, although negative in many ways, had a profound impact on my view of entrepreneurship. Indeed, at that moment I realised that the probability of success of the endeavour could have been improved had I employed a broader set of entrepreneurial concepts, tools, and theories. Or in other words, I became convinced that entrepreneurship could be taught…that entrepreneurs were made, not born.

Consequently, I spent the next several months engaged in the entrepreneurship literature. And shortly thereafter I had my first opportunity to teach entrepreneurship—more specifically, social entrepreneurship. It was a cross-listed course between the University's school of social work and business school, and I shared the teaching duties with a social work colleague. Students from both schools enrolled in the course.

I was quick to relay my experience as an entrepreneur, describing the story from above in great detail, and thereby admitting my weaknesses. But I also used the experience as a kind of live case study to help unpack the lessons of this failure for my would-be social entrepreneurs, not only in terms of entrepreneurial concepts, tools, and theories, but also mindset. It was probably this last idea, which was most obvious to me when teaching the course, and I am delighted to see chapters in this anthology which address it.

Anne

Made, not born—the emergence of entrepreneurship within universities has occurred rapidly over the past 30 years. It is not possible to imagine that the growth will not continue in the coming decades, and the twenty-first century is often called the century of entrepreneurs. But in my understanding, all human history is the story about entrepreneurs. I remember sitting in history class in my primary school reading and learning about how we as humans found new ways to survive the ice age changing landscapes, and about how the development of agriculture changed our entire existence.

Yes, I agree entrepreneurs are made, not born. So, with our human history in mind, the interesting question is what exactly does it take to become a successful entrepreneur in a globalised world? And more importantly, how can these skills be developed in Higher Education? As a result of multiple definitions of entrepreneurial mindsets and the lack of a universal understanding of how entrepreneurial skills can be learned, programmes which seek to teach entrepreneurship vary in their pedagogical approaches. In this anthology, we find twelve different approaches to teaching and learning entrepreneurship in higher education.

To me, the greatest challenge to teaching and learning entrepreneurship in higher education is in what Steve Jobs advised at the end of his speech to Stanford graduates in 2005: "Stay hungry. Stay foolish." Stories about successful college dropouts like Steve Jobs, Michael Dell, Bill Gates, and Mark Zuckerberg make it tempting, when you are young and brimming with ideas and dreams…to cut to the chase in order to follow the footsteps of the successful entrepreneurs. But data tell a different story, in which companies started by more highly educated founders tend to have more and prolonged success.

Back to my history class in primary school— human history told us that our entrepreneurial way of adapting to modern life was based on the transfer of knowledge and experience as a basis for new ideas and growth. Whereas our survival in the Stone Age depended on how families could develop new methods and hunting tools, we now depend on an education system which can encourage individual ideas and dreams based on knowledge and experience. And just as there has been a debate about whether or not entrepreneurial mindsets can be taught and how to teach them, there has also been disagreement about whether or not an entrepreneurial mindset can be assessed…and the best way to measure it. Increased attention ought to be paid to this critical issue in the field of teaching and learning entrepreneurship. When we believe that an entrepreneurial mindset can and ought to be taught and developed, we must develop a way to assess entrepreneurial skills which can support students who want to be entrepreneurs—to allow them to pursue their passions, their ideas, thereby driving human history into the twenty-first century.

Co-editing the chapters in this anthology and the symposium in Riga have given me the opportunity to explore how universities across the world are reaching out to teach tomorrow's entrepreneurs the things which they need to know in order to stay hungry…but not foolish.

Claus

I am an entrepreneur. I cannot help but start new projects. When I was a teenager in the late 80ies, I started a computer club, which grew to 230 members. It developed into a software company, in which I programmed some of the very first professional learning-software for the primary schools of Denmark. I went on to study business administration and wrote my bachelor thesis on entrepreneurship. Years later, when I did my Ph.D., I studied the effect of regional policy programmes on the choice of strategy of small- and medium-sized subcontracting companies. I was interested in knowing more about if and how we could grow business through public entrepreneurship programmes and public network programmes.

Working at Copenhagen Business School in the mid-90ies, I brought my interest of business strategy and entrepreneurship into my classroom, and started to teach using business cases. I became involved in the development of a case study about a Danish company in the hearing aid industry. We produced a CD-ROM with video interviews, annual reports, photos, podcasts (at that time podcasts were called tape-recordings), budgets, organisation charts, etc. All the material documented the life of the company. Students could analyse the company as part of their studies. It was a great success, because students became 'field researchers', and overall learned much more about the use of theory for analysing empirical situations. It was a great way to use technology to promote case-based learning, and to have students think like managers. I soon developed a concept of live cases, in which managers of businesses came into the business school and challenged my students to solve real problems. This was another effective way for getting students to think like managers. Because some of the live cases were about small entrepreneurial firms, the focus also became the entrepreneur, rather than the organisation. Through this it became natural to discuss entrepreneurial mindset, abilities, and skills.

I have no doubt that entrepreneurship is a set of skills which can be taught. In the making, such skills transform into entrepreneurial abilities, especially the ability to select the right context at the right time. And from that grows a certain entrepreneurial mindset, enabling you to see opportunities, to take chances, to aim for new horizons, to dare.

Reading the many wonderful examples in this book supports my view. Across disciplines, programmes, regions, and nations, engaged academics and teachers work to transform higher education into an arena for academic learning and personal development, thereby enabling students to take a leading role in their own professional lives. Some of them might become entrepreneurs and benefit the economy of their local society. To me that is the ultimate effect of teaching and learning entrepreneurship.

Chapter 1

A Framework for the Book

The chapters in this book are categorised in three sections: 1) policy; 2) practice; 3) mindset. Although all chapters touch upon all subjects, they each have a clear focus. Section one contains chapters whose main focus is entrepreneurial policy. Here you find chapters 2 to 5, all discussing the role of macro-political initiatives for encouraging and enhancing entrepreneurship education at the university level. Section two contains chapters whose main focus is entrepreneurial practice. Here you find chapters 6 to 11, showcasing university programmes and initiatives which bring entrepreneurship into the classroom. Section three contains chapters whose main focus is entrepreneurial mindset. Here you find chapters 12 and 13, where the main argument is that by teaching and learning entrepreneurship we change students' mindset.

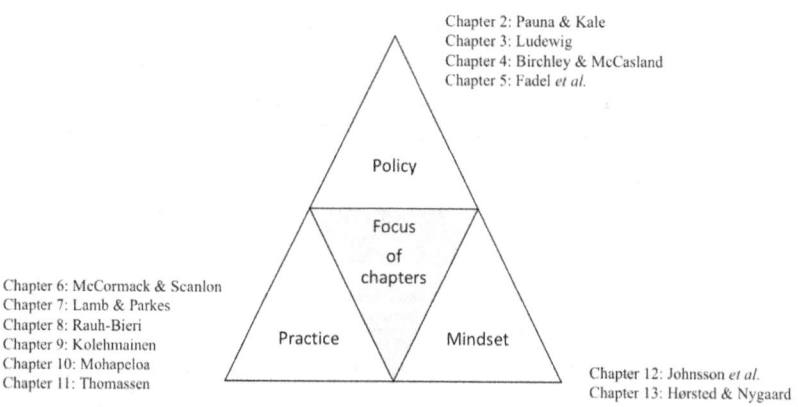

Figure 1: Sections and chapters of this book.

Chapters on policy

In Chapter 2, Pauna & Kale take us to Latvia. They reflect on the main approaches to the implementation of policy on entrepreneurship education in the EU and its consequences for Latvia. They present an overview of top-down and bottom-up policy approaches to entrepreneurship education in the European Union, and they provide a description of how top-down and bottom-up approaches influence entrepreneurship in higher education in Latvia.

In Chapter 3, Ludewig takes us to Germany. He argues for the importance of developing holistic and comprehensive entrepreneurship education approaches at the university level. He describes the policy of the nationwide German top-down programme EXIST, which he sees as a successful recipe for achieving that. To prove his point, he shows how Flensburg University of Applied Sciences has succeeded in developing holistic and comprehensive entrepreneurship education which combines the usage of top-down initiatives with bottom-up elements.

In Chapter 4, Birchley & McCasland take us to Japan. They wonder why Japan is failing to keep pace with other major world economies. Ranking 30th in the world and 5th in Asia in the Global Entrepreneurship Rankings, they find it difficult to understand why the country which gave us such global super-brands as Sony, Toyota, and Nintendo is producing so few entrepreneurs today. They see hope, and demonstrate how Japanese government policy on entrepreneurship and globalisation can be operationalised.

In Chapter 5, Fadel *et al.* take us to Saudi Arabia. They argue that entrepreneurship can well be taught at the university level, but only through practice supported by a robust entrepreneurial ecosystem starting at the university level. They cover both national entrepreneurial trends and tendencies in Saudi Arabia and give an overview of the current entrepreneurial ecosystem in Saudi Arabia. They conclude their chapter by discussing the case of entrepreneurship education at Taibah University, making a perfect transition to the section whose main focus is entrepreneurial practice.

Chapters on practice

In Chapter 6, McCormack & Scanlon take us to Australia. They provide a case study of how La Trobe University in Melbourne has implemented a strategy to make entrepreneurial education accessible to every undergraduate student as a standard part of coursework. They show how this has been driven by a number of interrelated factors: enhancing student employability in a highly competitive labour market, changing patterns of employment, and the demands of national economic competitiveness.

They argue that the success of La Trobe University rests not in educating students about innovation and entrepreneurship but rather on developing the knowledge, skills and mindset needed to be innovative and entrepreneurial, either for themselves in developing a start-up, or working for an employer.

In Chapter 7, Lamb & Parkes take us to England. Focusing on the design of an entrepreneurship module at Aston University in Birmingham, they provide three areas of value for readers who are planning to teach entrepreneurship. First, they demonstrate their 'research and design' approach to teaching entrepreneurship. Next, they account for the research which was commissioned in the context of entrepreneur-stakeholder engagement for the curriculum design. Finally, they provide a 'rough-guide' to curriculum design for other teachers of entrepreneurship.

In Chapter 8, Rauh-Bieri takes us to North America. He discusses two localised methods for teaching and learning entrepreneurship in higher education which occur outside the typical formal classroom setting: 1. a professional education workshop (PEW), and 2. multidisciplinary action projects (MAP). He argues that such entrepreneurial development benefits from the teaching and learning being applied, contextually-relevant, and experiential. And the outcomes, he says, are knowledge, skills, and abilities, which together yield student-practitioners with what he calls 'entrepreneurial acumen'.

In Chapter 9, Kolehmainen takes us to Finland. She shows how Metropolia University of Applied Sciences in Helsinki has promoted entrepreneurship as a project within social services and health care. There they have worked to develop teachers' entrepreneurial skills and competences, and created a foundation for policy-driven structural changes and networking. Not only does she address the skills and competences of teachers, but she also discusses the development of teaching methods and materials for entrepreneurship education.

In Chapter 10, Mohapeloa takes us to South Africa. She highlights how, in the context of Rhodes Business School, students can be stimulated intellectually, socially, and emotionally when being taught entrepreneurship by focusing on four core themes: ecology, economy, equity, and ethics. She argues that learning occurs through action, community engagement, and conversations with business practitioners, preparing students to meet global needs which respond to changing global markets.

In Chapter 11, Thomassen takes us to Denmark. In it she proposes a new role for educators at higher educational institutes, addressing a disharmony which has risen in relation to educating students *through* entrepreneurship, which challenges the traditional educator role. She argues that the origin of the disharmony can be traced back to the fact that the application of the most effective didactics in relation to developing students' entrepreneurial intention challenges the traditional role of educators at higher educational institutions. By identifying opportunities to circumvent the disharmony through a revision and redefinition of the role of educators in contemporary higher education, she shows a way forward for teaching and learning entrepreneurship. Her answer lies in the teacher being able to balance five capacities: domain expert, process facilitator, process consultant, coach, and co-creator. The discussion of these five capacities of entrepreneurship educators provides the perfect bridge between the practice and mindset sections.

Chapters on mindset

In Chapter 12, Johnsson *et al.* take us to North America. They present a novel teaching and learning approach, called the Berkeley Method of Entrepreneurship, which was developed at University of California— Berkeley. The authors stress the importance of including elements related to entrepreneurial mindset in the entrepreneurship curriculum, in addition to the traditional elements of theory and practice. The Berkeley-method uses behavioural games and debriefing sessions as tools, and results in students with an entrepreneurial mindset who, the authors argue, create more start-ups, ultimately leading to economic growth.

In Chapter 13, Hørsted & Nygaard take us to Denmark. They showcase an intensive course called Camp Future, which helps unemployed university graduates get a job in a tough job market. They argue that Camp Future is a success, because the course curriculum is designed to follow a process stream in which students work with real-life business challenges of companies over an intensive 10-week period. During the course, students are exposed to the everyday challenges of business owners and managers, which, when supported by focused teaching and learning activities, develop their entrepreneurial mindset. With their case, they, in a way, complete the circle back to the section on entrepreneurial

Chapter 1

policy, because Camp Future is a result of a Danish political process in which politicians have decided to support unemployed university graduates with further education directed to job-making initiatives.

In Summary

The week following the LiHE symposium at which this anthology was assembled, *A Seat at the Table*, the critically-acclaimed album by Solange (younger sibling of Beyoncé), debuted on the Billboard 200 charts at number 1. The album explored contemporary life as a black woman in America, and encompassed themes of rage, indignation, and survival. According to Solange, it was her "project on identity, empowerment, independence, grief, and healing". Incidentally, that same week, albums by Ariana Grande, Rihanna, and Adele were all in the top 20, with sister Beyoncé's *Lemonade* having just recently slipped from 16 to 22.

Although this anthology began with a rebuke of the *Born This Way* sentiment, these powerful female singer-songwriters continue to inspire this generation with their messages of self-discovery, vulnerability, and strength. It is perhaps unsurprising, therefore, that pundits also claim millennials as the first true entrepreneurial generation, citing their heady mixture of impatience, optimism, and social justice. The question of *how* to teach entrepreneurship and not *if* to teach entrepreneurship, therefore, is more crucial than ever. Consequently, this anthology ought to be considered a kind of rallying cry for the continued exploration of teaching and learning entrepreneurship. And maybe Lady Gaga even has some words of wisdom for would-be entrepreneurs *"Ignore all hatred and criticism. Live for what you create, and die protecting it."*

About the Authors

John Branch is Academic Director of the part-time MBA programmes and Assistant Clinical Professor of Business Administration at the Stephen M. Ross School of Business, and Faculty Associate at the Center for Russian, East European, & European Studies, both of the University of Michigan in Ann Arbor, U.S.A. He can be contacted at this e-mail: jdbranch@umich.edu

Anne Hørsted is Adjunct Professor at the University of Southern Denmark, Senior consultant at cph:learning in Denmark, and Adjunct Professor at the Institute for Learning in Higher Education. She can be contacted at this e-mail: anne@lihe.info

Claus Nygaard is executive director at Institute for Learning in Higher Education and executive director at cph:learning in Denmark. He can be contacted at this e-mail: info@lihe.info

Section 1: Policy

Chapter 2
Exploring the links between Policy Making and the Landscape for Entrepreneurship Education in Higher Education

Diana Pauna & Maija Kale

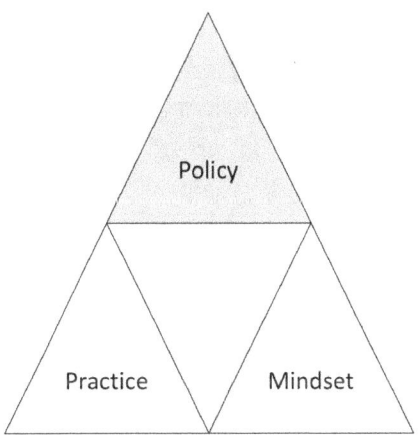

Introduction

It is a pleasure for us to open this section where chapters have their main focus on policy. Our chapter is an important contribution to this section – and to the book *Teaching and Learning Entrepreneurship in Higher Education* – because we explore the links between policy making and the landscape for entrepreneurship education in higher education. Dealing with entrepreneurship education, we address an important ambiguity that arises from the discussion of whether entrepreneurship education is to be considered an academic discipline on its own within social sciences or it is to be seen as a pedagogical practice which can be implemented in the curriculum across many different academic disciplines. As we address this ambiguity of entrepreneurship education, we draw our attention to the education policy governing higher education. This is the case, because universities in the European Union follow the supranational political decisions of EU as these are to be implemented at the national level by their member states.

Entrepreneurship education of higher education has been steadily addressed in EU policy documents for a decade and more profoundly over the last five years (EC 2012, 2013; EURYDICE, 2012). While EU institutions provide a policy framework, general guidelines, and an action plan (EC-OECD, 2012) at the supranational level, it is in the hands of national governments to decide on the policy framework for entrepreneurship education at national levels. In response to these policy initiatives at the supranational level, we explore the policy approaches that EU member states apply in designing entrepreneurship education at the national level. By choosing Latvia as a context for study, we aim to understand how countries *"at an early stage of development in terms of entrepreneurship"* (UNCTAD, 2010:4) develop their priorities and allocate scarce resources to entrepreneurship education.

The policy context for entrepreneurship education includes the general policy climate as well as the role of government (Hoppe, 2016; Pittaway & Cope, 2006) which are both interrelated with the economic, political, and cultural contexts (Valerio *et al.*, 2014; Welter *et al.*, 2011). Based on these contexts, an institutional framework is developed to provide laws and rules as the key to efficiency and sustainability (North, 1990). Overall, the EU documents on entrepreneurship education state what is to be changed, but there is very little guidance on how such changes should be implemented. Similarly, there is lack of academic research on policy initiatives promoting entrepreneurship education (Pittaway & Cope, 2006). Therefore, we attempt to fill this gap by answering the following two questions:

1. what policy approaches are applied in the EU to further develop entrepreneurship education within higher education?

2. what actions have been taken to fulfil the objectives stated in the current EU-policies on entrepreneurship education within higher education?

Reading this chapter, you will gain the following three insights:
1. insight into top-down and bottom-up approaches to policy implementation in regards to entrepreneurship education;
2. a description of how top-down and bottom-up approaches may influence entrepreneurship in higher education; and
3. insight into how Latvia as a country has dealt with entrepreneurship policy implementation.

Our chapter has two main sections. In the first section, we discuss approaches to policy implementation in the EU, and we look at the way in which member states have dealt with policies aimed at entrepreneurship education. In the second section, we present Latvia as a case, and discuss the political implications for entrepreneurship in higher education.

Section I: Approaches to Policy Implementation

The literature review on policy implementation in higher education offers a broad range of theoretical approaches. Given the focus of our study of policy approaches, and the research produced by the authors of other chapters included in this anthology, in this section we explore the top-down and bottom-up approaches and their application for implementing a policy change with a focus on entrepreneurship education. The top-down and bottom-up approaches explain different roles of policy designers and stakeholders and their interaction at different levels.

A top-down approach calls for a governmental policy with clear objectives and a legal structure for the implementation of policy. While this approach provides consistency across the country, it has been criticised for being too administrative and ignoring local contextual factors (Graham, 2014; Hoppe, 2016). In contrast, a bottom-up approach places responsibility in the hands of higher education institutions (Matland, 1995:148) and the local/regional community to learn about their goals and strategies, and the identified local network is further engaged in the policy planning and implementation process of governmental and non-governmental programmes. Based on the decision-making models, Matland (1995) identifies policy conflict and policy ambiguity as the key determinants of four policy implementation paradigms. Within this framework, the top-down approach is characterised by a low level of political conflict and low ambiguity because of clear policy goals and a structured implementation process; the bottom-up approach functions under high ambiguity and low conflict (Table 1).

Determinant	Top-down	Bottom-up
Level	Macro	Micro
Actors	Policy designers	Local target audience
Features	Prescriptive	Descriptive
Goals	Clear and consistent	Ambiguous

Table 1: Main features of top-down and bottom-up approaches (Cerna, 2013:17–19).

Several researchers have referred to top-down and bottom-up approaches (Shattock, 2003; Hoffmann et al., 2008; Graham, 2014). The interpretation of the top-down approach differs in relation to the level and actors engaged. Within a European context, the top-down approach refers to government intervention in producing and implementing a policy change (Shattock, 2003; Hoffmann et al., 2008; Hoppe, 2016), while Fadel et al. (in this volume) apply the top-down approach by looking at the university at a macro level, with university governance being the actors. The authors make reference to Graham (2014) who covers universities in Europe, the United States, and Russia in her research, and she uses two macro levels of the top-down approach with reference to governments, when analysing the case in Finland and to universities in the case study of the United States. Graham also shows that both top-down and bottom-up approaches are possible; however, with governments pushing economic growth, strengthening the role of the government may influence the implementation approach of entrepreneurship education by dealing with obstacles and creating a direction and structure that can be developed through further planning periods. Rinne & Koivula (2005) indicate that top-down policies should also be viewed through "cumulative change" by following up the new modes of action (Rinne & Koivula, 2005:105). In their study, both researchers refer to Shattock (2003) to highlight the importance of bottom-up initiatives, indicating the potential of a combined top-down and bottom-up approach.

Specific or Incorporated Strategies?

In the EU, entrepreneurship education is driven by two groups of institutions: national governments and regional/local governments. Depending on the economic, political, and cultural context, EU member states have chosen different pathways when integrating entrepreneurship education in their national strategies. The literature reviewed (Anderson et al., 2014; Chiu, 2012; EURYDICE, 2012; Hoppe, 2016; OECD, 2008; UNCTAD, 2010, 2012) and national reports of the selected countries show four different approaches to integrating entrepreneurship education in national policy documents:

1. launch a specific national strategy for entrepreneurship education;
2. embed entrepreneurship education into other national strategies;
3. encourage regional initiatives aimed at specific local needs; and
4. support individual university initiatives.

Based on the secondary research and literature review, the findings are summarised in Table 2, followed by a short reflection on the approaches.

Top-Down	Bottom-Up
Specific national strategies aimed at entrepreneurship education:	Regional initiatives related to entrepreneurship education:
• Denmark • Finland • Norway (not member of EU) • Sweden	• Germany • France • Spain • United Kingdom
Other national strategies with entrepreneurship education being incorporated:	Individual university initiatives related to entrepreneurship education:
• Bulgaria • Czech Republic • Hungary • Poland	• University of Munich in Germany • ESPCI ParisTech in France • INSEAD in France • The National Centre for Entrepreneurship in Education (NCEE) in the UK

Table 2: Different policy approaches to entrepreneurship education in the EU (EURYDICE, 2012:7–11).

Chapter 2

Top-Down Approaches

Specific national strategies aimed at developing entrepreneurship education, including in the higher education context, have been developed in Nordic countries. With the exception of Sweden, where the policy on entrepreneurship education is implemented through general education (Hoppe, 2016), the governments of Denmark, Finland, and Norway have supported the advancement of entrepreneurship education at all levels by setting up a national regulatory framework and thereby providing a clear direction for the coherent development of entrepreneurship education nationwide. In each context, the ministry in charge of education played a significant role, and the government intervention applied in Sweden, Finland, Denmark, and Norway was based on the cooperation between the ministries and other stakeholders. For example, developing the policy in Finland involved 16 external organisations working together, including representatives from universities, non-governmental organisations, local government, and professional associations. The Norwegian experience involved three ministries: the Ministry of Education and Research, the Ministry of Local Government and Regional Development, and the Ministry of Trade and Industry. Each ministry took responsibility for a total of 14 specific measures which were presented in Action Plan 2009–2014. By introducing the first strategic plan for entrepreneurship education in 2004 (MERN, 2014), Norway is recognised as being the most experienced country among the European countries in terms of entrepreneurship education policy.

Many countries have opted for embedding entrepreneurship education in different national strategies, such as in general education, lifelong learning, youth strategies, and growth strategies. For example, Bulgaria, the Czech Republic, Hungary, and Poland have included entrepreneurship as one of the key competencies in lifelong learning strategies (EURYDICE, 2012:7–9). Latvia has also adopted this strategy by incorporating entrepreneurship education in general education, higher education, lifelong learning, and youth strategies.

Bottom-Up Approaches

Regional initiatives on entrepreneurship education originating from the local community and aiming at specific local needs are seen in countries of a larger size that have a stronger federal government, such as Germany, France, Spain, and the United Kingdom (Anderson *et al.*, 2014). Regional activity in promoting entrepreneurship education at universities ranges from regional policy documents, such as "Determined to Succeed" developed by the Scottish government for the period of 2008–2011 (SG, 2008), to financial interventions and support from the local community of entrepreneurs that is practiced in all countries. Individual university initiatives related to entrepreneurship education set good practice models for other universities, and such universities can become instrumental in developing broader strategies either in the region or nationwide. A number of individual universities have become champions in entrepreneurship education (NIRAS Consultants *et al.*, 2008) either due to the commitment by the university management, such as at the Technical University of Munich in Germany and ESPCI ParisTech in France, or due to committed individuals such as at INSEAD in France.

Combined Top-Down and Bottom-Up Approach

With entrepreneurship being among the top priorities in national policy documents that are owned by a number of national agencies, evidence increasingly shows cases of a combined approach that each draw on their strengths. Ludewig (in this volume) describes the importance of the government programme EXIST in Germany that has provided support to entrepreneurial activities, including education since 1998 that in combination with federal support indicates to differentiation between implementation strategies (Cerna, 2013). Furthermore, Fadel *et al.* (in this volume) describe how governmental programmes, regional programmes, NGOs, and universities interact in providing entrepreneurship education, hence bringing together the top-down and bottom-up approaches in Saudi Arabia. The policy implementation approaches differ within a country and across countries. The research done by the authors of this anthology suggests that the policy implementation also differs based on the goals or intent of a policy.

Section 2: A Case Study of Latvia

In Latvia, three ministries and two governmental institutions are responsible for entrepreneurship education. The Ministry of Education and Science is responsible for the content of entrepreneurship education programmes, the Ministry of Economics provides for lifelong learning projects, and the Ministry of Welfare provides training for the unemployed. While the Latvian Investment and Development Agency provides financial support to universities through various funding programmes, the Council of Higher Education develops a national higher education strategy and the Ministry of Education and Science provides the regulatory framework.

A literature review of entrepreneurship education programmes in higher education in Latvia indicates deficiencies and improvements to be made in the general policy context, university context, programme context, and graduate employability. Over the last decade, the country's statistics have improved, especially regarding early stage entrepreneurship as indicated in the Global Entrepreneurship Monitor reports on Latvia (Krumina & Paalzow 2012, 2013/2014; Krumina & Rastrigina, 2010). However, in the same reports, reference is made to improvements in the quality of providing entrepreneurship education that echo other strategic assessment reports and recommendations for Latvia; for example, the Latvia Competitiveness Report, Europe 2020: Country-Specific Recommendations for Latvia, and most recently a recommendation made by the World Bank in *"Assessment of Current Funding Model's 'Strategic Fit' with Higher Education Policy Objectives"* to increase the quality of higher education, strengthen the links between universities and business, and enhance technology, innovation, creativity, and entrepreneurship.

In order to explore the policy climate for entrepreneurial education in higher education in Latvia and answer the proposed questions, we drew on the analysis of literature on entrepreneurship education and policy implementation research, national policy papers, and institutional websites, focusing on policy guidelines and implementation of entrepreneurship education in EU member states and Norway. Secondary research was complemented with focus group interviews in Latvia. Key stakeholders in entrepreneurship education (Table 3) were invited to three focus group discussions, engaging 17 participants in total.

We classified focus group questions into two large groups: the present outcomes of entrepreneurship education and the interaction between stakeholders to establish an agenda for entrepreneurship education in Latvia. Using the sequential exploratory pattern (Creswell & Plano Clark, 2007), we accomplished data analysis by processing (NViVo v.10) the material recorded during focus group discussions, followed by coding the transcribed material into thematic categories and reducing the data to key concepts (Hennink, 2013).

Ministries	Ministry of Economics
	Ministry of Education and Science
Governmental Institutions	National Centre for Education
	The State Education Development Agency
	National Industry Experts Council
	Investment and Development Agency of Latvia
Universities	Vidzeme University College
	Turiba University College
NGOs, Local Leaders	Junior Achievement Latvia
	TechHub Riga
	Mission Possible Riga
	Go Beyond
	Advisor to PM on economic matters
	Entrepreneur and entrepreneurship teacher

Table 3: Stakeholders in the focus group interviews.

The focus group discussions were structured around two blocks of questions to review the present outcomes of entrepreneurship education at university level and the interaction between the government, university, and businesses in order to make projections about areas for improvement in the future. In this section, we highlight the major themes and subthemes complemented with a range of opinions expressed during these discussions.

Chapter 2

Theme I: Varied Interpretations of Entrepreneurship Education

Even though the definition of entrepreneurship education was explained in writing in letters inviting participants to the focus group discussions and reinforced during the introductory part of each focus group discussion, a substantial amount of time in discussions was spent revisiting the concepts of education "about" and "for" entrepreneurship.

Entrepreneurship education for undergraduate or graduate students

The discussions ranged from a respondent stating that there should be no entrepreneurship in undergraduate programmes to the majority of respondents supporting entrepreneurship being taught in some way to students at all education levels. An underlying argument explaining these differences as perceived by the respondents was the importance of experience in understanding entrepreneurship. Two respondents representing business argued for entrepreneurship being taught to graduate students as being better targeted: *"I think that it is more reasonable to teach entrepreneurship to graduate students. Such students have acquired a profession, they have some working experience, they understand what real business is all about, and then they are ready for additional learning and knowledge helpful in setting up business."*

Four respondents referred to undergraduates, focusing on their discipline-specific studies to understand the subject-specific area first, be it biology, chemistry, or engineering, and later add entrepreneurship. Five respondents, however, highlighted the importance of gaining insights into entrepreneurship as early as possible. Eight respondents indicated that studies at universities were too theoretical. The discussion on the above alternatives concluded in accord that students at all levels and in all professions, need more entrepreneurial skills and exposure to real-life work experiences.

Education "about" and "for" entrepreneurship

In terms of education "for" entrepreneurship, it was broadly agreed that students at all levels and professions should develop an entrepreneurial mindset and a skill set that would allow students after graduation to become either entrepreneurs, self-employed, or entrepreneurial employees. Several participants mentioned that entrepreneurship should be integrated across the study programme. In relation to education "about" entrepreneurship, participants mentioned three alternatives: a core foundation course, an elective foundation course, and work experience with business incubators and mentors. The majority of respondents agreed on a foundation course in entrepreneurship as a necessary course for students in all study programmes: *"We should teach very practical things; and this is what we do – we teach practical and applied things based on an underlying assumption that students should master a general skill set to be applied in different contexts, including entrepreneurship."*

A few participants mentioned business incubators as perfect places for combining both education "about" and "for" entrepreneurship. A respondent provided an example of *Demola Latvia* – a university-business interface facilitating multidisciplinary teams of students to work on co-creation projects between university students and companies for which students and their faculty advisors were awarded credit points. A respondent from a regional university college mentioned a new initiative to engage with the local business community and bring their problems to the university laboratory to be solved by students.

Theme 2: Differences in Perceptions About Internship Requirements in Academic and Professional Programmes

All participants recognised the importance of internships in the related study area as an essential component in study programmes to expose students to a real working environment. However, a number of issues were identified in relation to formal requirements in professional and academic programmes and the institutional framework for employers. In relation to professional study programmes, all participants were aware of internships being a mandatory component both at undergraduate and graduate levels. The discussion about internships in academic programmes was reflective of two problem areas relating to deficiencies in the institutional framework. Respondents from ministries and governmental agencies noted that an internship was not required for students studying in academic programmes according to the regulations on higher education. Based on the current regulations, a respondent from the ministry stated: *"If we want to have entrepreneurs, then we have to create professional study programmes where internship is a mandatory component and would put students into real working environment."*

Three respondents were aware of internships being offered to students in academic programmes; however, they did not know how these internships were formalised within those universities. Several participants mentioned that the labour market needs a qualified workforce, irrespective of the academic or professional programme. A respondent from a sectoral council indicated that there was a gap between professional and academic programmes: *"I think that in real life we need both, let us say academic and professional '50 to 50' or '60 to 40' depending on the sector, and then something good will come out. Currently, I have a feeling that the ones work in one silo and the other ones are in a different silo. We should put them together."*

Discussions about internships indicated uncertainties and therefore substantial deficiencies in the legal framework for employers providing internships. A representative from the ministry mentioned two approaches that were applied: employers offer students either a job agreement or a specific internship agreement for an internship period. Several issues were mentioned in relation to internships and employers, including the extra time spent to supervise an intern and lack of efficiency, perceived as slowing down the regular work within the company. Different opinions expressed by participants from ministries and governmental agencies indicated the absence of a legal framework, as noted by a representative of a ministry: *"We have two different opposing viewpoints regarding internships. We will try bringing the different viewpoints, those of the Ministry Education and Science and the Ministry of Economy, closer. We all know that we have to do that, but the question remains which model to choose."*

In addition to contractual issues, the discussion revealed a knowledge gap on how to compensate employers providing internships. A respondent from the ministry suggested financial instruments such as grants, specially allocated tax money, or, alternatively, no compensation.

This discussion concluded in agreement that the government should make commitments to provide national policy guidelines for strengthening internship programmes.

Theme 3: Engagement with Business through Sector Councils and University or Regional Advisory Boards

The discussion regarding the university and business interface revealed three dimensions: creation and engagement of sector councils, involvement of representatives from employers on university advisory boards, and university representatives participating in local/regional business councils. Representatives from sectoral councils described their positive experience in cooperation with vocational schools and colleges, contributing to aligning study programmes with the needs of the labour market. Participants were certain that universities should also become involved with sectoral councils. A representative from a ministry noted: *"We are currently working on a new system, and engagement of sectoral councils in higher education is next on our agenda. I am just concerned whether higher educational institutions will accept that."*

Engaging business representatives in university advisory boards (conventions) was mentioned as another pathway for involving external stakeholders in university strategic planning and providing better understanding of the labour market. Concerns were expressed regarding the efficiency of these boards because of the long list of board members and unclear expectations, responsibilities, and tasks assigned. A participant from a regional university college mentioned positive outcomes of cooperation with the local business council. Finally, a representative from a ministry mentioned intentions to create study field councils in, for example, engineering, the natural sciences, information technologies, and similar fields.

Theme 4: Linking up Schools and Universities for Better Entrepreneurship Education Outcomes

Respondents from a ministry, governmental agencies, and NGOs highlighted the significance of continuity in entrepreneurship education, starting from school and continuing all the way to university. While a participant from a ministry noted that entrepreneurial skills were included in schooling from elementary to secondary year groups, a representative from Junior Achievement Latvia stated that general guidelines for schools were, however, adopted: *"The government should clearly describe the learning outcomes of entrepreneurship education for each stage of schooling, for example what pupils should know and be able to do at the elementary and secondary stage, and similarly students in higher education. The government should take action and develop policy guidelines so that it is clear for everybody."*

Representatives from sectoral councils agreed that secondary school students well equipped with entrepreneurial skills would develop into entrepreneurial students who would be able to start their entrepreneurship programmes at a higher level. Several respondents referred to the experience of Junior Achievement Latvia, stating that Junior Achievement programmes should be introduced in all schools because of their internationally recognised and well-structured content and approach.

Theme 5: Impact of Financial Constraints in the Current and Future Development of Entrepreneurship Education

Participants mentioned funding as an essential instrument for sustaining sector councils, establishing study field councils, providing internship programmes, developing entrepreneurship programmes and business incubators, and organising entrepreneurial activities. Responses from representatives of governmental institutions differed from responses from representatives of universities, business, and NGOs. Representatives from governmental institutions referred to the state budget constraints, stating that since entrepreneurship is part of social sciences and since funding is being decreased in social sciences in favour of science, engineering, and technology, funding for entrepreneurship education would not be available. A representative from the ministry noted: *"To address this issue, we are currently in a process looking for solutions. It cannot be done, however, as a revolutionary change over a year, because it is a process of gradual change. We should look at entrepreneurship programmes as integrated in engineering and natural sciences programmes."*

Proportions and configuration of state budget funding were suggested as solutions to provide continuity for successful projects such as sectoral councils and to introduce changes as needed. With funding being linked to regulations and policy guidelines, respondents noted the importance of specific guidelines for entrepreneurship education, including entrepreneurship programmes and internships. Small grants for student entrepreneurial projects and events such as business idea competitions were recommended by representatives from business and NGOs.

Theme 6: Lack of Coordination among the Engaged Stakeholders

Representatives from ministries outlined the responsibilities shared between ministries in entrepreneurship education. Even though a representative from a ministry mentioned substantial improvements in coordination between the ministries over the last five years, he could not provide any examples of present projects, mentioning that there were a few task force groups working together, yet the details were vague. A few representatives from governmental institutions stated that there was no need to launch a new institution or special interface to coordinate entrepreneurship education.

Representatives from business and NGOs mentioned that universities should also be more active in connecting with industries instead of "waiting until the company goes to the university". Regarding entrepreneurship programmes and the entrepreneurship faculty, respondents could not name any platform or interface for sharing resources and experiences.

Theme 7: Sine qua non-for Standardisation of Coherent Entrepreneurship Education Nationwide

During the discussion, a majority of respondents referred to standards either established or to be established in entrepreneurship education by the government. In relation to the present higher education context, certain standards were referred to as barriers; for example, restrictions on awarding credit points for student entrepreneurial learning in projects linked with business incubators or similar projects. Speaking about changes and innovations in study programmes and curricula, representatives from universities referred to standards provided by governmental institutions as constraints, indicating the need to develop specific standards for entrepreneurship education. Representatives from governmental institutions referred to systemic changes to "remove entrepreneurship from social sciences" and integrate it as an entrepreneurial competence embedded across higher education. A respondent from a ministry noted: "*First, entrepreneurship should be linked to the academic discipline students are studying, and then study programmes should be designed integrating entrepreneurial competence as one of the basic components. Second, studies in academic disciplines should be linked to internships within a standardised framework for cooperation. These are the tools that should be used in developing standards and building study programmes.*"

A respondent suggested that the government should develop specific policy guidelines on entrepreneurship education covering all age groups, from kindergarten and school to higher education and lifelong learning. However, a few representatives from sectoral councils referred to a number of policy documents that concluded that there was no need to create a new policy; the most important issue was implementing the present guidelines more efficiently.

Findings

The analysis of secondary sources indicates the features of the top-down approach currently prevailing in the EU, with policy designers being the central actors. With entrepreneurship education being a fairly new concept in EU member states, implementing a policy change in the national environment calls for a top-down approach (Graham, 2014; Hoppe, 2016) that helps to increase the overall understanding in all social layers over time and underpin the importance of the economic, political, and social contexts. The determinants of the top-down approach, such as prescriptive policy documents and a clear and consistent message, vary across EU member states. Firstly, the experience in Nordic countries, notably in Norway, demonstrates a low level of political conflict and low ambiguity through applying a specific national strategy on entrepreneurship education that also signals the importance of entrepreneurship (UNCTAD, 2010). The national strategy serves as a framework for setting standards and objectives, allocates policy resources, and establishes implementing agencies and inter-organisational communication, and this framework has been developed over twelve years. Secondly, by having entrepreneurship education embedded in different national strategies, the governments of new EU member states, including Latvia, do not send a clear message about the significance of entrepreneurship education that is recognised by UNCTAD (2010) as characteristic of developing countries. Following this, the pattern is characterised by a combined approach applying the top-down level at an early stage with the potential to gradually transfer to a bottom-up model in which higher education institutions play a central role. Thirdly, regional initiatives as a typical bottom-up approach in extending entrepreneurial culture may result in a "cumulative change" (Rinne & Koivula, 2005) by readdressing entrepreneurship at a national level over time (Anderson et al., 2014). The overview of policy approaches in EU member states indicates the importance of interaction between the policy designers at the macro level and the local community and higher education institutions at the micro level.

In Latvia, the top-down approach is implemented by embedding entrepreneurship education in four different national strategies that might be perceived as embracing larger groups of the population (UNCTAD, 2010). However, without a strong and clear message about the importance of entrepreneurship education in Latvia, the engaged stakeholders experience ambiguity due to each of the national strategies having their specific policy objectives, with entrepreneurship failing to be an obvious policy objective (Matland, 1995). The data analysis of focus group discussions confirms lack of coordination and communication between governmental institutions, notwithstanding formal task force groups set up for the task. The data from focus group discussions presents entrepreneurship education as "floating" in between institutions while higher education institutions try to "grab" all the resources available. In this vein, the secondary research highlights the top-down approach to implementing entrepreneurship education in Latvia, while the data analysis shows ambiguity and descriptive policy documents that are signs of a bottom-up approach.

The findings confirm that a successfully implemented top-down approach at the macro level establishes foundations for a transition to a bottom-up approach at the micro level, with the local target community fully engaged. The case of Latvia suggests that a bottom-up approach with different stakeholders involved and pressure from universities may result in a top-down approach and an active local target community at the micro level. The actions taken to achieve the policy objectives are represented in creating sectoral councils, engaging external stakeholders on university advisory boards, and establishing business incubators; however, the majority of plans are not yet in action but are planned for implementation in the near future.

Conclusion

In this study, we attempted to explore the landscape of entrepreneurship education in general in the EU, and Latvia in particular with a focus on higher education. We explored the policy approaches applied to developing entrepreneurship education at higher education institutions and identified the actions taken. The findings show that there is still ambiguity regarding entrepreneurship education, and it can be addressed by 1) policy implementation using a top-down approach that is perceived as sending a clear message to the wider society, and it is more efficient and easier to monitor; 2) communication and coordination, which are essential in the policy implementation process both in top-down and bottom-up approaches; and 3) there is evidence that bottom-up and top-down approaches overlap and support each other. We hope this study contributes to building case studies on entrepreneurship education policy context in EU member states. We have also attempted to provide the context for other authors of this anthology to share their research on teaching and learning entrepreneurship in higher education.

* This study has been performed within the project "*EU policies impact to the transformations of the higher education and research system in Norway and Latvia*" No. NFI/R/2014/006, EEA and Norway Grants 2009–2014.

About the Authors

Diana Pauna is Dean of Arts & Sciences at University of Central Asia, and the former Pro-Rector of the Stockholm School of Economics in Riga, Latvia. She can be contacted at this e-mail: diana.pauna@ucentralasia.org

Maija Kale is Adviser at Nordic Council of Ministers' Office in Latvia. She can be contacted at this e-mail: maijakale@gmail.com

Bibliography

Anderson, S.; N. Culkin; A. Penaluna & K. Smith (2014). *An Education System fit for an Entrepreneur: Fifth Report by the All Party Parliamentary Group for Micro Businesses*. Online Resource: http://www.enterprise.ac.uk/index.php/resources [Accessed on 3 August 2016].

Bikse, V. & I. Riemere (2013). The Development of Entrepreneurial Competences for Students of Mathematics and the Science Subjects: The Latvian Experience. *Social and Behavioral Sciences*, No. 82, pp. 511–519.

Bikse, V.; B. Rivža & I. Brence (2013). Competitiveness and quality of higher education: graduates' evaluation. *Journal of Teacher Education for Sustainability*, Vol. 15, No. 2, pp. 52–66.

Cerna, L. (2013). *The Nature of Policy Change and Implementation: A Review of Different Theoretical Approaches*. OECD Publishing.

Chiu, R. (2012). *Entrepreneurship education in the Nordic countries – strategy implementation and good practices*. Oslo: Nordic Innovation Publication 2012:24.

Creswell, J. & V. Plano Clark (2007). *Designing and Conducting Mixed Methods Research*. Thousand Oaks, CA: Sage.

Cunska Z.; C. Ketels; A. Paalzow & A. Vanags (2012). *Latvian Competitiveness Report 2011*. Riga: Stockholm School of Economics.

Daniels, C. & C. Brush (2013). *Babson College Career Pathways Alumni Study*. Wellesley, MA: Babson College.

EC (European Commission) (2006). *Entrepreneurship Education in Europe: Fostering Entrepreneurial Mindsets through Education and Learning*. Online Resource: http://www.eesc.europa.eu/?i=portal.en.soc-opinions.18027 [Accessed on 3 August 2016].

EC (European Commission) (2007). *Key Competences for Lifelong Learning: A European Framework*. Luxembourg: Office for Official Publications of the European Communities.

EC (European Commission) (2012). *Building Entrepreneurial Mindsets and Skills In the EU*. Brussels: Directorate-General for Enterprise and Industry, European Commission.

EC (European Commission) (2013). *Entrepreneurship 2020 Action Plan. Reigniting the Entrepreneurial Spirit in Europe*. Brussels: COM (2012) 795 final.

EC-OECD (2012). *A Guiding Framework for Entrepreneurial Universities*.

EURYDICE (2012). *Entrepreneurship Education at School in Europe: National Strategies, Curricula, and Learning Outcomes*.

Fayolle, A. & D. T. Redford (Eds.) (2014). *Handbook on the Entrepreneurial University*. Cheltenham: Edward Elgar Publishing, Incorporated.

Graham, R. (2014). *Creating University-based Entrepreneurial Ecosystems – Evidence from Emerging World Leaders*. Massachusetts Institute of Technology.

Hennink, M. M. (2013). *Understanding Focus Group Discussions*. Oxford University Press.

Hoppe, M. (2016). Policy and Entrepreneurship Education, *Small Business Economics*, Vol. 46, No. 1, pp. 13–29.

Kitagawa, F. (2005). Entrepreneurial Universities and the Development of Regional Societies: A Spatial View of the Europe of Knowledge, *Higher Education Management and Policy*, Vol. 17, No. 3, pp. 65–89.

Kozlinska, I.; T. Mets; A. Paalzow; A. Gustafsson-Pesonen & the CB Entreint project team (2013). Analysis of entrepreneurship educators' training needs and practices, Research Report, *Central Balticum Entrepreneurship Interaction (Entreint)*, Aalto University, pp. 15–29.

Krumina, M. & A. Paalzow (2012/2013). *Global Entrepreneurship Monitor 2012/2013 Latvia Report*. TeliaSonera Institute at the Stockholm School of Economics in Riga.

Krumina, M. & A. Paalzow (2013/2014). *Global Entrepreneurship Monitor 2013/2014 Latvia Report*. TeliaSonera Institute at the Stockholm School of Economics in Riga.

Krumina, M. & O. Rastrigina (2010). *Global Entrepreneurship Monitor, 2010 Latvia Report*. Stockholm School of Economics in Riga.

Levin, J. & P. Milgrom (2004). *Introduction to Choice Theory*. Online Resource: https://web.stanford.edu/~jdlevin/Econ%20202/Choice%20Theory.pdf [Accessed on 29 April 2016].

Matland, R. E. (1995). Synthesizing the Implementation Literature: The Ambiguity-Conflict Model of Policy Implementation. *Journal of Public Administration Research and Theory*, Vol. 5, No. 2, pp. 145–174.

MERN (Ministry of Education and Research et al., Norway) (2004). *See the Opportunities and Make them Work! – Strategy for entrepreneurship in education and training 2004–2008*. Strategy Plan.

MERN (Ministry of Education and Research, Norway) (2009). *Entrepreneurship in Education and Training – from compulsory school to higher education 2009–2014*. Oslo, publication code: F-4251 E.

Ministry of Education, Finland (2009). *Guidelines for Entrepreneurship Education*. Publications of the Ministry of Education, Finland 2009:9.

NIRAS Consultants; FORA; ECON Pöyry (2008). *Survey of Entrepreneurship Education in Higher Education in Europe*.

North, D. C. (1990). *Institutions, Institutional Change, and Economic Performance.* Cambridge University Press.

Pittaway, L. & J. Cope (2006). Entrepreneurship Education: A Systematic Review of the Evidence. National Council for Graduate Entrepreneurship, Working Paper 002/2006.

Rinne, R. & J. Jenni Koivula (2005). The Changing Place of the University and a Clash of Values. The Entrepreneurial University in the European Knowledge Society. A Review of the Literature. *Higher Education Management and Policy,* Vol. 17, Nr. 3, pp. 91–125.

SG (Scottish Government) (2008). *Determined to Succeed.* Online Resource: http://www.educationscotland.gov.uk/images/CommunicationsLAGuidancephase2_tcm4-492583.pdf [Accessed on 3 August 2016].

Shattock, M. (2003). *Managing Successful Universities.* SRHE and Open University Press, Buckingham.

OECD (2008). *Entrepreneurship and Higher Education.* OECD Publishing.

UNCTAD (United Nations Conference on Trade and Development) (2012). *UNCTAD entrepreneurship policy framework and implementation guidance.* New York: United Nations.

UNCTAD (United Nations Conference on Trade and Development) (2010). *Entrepreneurship education, innovation and capacity-building in developing countries.* New York: United Nations.

Valerio, A.; B. Parton & A. Robb (2014). *Entrepreneurship Education and Training Programs around the World: Dimensions for Success.* Washington, DC: World Bank.

Welter, F. & D. Smallbone (2011). *Handbook of Research on Entrepreneurship Policies in Central and Eastern Europe.* Edward Elgar Publishing.

World Bank Reimbursable Advisory Service on Higher Education Financing in Latvia (2014). *Assessment of Current Funding Model's 'Strategic Fit' with Higher Education Policy Objectives.*

Chapter 3
Developing Holistic and Comprehensive Entrepreneurship Education Approaches in Germany

Dirk Ludewig

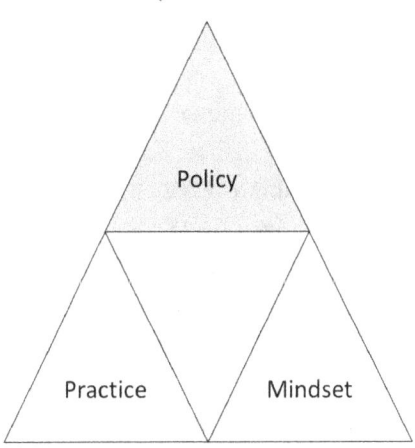

Introduction

My chapter is an important contribution to this section on policy – and to the book *Teaching and Learning Entrepreneurship in Higher Education* – because I stress the importance of holistic and comprehensive entrepreneurship education approaches at university level. Furthermore, I highlight successful recipes for both nationwide initiatives and university-level initiatives that aim for the development of entrepreneurship education in higher education. Reading this chapter, you will gain the following three insights:

1. an understanding of the importance of developing holistic and comprehensive entrepreneurship education approaches at university level;

2. a successful recipe for a nationwide initiative that aims to develop holistic and comprehensive entrepreneurship education approaches at university level using the example of the German top-down programme EXIST;

3. a successful recipe for developing holistic and comprehensive entrepreneurship education approaches at university level using the case study at Flensburg University of Applied Sciences which combines the usage of top-down initiatives with bottom-up elements.

I have divided the chapter into three main section. First, I start by stressing the importance of applying a more holistic and comprehensive view on teaching and learning entrepreneurship in higher education. Here I touch on contemporary research within the field of entrepreneurship education and define key terms of the chapter.

Second, I present the German top-down programme EXIST. It is a major support programme run by the German Federal Ministry for Economic Affairs and Energy, that aims to improve the entrepreneurial environment at universities and research institutions. EXIST has proven to be a successful nationwide initiative which has led to the development of holistic and comprehensive entrepreneurship education approaches at university level. With EXIST, entrepreneurship became widespread in the German university context. The following subsection covers further support programmes and sources that were implemented at German universities to establish and maintain entrepreneurship education approaches in addition to the EXIST programme. The section closes with a picture of the quantitative development of the entrepreneurship education environment in Germany.

Third, I highlight a successful four-phase approach at university level by using the case study from Flensburg University of Applied Sciences, the northernmost university in Germany, which combines the usage of top-down initiatives with bottom-up elements. These phases are highly representative of the development at many German universities and offer detailed insights of the level of an individual university. In a German ranking of entrepreneurship activities in the field of organisation, activation, teaching, and support, Flensburg University of Applied Sciences ranks at the top among universities in Schleswig-Holstein and Hamburg.

Finally, the chapter closes with a conclusion addressing the key findings and lessons presented in the chapter.

Section 1: The Importance of Holistic and Comprehensive Entrepreneurship Education Approaches in the University Context

Inspired by the well-known entrepreneurship definition by Shane & Venkataraman (2000), Bager (2011:303) defines entrepreneurship education as *"the transfer and facilitation of knowledge and competences about how, by whom and with what effects opportunities to create future goods and services are discovered, evaluated and exploited"*.

He distinguishes between two perspectives of entrepreneurship education. In the narrow perspective, entrepreneurship research and education is regarded as another discipline implemented by new research initiatives and courses. Following the idea of Gibb (2006), Bager (2011:312) regards a rather holistic approach as comprising much more than just a few courses and research activities; that is, *"a core strategic activity, which aims to reach out to all students, revolutionise teaching practises, strengthen university-business collaboration and install an entrepreneurial culture instead of the dominant bureaucratic culture at universities – in short, to develop The Entrepreneurial University"*.

Lilischkis *et al.* (2015) use a comprehensive conceptual framework in their study "Supporting the entrepreneurial potential of higher education" which comprises:

- curricular aspects of entrepreneurship education (i.e., learning within the formal curriculum of the university);

- extracurricular aspects (e.g., business plan competitions, start-up consulting and mentoring, start-up information days and campaigns);

- institutional aspects (i.e., organisational set-up/change, regulation, and mindsets that effect entrepreneurship education).

Following the ideas of Bager (2011) and Lilischkis *et al.* (2015), I regard the holistic and comprehensive entrepreneurship education approach as central for the success in teaching and learning entrepreneurship in higher education. This chapter is therefore consistent in following this logic.

Chapter 3

Section 2: Developing Holistic and Comprehensive Entrepreneurship Education Approaches – Highlighting the Successful Example of the Nationwide German Top-Down Initiative EXIST

In 1998, the German Federal Ministry for Education, Science, Research and Technology identified the following deficits in Germany (Bundesministerium für Bildung, Wissenschaft, Forschung und Technologie, 1998):

- compared to the high number of graduates, only a very few became entrepreneurs;
- despite an excellent education in the respective subject, entrepreneurship was not part of the curriculum and an entrepreneurial culture did not exist in teaching, research, and university administration;
- compared to a growing number of innovative start-ups in the 1990s in general, the start-up potential within the universities was not activated and only a few university start-ups were present as positive benchmarks.

German Top-Down Programme EXIST for Supporting Holistic and Comprehensive Entrepreneurship Education Approaches

Against this background, the Germany-wide support programme for university-based start-ups and approaches EXIST was established (for an overview of approaches in other EU member states see Pauna & Kale in this volume). The name is derived from the German word "Existenzgründungen".

Being a nationwide initiative driven by policy designers who are central actors, EXIST can be characterised as a top-down approach (Cerna, 2013). The programme's goals and the content clearly aim at supporting holistic and comprehensive entrepreneurship education approaches.

According to Kulicke (2014), the goals of EXIST are:

- a permanent establishment of an entrepreneurial culture in teaching, research, and university administration;
- a consistent transfer of research results into economic value added;
- a focused support of the great potential of business ideas and entrepreneurial personalities at universities and research institutions;
- a significant increase of innovative start-ups and thereby the creation of new and sustainable jobs.

The top-down support programme consists of three main pillars (EXIST, 2016):
- EXIST culture of entrepreneurship;
- EXIST business start-up grant;
- EXIST transfer of research results.

Temporarily, further programmes, such as EXIST-HighTEPP (High Technology Entrepreneurship Postgraduate Programme) and EXIST-PrimeCUP (business plan competition) were included (Kulicke, 2014). However, the focus in the following sections will be on the three main pillars.

EXIST culture of entrepreneurship aims at supporting universities to define and sustainably implement holistic and comprehensive strategies for an entrepreneurial culture and entrepreneurship education approach. Supporting the universities since 1998, the EXIST cultural programme has not been a homogeneous programme throughout. Up to now, four different phases with a clear variation in the number of universities receiving support and with a "learning" approach to its core content have been offered (Kulicke, 2014; EXIST, 2016):
- 1998: EXIST I – 5 example initiatives with 20 universities – focus on networks of universities with partners in science, business, and politics to lay the foundations and create services for motivating, training, and the assistance of entrepreneurial personalities;
- 2002: EXIST II – 10 transfer network initiatives with 37 universities – an additional 10 networks with the same content as EXIST I were supported;

- 2006: EXIST III – 47 projects with 86 universities – at this stage, remaining gaps in qualification and assistance services were to be closed, whereby a focus was placed on clearly defined and differentiated projects with partners;
- 2010: EXIST IV – 22 projects with 24 universities – here the focus has been on university-wide approaches and a positioning as truly entrepreneurial universities.

The second and third main pillars, namely the EXIST business start-up grant and the EXIST transfer of research results emerged from the EXIST-SEED programme which became effective in 2000. EXIST-SEED funded individual start-up projects at universities for a duration of one year. In 2007, the idea of EXIST-SEED was amplified through the definition of the separate programmes of start-up grants and transfer of research results (EXIST, 2016).

With the EXIST business start-up grant, students, graduates, and scientists from universities and research institutes are supported in translating their business idea into a viable business plan. Prerequisites are an innovative and knowledge-based character of the idea together with a clear and unique advantage and a high business potential. Living expenses for up to one year along with a certain amount of money for material, equipment, and coaching is funded (EXIST, 2016).

EXIST transfer of research results focuses on excellent research-oriented projects that prove to be more expensive and involve a higher degree of risk. The programme has two stages. In stage one, research results are translated into products and processes. A solid business plan should also be developed. In the second phase, measures for starting up the business and the acquisition of external financing are the focus of the support programme (EXIST, 2016).

Further Sources to Support Holistic and Comprehensive Entrepreneurship Education Approaches

EXIST is the single most important top-down programme and financial source that has initiated and maintained holistic and comprehensive entrepreneurship education approaches at German universities. However, there are more financial sources and programmes supplementing and replacing the EXIST programme. Looking at the large number of universities that received financial support during EXIST I–III and comparing it to the small number in the EXIST IV programme shows the challenge of maintaining an own entrepreneurship education approach without permanent financial assistance from EXIST.

Further sources helping to finance sustainable entrepreneurship education approaches can be identified:

- university resources – establishing chairs and study programmes for entrepreneurship, implementing reward programmes for staff participating in the programme (Kulicke et al., 2012);
- state resources – funding university activities with own state resources or with acquired international funds (e.g., European funds such as the EFRE/ESF funds) offering state entrepreneurship education programmes and thus assisting individual universities (e.g., student grants and start-up funds) (Kulicke et al., 2012);
- public third-party funds – acquiring public third-party projects to finance extra university services in the field of entrepreneurship education (e.g., the cross-border programme Interreg);
- private third-party funds – acquiring private third-party funds to finance extra university services in the field of entrepreneurship education (e.g., from private companies and foundations);
- paid services – charging students, graduates, and scientists receiving support for the services or financing the programme by holding and selling shares in the start-ups;
- shared networks – sharing the task and thus the resources with other partners in the entrepreneurship support environment.

Chapter 3

Quantitative Development of the Entrepreneurship Education Environment at German Universities

Before 1998 (and thus before the top-down EXIST programme was introduced), the topic of entrepreneurship as well as holistic and comprehensive entrepreneurship education approaches were rather rare at German universities, as the study by the German Federal Ministry for Education, Science, Research and Technology found out (Bundesministerium für Bildung, Wissenschaft, Forschung und Technologie, 1998). As an example, according to Günther et al. (2007), the first entrepreneurship professorship in Germany (an endowed professorship) was introduced in 1997.

After the EXIST programme had been active for a certain period, its effects became visible. In 2007, Günther et al. (2007) already identified 49 universities with 54 entrepreneurship professorships and offering roughly 250 courses. Full incubators could be found at 19 universities, whereas consulting for potential entrepreneurs was offered at 41 universities. Through further EXIST phases and with the application of additional financial sources and programmes to support holistic and comprehensive entrepreneurship education approaches, the extent of the university services has been increased further. The study "Gründungsradar 2013" (entrepreneurship radar 2013) by Grave et al. (2014) ranks 139 universities in Germany (39 larger universities, 50 medium-sized universities, and 50 smaller universities) with entrepreneurship activities in the field of organisation, activation, teaching, and support. All in all, 168 universities with entrepreneurship activities participated in this study. However, 29 of them did not offer a full set of data and could not be ranked. Furthermore, not all universities participated in the study, and it can be expected that more universities in Germany engage in the field of entrepreneurship. However, the number of 168 universities that offer entrepreneurship education approaches is a good indicator. They provide a total of 1,474 curricular and 3,028 extracurricular courses. Seventy-six universities have a total of 103 entrepreneurship professorships. Furthermore, nearly all of the 168 universities provide consulting and support for entrepreneurs at different levels of intensity, ranging from rough information formats to large-scale incubators with high manpower.

There has been a tremendous development in comprehensive

entrepreneurship education approaches at German universities following the introduction of the EXIST programme in 1998 and the identification of further financing sources (see Figure 1). Before the top-down EXIST programme was established, only a few services in the field of entrepreneurship education approaches were available (exact numbers could not be found, which is expressed by the "?" in Figure 1). From 1998 onwards, the EXIST culture of entrepreneurship programme supported universities in four phases, starting with 20 universities in the first phase, 37 in the second, 86 in the third, and currently 24 universities in the fourth phase. Comparing the small number of 24 universities supported by EXIST today with the at least 168 universities that offered entrepreneurship education approaches in 2013, I conclude that the initial funding of EXIST in four phases has had a sustainable influence on the entrepreneurship education environment in Germany. A lot of universities benefitted from the different phases of the top-down EXIST support. These universities now use other sources for financing their services. In addition, further universities not taking part in EXIST provide services as well.

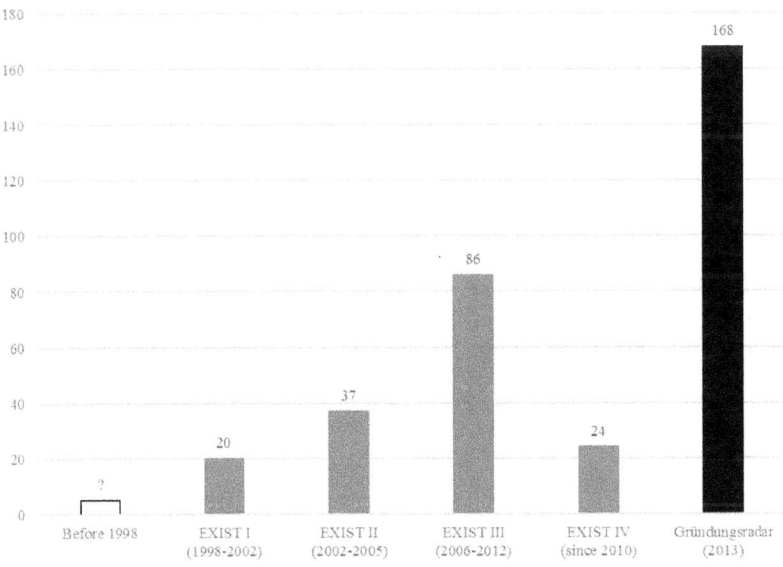

Figure 1: Number of universities in different phases.

According to Grave *et al.* (2014), this positive development of holistic and comprehensive entrepreneurship education approaches at university level in Germany has been very dynamic in recent years. In all four measured factors of entrepreneurship organisation, activation, teaching, and support, the universities were rated better on average in the latest study than in the study two years earlier. This is not just true for the entire group of universities but also in the three subgroups of larger, medium-sized, and smaller universities.

Section 3: Developing Holistic and Comprehensive Entrepreneurship Education Approaches – Highlighting the Successful Example of the Approach at Flensburg University of Applied Sciences

Flensburg University of Applied Sciences ranks 9th out of the 50 smaller universities in the study "Gründungsradar 2013" (Grave et al., 2014). No other university in the region of Schleswig-Holstein and Hamburg ranks higher in any of the three groups of larger, medium-sized, and smaller universities. In recent years, 39 companies were founded out of this university. Several idea competitions were won by campus start-ups and a lot of scholarships as well as start-up funding could be raised. In a recent article in the Handelsblatt, the entrepreneurship activities at Flensburg University of Applied Sciences were highlighted as a good Germany-wide example of the positive impact of these activities for the local economy (Wermke, 2016).

In this section, we highlight a four-phase case study of the development of the holistic and comprehensive entrepreneurship education approach at this northernmost university in Germany which combines top-down and bottom-up elements.

Phase 1.0: "Early beginnings"

Until 2007, the only entrepreneurship education offered at Flensburg University of Applied Sciences was a course called "young management" consisting of two modules in the field of consulting and entrepreneurship.

The course was only available to business students. In the entrepreneurship module, the students had the task of writing a business plan.

Further services, such as additional curricular or extracurricular courses or a consulting programme for entrepreneurship, were not available.

Phase 2.0: "Start-up" – EXIST III and First Robust Steps

In 2008, Flensburg University of Applied Sciences positioned itself with the definition of entrepreneurship goals as part of the strategic target agreement with the responsible ministry. One first cornerstone measure was the creation of a permanent entrepreneurship professorship at the end of 2008. This decision was taken at the same time as the acquisition of one of the top-down EXIST III projects on entrepreneurship culture at the end of 2008 which was carried out in a network with four other regional universities.

In this period, the entrepreneurship approach at Flensburg University of Applied Sciences developed much further than the original single course. For the first time, a holistic and comprehensive three-step approach was established. In the first step, called "information and motivation", students, scientists, and employees of Flensburg University of Applied Sciences were informed via newsletters, information on the website, events for first semester students, and an online business-platform. Furthermore, motivation events were established such as the participation in regional and Germany-wide idea and business contests.

In the second step, "qualification", the course "young management" was replaced by a more comprehensive curricular course for business students and an extracurricular course for non-business students. Beside this, the students at Flensburg University of Applied Sciences were able to participate in a course at the Europa-Universität Flensburg and a summer school that was offered together with all universities in the regional EXIST III project. Also, services, classes, and similar activities at the nearby University of Southern Denmark, were made available to them. In addition, the students had the possibility to write their theses on entrepreneurship topics.

The third "support" step was aimed at those students and scientists who had the ambition to establish their own business. A first consulting approach, contacts to the regional support network, assistance with applications for scholarships, and the possibility to get a small office were introduced.

Phase 2.0 of the entrepreneurship education approach at Flensburg University of Applied Sciences was financed by the university itself (bottom-up) and by the top-down EXIST III project. What became very important was the early embedment of the concept into the regional network consisting, for example, of the chamber of industry and commerce, the regional business development agency, and the regional entrepreneurship network. From the beginning, the objective was to bring students and scientists together with this network.

Phase 3.0: "Growth" – Dr Werner Jackstädt Center for Small and Medium-Sized Companies and Entrepreneurship Flensburg

In April 2011, the Dr Werner Jackstädt Center (DWJC) for small and medium-sized companies and entrepreneurship Flensburg was founded by Flensburg University of Applied Sciences and the Europa-Universität Flensburg. Since then, the DWJC has been financed by the Dr Werner Jackstädt Foundation, the regional business community, the two local universities, and the state of Schleswig-Holstein. Furthermore, third-party funded projects have been acquired to supplement the financing of the DWJC. In phase 3.0, the holistic and comprehensive entrepreneurship education approach at Flensburg University of Applied Sciences can be characterised as purely bottom-up.

Today, the DWJC is made up of a group of roughly 20 professors, assistants, and research associates who cover a large range of topics in the fields of small and medium-sized companies and entrepreneurship in research, teaching, and transfer. In the field of entrepreneurship, the team is grouped under the name Jackstädt Entrepreneurship Center (JEC). It covers four topics:

- academic entrepreneurship;
- entrepreneurship in teachers' education;
- green entrepreneurship;
- women's entrepreneurship.

Here, the focus will be on the programme in the field of academic entrepreneurship, which stands for the holistic and comprehensive entrepreneurship education approach that gathers the main elements that are used to inform, motivate, qualify, and support students, scientists, and employees of the universities in their entrepreneurship efforts. The services in the fields of teachers' education, green entrepreneurship, and women's entrepreneurship focus on special groups and ideas in this larger group of students, scientists, and employees of the universities. They can be used by the special groups on top of the academic entrepreneurship programme and are also available for cross-border German-Danish entrepreneurs and/or entrepreneurs in Schleswig-Holstein. The components of the academic entrepreneurship programme in phase 3.0 are highlighted in Figure 2.

Motivation & Information	Qualification	Support
1. Motivation: • CampusCup and MasterCup Competitions; • Idea Contest Schleswig-Holstein and Flensburg; • Weekend Events; • Encounters; • Lounge Event; • Wall of Fame. 2. Information: • First semester information; • Homepage; • "XING"- Network; • E-Mail-Newsletter. 3. Public Relations. 4. Screening/Scouting.	1. University of Applied Sciences: • Major in master program; • Bachelor module; • Course "MINT- Green Entrepreneurship". 2. Europa-University: • Major in master program; • Bachelor module; • Course "Entrepreneurship Personality"; • Course in teacher education. 3. Different shared Summer Schools offered with partners. 4. Thesis/Internships.	1. Founder's room and workspace. 2. Support: • Consulting hours; • Idea development; • Business modelling and planning; • Partner matching. 3. Network: • Consulting hours of regional business network partners; • University networks; • Project networks. 4. Financing: • Scholarship and funds access; • Business angels and venture capital.

Figure 2: Components of the entrepreneurship approach in phase 3.0.

Chapter 3

Again, the entrepreneurship education approach was largely broadened in comparison to the former phase, as Figure 2 shows. The financing of the concept is shared among different sources today, which makes it much more sustainable. Also, the partner base was extended by the inclusion of further public and private regional, state, national, and international partners into the JEC network. Their services are available to students, scientists and employees of the universities on top of the highlighted programme.

Figure 3 highlights the effects of phases 2.0 and 3.0 on the entrepreneurial activities at Flensburg University of Applied Sciences (most of the campus start-ups and new projects originate from Flensburg University of Applied Sciences). It shows the number of actual new entrepreneurial projects (not including projects that are just being pursued for learning purposes in curricular and extracurricular courses) and the number of start-ups deriving from these projects. These numbers are minimum numbers. It is possible that further projects are being pursued without the JEC knowing about it. Starting from a low level, the entrepreneurial activity clearly increased during phase 2.0. Then, after starting the phase 3.0, the activity accelerated to an even higher level (note that in 2016, only the numbers for the first half year are shown).

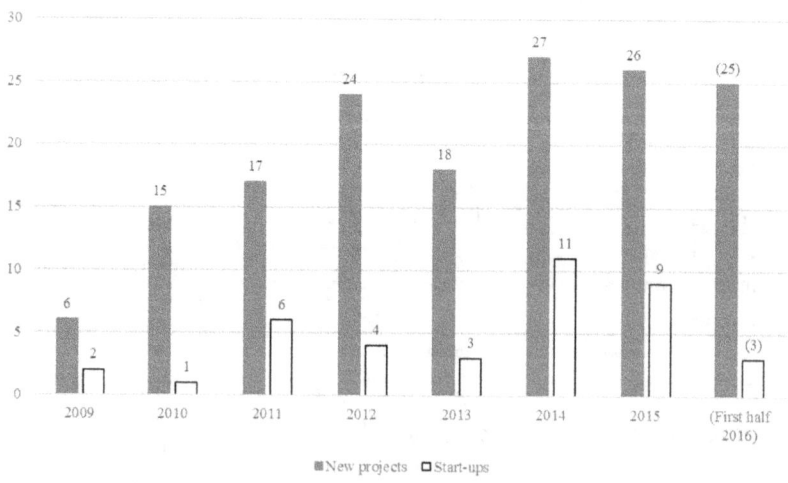

Figure 3: Number of new projects and start-ups at the Flensburg University of Applied Sciences.

Phase 4.0: "Optimized growth" – VentureWerft – Start-Up Campus and Region Flensburg

Today, the JEC is in the middle of a strategy process with regional and state partners, as well as start-ups, for shaping the future of the holistic comprehensive entrepreneurship education approach on the campus and within the region of Flensburg under the umbrella brand "VentureWerft". The goals of the process are to evaluate and to improve the concept as well as to secure its long-term existence, and the concept is entering a fourth phase of optimisation and qualified growth.

In particular, the following agenda was identified within the first meetings:

- programme – optimising the existing services, creating new services in identified gaps, and sharing the responsibilities among the partners;
- integration – achieving the highest possible level of integration of the campus programme into the entire entrepreneurship environment of the region of Flensburg and a good level of integration into further cross-border and regional networks;
- partnering – winning new partners on campus (such as more professors and staff) to promote and support the services and courses as well as integrating the existing young start-ups and experienced entrepreneurs into the concept;
- improving the marketing effort and the visibility of the programme;
- improving the start-up community and culture.

This agenda has to be worked on, specified, and then implemented over the next couple of years.

The four-phase case study of the development process of the holistic and comprehensive entrepreneurship education approach at Flensburg University of Applied Sciences offers a successful example and a recipe for including both top-down and bottom-up elements. These phases are highly representative of the development at many German universities and are also applicable to international universities with similar conditions.

Conclusion

In my chapter, I provided the reader with an understanding of holistic and comprehensive entrepreneurship education approaches at university level and highlighted successful recipes for both nationwide and university-level initiatives that aim for the development of these approaches.

I started by showing the critical importance of integrating the aspects of teaching and learning entrepreneurship in higher education into more holistic and comprehensive entrepreneurship education approaches at universities.

Then I described the nationwide German top-down initiative EXIST with its main components and its dynamic learning approach as a successful recipe for a nationwide initiative that aims at developing holistic and comprehensive entrepreneurship education approaches at university level. Furthermore, additional sources for financing new and maintaining established services were highlighted, along with figures on the development of entrepreneurship education approaches in Germany over time. An important lesson here is that major public top-down initiatives can have a successful and sustainable impact on the widespread diffusion of holistic and comprehensive entrepreneurship education concepts if they are managed dynamically and coincide with other additional sources of financing, as the example of EXIST in Germany has proven.

The last section presented a successful recipe for developing holistic and comprehensive entrepreneurship education approaches at university level using Flensburg University of Applied Sciences as a case study that combines the usage of top-down initiatives with bottom-up elements. The four-phase approach is highly representative for the development at many German universities and is also applicable to international universities with similar conditions.

About the Author

Dirk Ludewig is a professor at Flensburg University of Applied Sciences. He can be contacted at this e-mail: dirk.ludewig@hs-flensburg.de

Bibliography

Bager, T. (2011). Entrepreneurship education and new venture creation: A comprehensive approach. In K. Hindle & K. Klyver (Eds.), *Handbook of Research on New Venture Creation*. Cheltenham: Edward Elgar Publishing Limited, pp. 299–315.

Bundesministerium für Bildung, Wissenschaft, Forschung und Technologie (1998). *Existenzgründer aus Hochschulen. 12 regionale Netzwerke für innovative Unternehmensgründungen*. Bonn: BMBF.

Cerna, L. (2013). *The Nature of Policy Change and Implementation: A Review of Different Theoretical Approaches*. OECD Publishing.

EXIST (2016). Online Resource: http://www.exist.de/DE/Programm/Ueber-Exist/inhalt.html [Accessed on 28 July 2016].

Gibb, A. (2006). *Towards the entrepreneurial university. Entrepreneurship education as a lever for change*. Birmingham: NCGE Policy Paper Series.

Grave, B.; P. Hetze & A. Kanig (2014). *Gründungsradar 2013. Wie Hochschulen Unternehmensgründungen fördern*. Essen: Stifterverband für die deutsche Wirtschaft.

Günther, J.; K. Wagner & I. Ritter (2007). Zehn Jahre Entrepreneurship-Ausbildung in Deutschland: Eine positive Zwischenbilanz. *Wirtschaft im Wandel*, Year 2007, No. 9, pp. 350–356.

Kulicke, M. (2014). *15 Jahre EXIST "Existenzgründungen aus der Wissenschaft". Entwicklung des Förderprogramms von 1998 bis 2013*. Karlsruhe: Fraunhofer.

Kulicke, M.; F. Dornbusch; K. Kripp & M. Schleinkofer (2012). *Nachhaltigkeit der EXIST-Förderung. Gründungsunterstützung an Hochschulen, die zwischen 1998 und 2011 gefördert wurden*. Karlsruhe: Fraunhofer.

Lilischkis, S.; C. Volkmann; M. Gruenhagen; K. Bischoff & B. Halbfas (2015). *Supporting the Entrepreneurial Potential of Higher Education. Final Report*. European Commission.

Shane, S. & S. Venkataraman (2000). The promise of entrepreneurship as a field of research. *Academy of Management Review*, Vol. 25, No. 1, pp. 217–226.

Wermke, C. (2016). Heimlicher Aufstieg. *Handelsblatt*, Year 2016, No. 100, pp. 50–51.

Chapter 4
A Global Approach to Teaching Entrepreneurship in Japan

Sarah Louisa Birchley & Philip McCasland

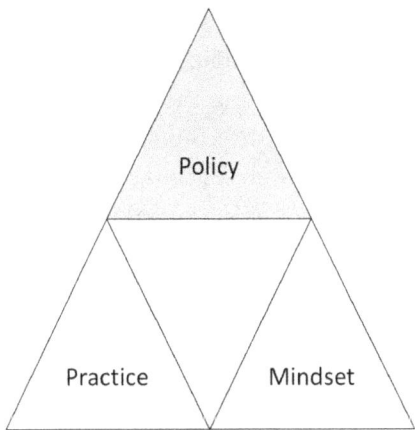

Introduction

Our chapter is an important contribution to this section on policy – and to the book *Teaching and Learning Entrepreneurship in Higher Education* – because we demonstrate with our reference to courses at Toyo Gakuen University in Tokyo and Fukushima University in Fukushima, how Japanese government policy on entrepreneurship and globalisation may be operationalised in order to advance innovation and entrepreneurship within higher education. In our view, there is an urgent need for this chapter and for a discussion of entrepreneurship education in Japan. While Japan is recognised as a major global economy, ranking 3rd for GDP according to the World Bank, and still considered a financial powerhouse in the areas of innovation and entrepreneurship, Japan is failing to keep pace with other major world economies. Ranking 30th in the world and 5th in Asia in the Global Entrepreneurship Rankings, it is difficult to understand why the country that gave us such global brands as Sony, Toyota, Nintendo, and Panasonic, which represented innovation in different industries in the past, is producing so few entrepreneurs today.

Some may say that this lack of innovative thinking and entrepreneurial activity is due to a prolonged stagnant economic environment coupled with a risk-averse culture that permeates both corporate world and personal mindset in Japan today. The Global Entrepreneurship and Development Institute reports that start-up skills and opportunity perception are improvements necessary to create an environment conducive to entrepreneurial growth. In addition, the Japanese Ministry of Education has identified this lack of entrepreneurship as a problem, resulting in new policies being put forward to tackle a lack in development and implementation of entrepreneurial education. Nevertheless, these educational policies are slow to be implemented in the tertiary curriculum.

In our chapter, we bridge the macro-political policy section with the micro-level practice section, as we present our courses "Professional Skills", which is part of the curriculum at Toyo Gakuen University, Tokyo. In our course, we use "Content and Language Integrated Learning" (CLIL) as our vehicle for teaching entrepreneurship. It may seem unusual at first, but we have found a great benefit for students, when we integrate entrepreneurial education and language education. In our course, we teach the professional skills required for entrepreneurs through Content and Language Integrated Learning that is framed in research on international posture and possible selves. We believe that tertiary education CLIL courses in Japan can provide students with the opportunity to develop more than just an international perspective and foreign language skills. In our view, CLIL courses can provide students with learning opportunities where they visualise themselves as entrepreneurs. This is what we aim to show in this chapter. Reading this chapter, you will gain the following three insights:

1. an understanding of entrepreneurship education in Japanese higher education;

2. an introduction to the literature of possible selves, content and language integrated learning, and international posture as they relate to entrepreneurship education; and

3. a set of activities to be used in the CLIL classroom for teaching entrepreneurship.

Our chapter has four main sections. First, we begin by examining the government policies on entrepreneurship education and *global jinzai*.

This section clarifies the political focus of entrepreneurship education in Japan. Second, we introduce the theoretical frameworks of international posture and imagined selves, arguing that these can be combined to develop curriculum for entrepreneurship education. Third, we describe the teaching method of Content and Language Integrated Learning (CLIL) as a way of teaching entrepreneurship. Fourth, we share three practical classroom activities, which have enabled us to introduce entrepreneurship with success in the curriculum. And fifth, we highlight our advice for developing CLIL-style lessons for entrepreneurship. The key lesson from our chapter is that policies can be operationalised through sound theoretical and methodological frameworks.

Section I: Policy

In this section, we introduce two current policies in Japanese higher education: 1) Japanese entrepreneurship education policy, and 2) Global Jinzai Policy.

Japanese Entrepreneurship Education Policy

In Japan, the phrase *"ikiru no chikara"*, often translated "zest for living", has been a building block of education since the mid-1990s (MEXT, 2008). The Ministry of Education more clearly defines this holistic concept as an individual who has solid academic achievement, meaningful personal relationships, and good health and physical fitness. This zest for living has been applied to entrepreneurship education because it relates to an individual's problem, discovery, and resolution capability, along with creativity, sensibility, motivation, and the ability to engage in active learning (METI, 2009).

We use the following working definition of entrepreneur education taken from the Ministry of Trade and Industry Study policy paper, produced by the Group for the Creation and Development of Start-ups (2008:19): *"Entrepreneurship education refers to education provided to train people to develop 'entrepreneurship' and 'entrepreneurial skills' and to be able to 'find their own mission, discover themselves what to do with it, and carry it out themselves.'"* According to the policy, the skills entrepreneurs are expected to develop are:

Chapter 4

Entrepreneurship characteristics:
- A spirit of challenge: a forward-looking attitude to try something new and address the challenges that emerge;
- Ambition: motivations and causes;
- Passion: zeal;
- Courage: willingness to expose themselves to certain risk.

Entrepreneurial skills:
- Ability to dream: imagination, creativity, problem-finding, positive attitudes, optimism;
- Ability to explain a dream: communication skills, logical thinking, presentation skills, personality, and honesty;
- Ability to realise a dream: skills to collect information, problem-solving, ability to make plans, vitality, judgment/decisiveness, patience.

Similar to the Japanese Ministry of Economy Trade and Industry (METI), we also define entrepreneurial spirit as a passion for challenge, creativity, and curiosity, while entrepreneurial qualities are defined as the ability to gather and analyse information, make judgments, and lead. We are therefore seeking to provide an education that fosters human resources with strong communication skills.

The Japanese government recommends the following approaches to entrepreneurial education in higher education:
- external lectures by entrepreneurs and managers;
- opportunities to examine corporate activities through visiting companies, watching videos, and analysing management in these contexts;
- use of case studies and business games;
- creation of business ideas, plans, and business contests;
- setting up joint projects with companies in local areas.

The government has been most supportive in embedding entrepreneurialism in schools and universities since 2009. Firstly, it established the "University Entrepreneur Education Promotion Network". The aim of this programme was not only to connect students with university faculty, but more importantly to connect students with entrepreneurs who would relay corporate experience to the next generation in support of entrepreneurial education (METI, 2009; MEXT, 2010).

Secondly, the Japanese government conducted a significant large-scale research study on entrepreneurship in higher education in 2009. This comprises the most comprehensive look at Japanese university entrepreneur education in the past 20 years. This research found that entrepreneurship education consists of approximately 50% coursework in classes such as Corporate Management, Intellectual Property and Strategy, An Introduction to Venture Companies, and The Need for and Methods of Marketing. On the other hand, 30% of courses engaged students in business planning exercises by developing knowledge of markets, business performance analysis methods, along with tax and practical knowledge in the areas of funding, labour needs, and legal aspects. While less than 20% of courses included business etiquette and soft skills, and effective communication strategies. Table 1 shows the types of classroom activities that are currently being used in Japan.

Business plan contests—co-sponsored with industry

Symposiums and seminars—jointly organised

Workshops—by guest lecturers

Entrepreneurship workshops

Funding consultations— with financial organisations

Business internships—with local industry

Seminars and meetings

Table 1: Typical classroom activities in entrepreneurship education in Japan.

In entrepreneurial education, teachers in business and management faculties are the most common lecturers in nearly 50% of institutions, while business people with entrepreneurial experience are lecturing in 40.3% of institutions. Fifty-three percent utilised faculty from the humanities and sciences, while 5.5% utilised the skills of non-teaching staff from the university careers centres. Therefore, it appears that the development of entrepreneurial education is being undertaken by faculty and staff members from a variety of different backgrounds (Nufufu.com, 2014; Co-media.com, 2016).

The Ministry of Economy, Trade and Industry (METI) ascertain that the content directly linked to actual entrepreneurial activity is presumed to be small. Therefore, the curricula may be fragmented as it is not clear within which faculty or programme entrepreneurial education is based, and according to the research conducted by METI in 2009, no university had integrated entrepreneurial education with language studies. The government nevertheless lists four points that need to be addressed for entrepreneurship education to be more successful:

- the purpose of entrepreneurship education is often unclear;
- there must be a link between theory and practice;
- universities are not taking full advantage of external human resources, resulting in weak relationships with industry;
- cooperation with external organisations of the region is not sufficiently developed.

We argue that there is an additional issue to be addressed: how to develop entrepreneurs that can function outside Japan. Entrepreneurs need to develop networks and partnerships both internally and externally; and for this to happen, students need effective communication skills in English (Shinato et al., 2013). Current research in Japan brings out what we have suspected: there is a lack of general confidence in Japanese entrepreneurs; a lack of entrepreneurial role models and mentors for young people, specifically women; a lack of confidence in foreign language ability to work outside Japan; and a lack of appropriate education for entrepreneurship (Wharton School, 2013; Kagami, 2015; Ito et al., 2015). Work by Yokoyama & Birchley (2014) and Yokoyama (2015) on 30 Japanese self-initiated expatriate entrepreneurs (SIEEs) working across Southeast Asia found that successful Japanese SIEEs had exposure overseas in the exploration stage of their career, with males beginning their entrepreneurial activities in their twenties. Additionally, these individuals demonstrated flexibility, were able to articulate a strong career anchor, developed mentor relationships, and had high levels of intrinsic motivation.

Global Jinzai Policy

In 2013, the Japanese Ministry of Education developed a set of new goals for English education. These included a renewed focus on content learning through English, particularly with classes taught entirely in English. Also included was a mandate to cultivate global human resources (MEXT, 2012), commonly referred to in Japanese as *global jinzai*. The policy highlighted three factors and five linguistic skills (METI, 2012; Ashizawa, 2012) necessary to become a *global jinzai*:

Factor I: Linguistic and communication skills

(1) for travels abroad;

(2) for interactions in daily life abroad;

(3) for business conversation and paperwork;

(4) for bilateral negotiations;

(5) for multilateral negotiations.

Factor II: Self-direction and positiveness, a spirit for challenge;

Factor III: Understanding of other cultures and a sense of identity as a Japanese.

Students need an active attitude toward communication with the confidence and ability to present their own ideas. Research suggests that demand for *global jinzai* by Japanese companies will grow by 240% between 2012 and 2017 to make up 8.7% of the employed population (MEXT, 2013), yet it can be argued that the skills for *global jinzai* are synonymous with those necessary for successful entrepreneurship and even intrapreneurship, and thus universities should be developing programmes that support these aims. If, as Shinato *et al*, (2013) argue, *"entrepreneurship education needs to contribute to a change of culture and consciousness towards entrepreneurs in Japan"* and if the Japanese government has identified a need for universities to produce *global jinzai*, what kind of entrepreneurial education could meet these goals? We argue that there is a clear need to develop a new, more globalised approach to entrepreneurial curriculum development that is informed by research on possible selves and international posture and that can effectively operationalise government policy.

Table 2 maps how the *global jinzai* factors align with with entrepreneurial skills and entrepreneurship characteristics according to the definition from METI (2009):

Global Jinzai Factors	Entrepreneurship Characteristics and Entrepreneurial Skills
Factor I	Ambition, passion, courage, ability to explain a dream problem-solving, ability to make plans, vitality, judgment/decisiveness, patience.
Factor II	A spirit of challenge, passion, ambition, courage, ability to dream, imagination, creativity, problem-finding, positive attitudes, optimism.
Factor III	Personality, honesty, communication skills.

Table 2: Mapping across policies.

Section 2: Theoretical Framework

In this section, we introduce two theoretical frameworks, that we use to ground our practice of teaching entrepreneurship in current educational and sociological theory: 1) Possible Selves, and 2) International Posture.

Possible Selves

We suggest that the concept of possible selves, as advocated by Markus & Nurius (1986) and developed by Meara *et al.* (2005), can represent students' ideas of what they might become (employees of a well-known company), what they would like to become (entrepreneurs), and what they are afraid that they may become (generic office workers). This provides a conceptual link between cognition and motivation. The development of a possible self can provide *"an evaluative and interpretive context for the current view of self"* (Markus & Nurius, 1986:962) and is *"cognitive manifestations of enduring goals, aspirations, motives, fears, and threats"* (Markus & Nurius, 1986:954). Awareness raising of the possible self can in some ways act as an incentive for future behaviour as it helps students visualise an interpretive context for their current view of themselves; it can help us to see what the students aspire to and/or their not yet realised identities

(Cross & Markus, 1994). Considering one's possible self relates to understanding and conceptualising goals, aspirations, motives, and behaviour. Thus, we argue that when students perceive that the class content is relevant to a desired identity, they are more motivated to learn.

In research on entrepreneurship, scholars have also begun to explore the idea of self-concept as a means of predicting future entrepreneurial outcomes (Cardon *et al.*, 2009). Hoang & Gimeno (2015:4) state that thinking about possible identities can *"guide and motivate goal-oriented behavior, often to the extent that a possible role becomes an actual one"*. Oyserman *et al.*, (2006) refer to possible selves as trajectories or roadmaps that could get the individual to where they want to be. Research on entrepreneurs shows that there are many individuals who express intent to become an entrepreneur but have not taken any concrete steps (Van Gelderen *et al.*, 2005); therefore, it is necessary for us to consider which factors and forces move individuals to become entrepreneurs that we should share with our students (see Johnsson *et al.*, in this volume).

Through the activities introduced in this chapter, we provide opportunities for students to identify their aspirations about who they want to become, asking them to analyse what actions they need to take to be able to fulfil that desire. These activate a students' schema about themselves to assist them in building cognitive maps that help them understand and process such information. Thus, we concentrate our efforts on offering an entrepreneurship education in which the students are presented with real opportunities to take entrepreneurial action.

International Posture

Research on international posture became mainstream through Nakata's (1995) work on international orientation and Yashima's (2002) development of international posture and willingness to communicate. She defined the construct of international posture as the tendency of some learners to be *"more interested in or have more favorable attitudes toward ... interest in foreign or international affairs, willingness to go overseas to stay or work, readiness to interact with intercultural partners, and, one hopes, openness or a non-ethnocentric attitude toward different cultures, among others"* (Yashima, 2002:57). International posture is considered to be a positive international attitude made up of at least three dimensions: 1) interest in an international vocation or activities; 2) tendency to approach rather than avoid dissimilar others, such as non-Japanese in Japan; and 3) interest in foreign affairs. Students who are conscious of how they relate to the world tend to be more motivated when studying and seeking employment. In Yashima's work, she theorised that the presence of international posture in young Japanese students could also represent the favourable attitudes they have towards English and what English symbolises. Therefore, we see it as a way to explore how connected students feel to the international community, specifically in terms of business and work. We speculate that the presence or absence of international posture affects a learner's motivation, which in turn leads to proficiency as well as self-confidence. We suggest that international posture could be a strong predictor of students' interest in entrepreneurship.

Through the activities in this chapter, we show how to stimulate students' interests in international activities. We show how to develop pedagogical practices that support the development of student possible selves and their international posture in relation to entrepreneurship and their future careers.

Section 3: Method

The following section explains the teaching method of Content and Language Integrated Learning (CLIL) and how this method can be used as vehicle through which we can teach entrepreneurship.

CLIL

The CLIL framework used in Japan and Europe is based on Coyle's work integrating culture, cognition, communication, and content (Coyle, 2006, 1999; Coyle et al., 2010), more commonly known as the 4 C's, into each lesson. In the context of entrepreneurship education in Japan, the content covers business knowledge necessary for the effective management of business opportunities' along with knowledge on the mechanics of developing a business plan, marketing, and leadership. When considering cognition, the teacher needs to predict what kind of questions the students will ask and how the activities activate the student's higher and lower order thinking skills, especially critical thinking, curiosity, analysis, and logical thinking skills. In terms of communication, English is the medium of learning through which students develop and practice content-related language (specifically business language) through activities. Finally, for culture, a CLIL business lesson would focus on intercultural business communication, global business strategies, and border crossing of goods, services, and people. The goals of this business lesson would be to increasing students' intercultural understanding of business, since entrepreneurs need to network, forge partnerships, collaborate, and effectively communicate ideas. What we would like to see is the expansion of similar CLIL Professional Skills courses integrated into entrepreneurial programmes.

This research acknowledges the work being conducted in Europe, namely the Edison project which uses CLIL in entrepreneurial education in Austria, and seeks to suggest policy borrowing and development in an Asian context (see Kolehmainen, in this volume). In Japan, the growth of CLIL programmes and English as a medium of instruction (EMI) is phenomenal (Brown, 2014). However, it is an underdeveloped area in the context of business English, business skills, and career courses, and almost non-existent in entrepreneurial education courses in Japan.

Section 4: Practice

In the following section, we share three example activities used in classroom practice that operationalise the government policies outlined above. The activities are part of two courses. One initially developed in 2009 called "Professional Skills" at Toyo Gakuen University, Tokyo and the other titled "Japan Studies Program I" taught at Fukushima University. These courses are part of a 60-week course for 3rd and 4th year university students from a variety of academic fields. The intended learning outcomes of the Professional Skills course are that students are expected to understand the main concepts of business, understand the value of thinking globally, be able to demonstrate the ability to communicate effectively, think critically, have an awareness of entrepreneurism, and understand and utilise business-related professional skills in a variety of tasks both inside and outside the classroom. As the course is skills based, we looked at how to define professional and entrepreneurial skills from the outset. The work of Payne (2000:354) gives the definition of "skills" as being *"broader and more equivocal than it has ever been"*. A "skill" can mean whatever *"employers and policy makers want it to mean"* (Payne, 2000:361). In their research, Shuman et al. (2005) defined professional skills in two categories: process skills (communication, teamwork) and awareness skills (knowledge of contemporary issues). Although theses definitions are quite clear, for the purpose of this course, professional skills were broadly defined as a core set of competencies—both innate and acquired—necessary to successfully function and thrive in a corporate environment (Birchley, 2012). A list of skills (or competencies) was drawn up based on government policies and research from the fields of career design, business, leadership, and management. Recently, the skills list has been adapted and enhanced in line with the literature on the 21st Century Skills. Moreover, a second set of courses called the "Japan Studies Program" has been developed at Fukushima University which follows a similar syllabus design. The activities described in the next section are taught in English using the CLIL methodology. The table below shows how each activity targets the characteristics and skills that are described in the policies of the Japanese Ministry of Education.

Activity	Characteristics	Skills
HSBC Commercial	Challenge, motivation, zeal, risk-taking.	Imagination, creativity, attitude, optimism.
Dragons Den	Challenge, ambition, passion, courage.	Communication, presentation, research, planning, decisiveness.
Buying and Selling	Challenge, ambition, courage.	Research, problem-solving, planning, judgement, patience.

Table 3: *Activity targets from policy descriptors.*

HSBC Commercial Activity

The Hongkong (sic) and Shanghai Banking Cooperation (HSBC) developed a series of commercials in the 2000s that endeavoured to position itself as "the world's local bank". These commercials serve as excellent teaching materials (McCasland, 2010) for developing knowledge of entrepreneurship and particularly imagined possible selves. Students are shown a commercial and through guided activities are asked to identify with a narrative about a young successful entrepreneur, a self-made business person; to see the type of business traits it takes to be a successful entrepreneur; to visualise the steps it takes to become a successful, self-made business person; to identity the challenges and difficulties that an entrepreneur faces when breaking out of the norm—taking a new idea from concept to reality; to contemplate definitions of success; and to introduce, primarily intuitively, the nomenclature of entrepreneurship and start-up business ventures. The commercial featuring a young Egyptian entrepreneur is particular affective for helping students to query, imagine, co-create, and identify with the qualities of entrepreneurship (HSBC AMANAH—Tour Guide, 2009). By watching a narrative of a young entrepreneur in Egypt who, over the course of many years, goes from being a taxi driver to starting a tour company and finally expanding to be a major tour agency executive, students experience vicariously the joys of success. Students can see that entrepreneurial spirit is more than having a dream, it is about finding a gap in the market—the difference between *"I can do that"* and *"I can do that better than anyone else is doing it in the current market"*. Furthermore, in order to develop a possible self, students are asked to step into the role of the character by constructing an interior dialogue with that person. Students work through the steps the entrepreneur must make in order to be successful in business by imagining what that person thinks and feels. Through in-depth discussions, students are then asked to draw comparisons with their possible future. By answering prescribed questions of application, students reach a deeper level of understanding about their own identity while identifying with the person in the narrative. By drawing on the emotive side of a successful narrative, students are confronted with the emotional fortitude it takes to be a successful entrepreneur, and thus they become aware of the gap in their experience and knowledge. The template outlined in Table 4 is designed to be applied to other HSBC commercials in this series as well as Tour Guide (2009); for example: Veterinarian, Family Business, Lemonade Stand, Taxi, and Shop Keepers.

1) Watch commercial;
2) Imagine and co-create background information—through answering prompts;
3) Develop a personality and trait profile;
4) Chart the events by breaking down the narrative into steps of opportunities, successes, and failures, while assigning a timeline;
5) Analyse the character for business skills and acumen;
6) Identify with characters. Contemplate how they are similar and different to you.
7) Expand the narrative by creating detailed scenarios of what happened before and after;
8) Research the business sector, the county, the geography, and the culture;
9) Apply to your current situation.

Table 4: HSBC commercial activity structure.

Dragons' Den-style Business Pitch Activity

The television entrepreneurial game show *Tigers of Money* was originally made and broadcast in Japan (Nisen, 2013). Its premise was that in order to obtain funding from an angel investor, potential entrepreneurs must pitch their business ideas within a certain time limit and then field questions about their idea (potential business plan). After a successful run in Japan, the rights were bought by overseas companies and the show was produced and aired in Europe as *Dragons' Den* (BBC, 2016) and in America and Australia as *Shark Tank*. Through this television show, a number of activities, both business and language related, can be utilised.

Remarkably, at least from our experience, Japanese students are unable to list the names of any successful Japanese entrepreneurs, particularly those under the age of 30. During the lesson, students are introduced to entrepreneurs from Forbes magazine 2016 successful female entrepreneurs under 30 (Forbes, 2016). Students cite funding as a major barrier to setting up a business, thus the lesson follows by exploring Kickstarter.com, crowdfunding, and the concept of angel investors. This helps students to see that not only selling goods and services goes beyond borders but also opportunities for investment and not just restricted to domestic investors.

Through watching and analysing a case study from *Dragons' Den*, in an episode where three young British gentlemen successfully pitch their idea for a company called "Pop da Pop", students are able to imagine the possibility of taking an idea from concept to pitch. Observing the role models in the show, the students learn the skills necessary to pitch an idea. The ultimate goal of the lesson is for students to imagine themselves as entrepreneurs; they develop a product and pitch it for investment. Therefore, students develop not only knowledge about investment but also the language for presentation, creativity, and teamwork skills. This activity encompasses the METI (2009) definitions of entrepreneurship, particularly entrepreneurial spirit as a passion for challenge, creativity, and curiosity, and the entrepreneurial qualities such as the ability to gather and analyse information, make judgments, and lead.

1) Introduce successful entrepreneurs from Forbes; highlighting the young, Japanese entrepreneurs; discuss the concept of entrepreneurship in Japan;
2) Discuss the concept of investment, putting particular attention on Kickstarter, crowdfunding, and angel investors;
3) Show an episode of *Dragons' Den*; analyse the products, the people, the performance, the presentation;
4) Task students with working in pairs to develop a product/service to pitch to an investor (without using PowerPoint);
5) Present, watch, give feedback on ideas and practicalities of the business idea;
6) Students are encouraged to use Kickstarter if they believe their idea is very viable, in order to take the idea from the classroom to the real world.

Table 5: Dragons' den activity structure.

Buying and Selling Activity

In the examples above, it is one thing to teach principles of business and entrepreneurial spirit in the classroom and quite another to take it out of the classroom where things get a bit more complex. In this activity, students test their skills in the real world by purchasing something in Japan, and reselling it for a profit in the USA. This activity helps to inspire entrepreneurial spirit; introduces business concepts through practical application; demonstrates value-added as it relates to border-crossing; and gives students an opportunity to develop their sales, marketing, and communication skills (in a foreign language).

1) Students buy one or more items valued at 10-10,000 yen in Japan (approximately $.10 to $100);
2) Take the item(s) to the USA;
3) Develop strategies for marketing and selling the item in the USA;
4) Sell for a profit;
5) The winners are the students who make the most profit in monetary value and mark-up value;
6) Provide feedback on student surveys and reflect for future application.

Table 6: Structure for buying and selling activity.

The context of this activity was very unique and may not be so easily replicated. Six university students were travelling to the USA for an eight-week business internship in a large city in the south. Thus, they already had a clear purpose as well as funding to travel across international borders. In after-task interviews and through surveys, we found that students used a variety of marketing methods such as face-to-face (friends and colleagues), posters, Internet auction sites (e.g., E-bay), and cold calling direct to outlets. In each instance, students had to write their own text in English and develop communication skills with potential customers. They developed their own strategy for selling, worked independently and asked for advice when needed, integrated technologies (such as using online apps for monitoring mark-ups and profits), and used their personality traits to sell. There were students who were also unsuccessful in their attempts to sell overseas. This was primarily due to poor time management in addition to a lack of structure and understanding of the challenge. In this case, failure was seen as a key learning opportunity and teachable moment.

The original idea was to help students comprehend the essence of business—or at least, one part of business: buying low and selling high—with profit as the first motivator. In hindsight, it may seem that this activity was basically a marketing exercise, but it was surprising to find that four of the six students had never tried any form of entrepreneurial activity such as buying or selling any product or service.

The activities highlighted above attempted to fulfil the goals of CLIL classes according to Coyle's (1999) framework by having the students develop business knowledge, entrepreneurial spirit, a passion for challenge, creativity, and curiosity; as well as entrepreneurial qualities such as the ability to gather and analyse information, make judgments, and lead. Moreover, they help to foster human resources with strong communication skills. Alongside developing these entrepreneurial skills and language skills, students are simultaneously imagining themselves as successful entrepreneurs in an intercultural, global context.

Section 5: Advice for Developing Class Activities

The activities above require much preparation to be successful, thus the following section provides advice on developing CLIL-style lessons for entrepreneurship. Moreover, in these kinds of lessons, a lot of learning happens unexpectedly. These surprising moments bring out the students with innate ability and talent—sometimes discovered for the first time. For teachers who require a great deal of control, this style of teaching may prove difficult, since flexibility and agility are necessary to teaching language as it occurs whilst also demonstrating a mastery of business. Below is a checklist for developing such activities:

- Develop clear principles that organise the aims and goals of the activity;
- Develop and communicate clear guidelines and educational objectives for students;
- Find a balance of how and when to advise students and when to let them work independently—and even fail;
- Balance freedom and form when teaching both language and content;
- Encourage students to research marketing outside of class and provide structures for them to accomplish this;
- Publicise such activities and contests in a way that does not interfere with the class, thus helping develop a spirit of entrepreneurship on campus;
- Encourage and promote team building amongst students;
- Help students develop their own business identity, sense of self, and capabilities while nurturing their visions;
- Share examples of your (the teacher's) own entrepreneurial history, including both the successes and failures;
- Use various media and technology, such as apps, to give students multiple real-world examples by tapping into their generation's need to be connected;
- Use humanistic principles of teaching in order to coach students in discovering their possible selves.

Table 7: Advice for developing activities.

By connecting entrepreneurship with language study, students can become engaged with authentic materials and situations; they can develop soft skills while studying about concepts and immediately put their knowledge into practice. These activities engage students and encourage the development of international posture and raise awareness of imagined selves.

Conclusion

Further research needs to be conducted in this area, particularly in Japan. Curriculum designers in Asia would do well to look to European models to develop more globally focused entrepreneurial programmes (Garcia et al., 2015; Raposo & de Paco, 2011) and look to the examples in this volume. We have shown that government policies can be operationalised through sound theoretical and methodological frameworks such as international posture, imagined selves, and CLIL. Finally, we urge academics, policy makers, and industry professionals to engage in more interactive discussions to ensure that sufficient opportunities are provided to foster entrepreneurship among young people in Japan.

About the Authors

Dr. Sarah Louisa Birchley is an associate professor in the Faculty of Business Administration, Toyo Gakuen University, Tokyo, Japan. She can be contacted at this e-mail: sarah.birchley@tyg.jp

Philip McCasland is an associate professor in the Department of Economics and Business Administration at Fukushima University in Fukushima, Japan. He can be contacted at this e-mail: mccasland@econ.fukushima-u.ac.jp

Bibliography

Ashizawa, S. (2012). *Why Now? Global Jinzai and Gap Year*. Paper presented at Meiji University Research Institute of International Education Inaugural International Symposium Series 3, Tokyo.

BBC Dragons' Den. (2016). Online Resource: http://www.bbc.co.uk/programmes/b006vq92 [Accessed 3 October 2016].

Birchley, S. L. (2012). Japanese Students' Perceptions of Soft Skills: Teaching Professional Skills and CLIL. *Bulletin of Toyo Gakuen University*, Vol. 21, pp. 182–207.

Brown, H. (2014). Contextual factors driving the growth of undergraduate English –medium instruction programs at universities in Japan. *Asian Journal of Applied Linguistics*, Vol. 1, No. 1, pp. 50–63.

Cardon, M.; J. Wincent; J. Singh, & M. Drnovsek (2009). The nature and experience of entrepreneurial passion. *Academy of Management Review 2009*. Vol. 34, No. 3, pp. 511–532.

Co-media (2016). The Era of Women. Eight Entrepreneurs in their Twenties.

Coyle, D. (1999). Theory and planning for effective classrooms: supporting students in content and language integrated learning contexts. Masih, J. (Ed.) *Learning Through a Foreign Language*. London: CILT.

Coyle, D. (2006). *Developing CLIL: Towards a Theory of Practice*. In Monograph 6, APAC Barcelona.

Coyle, D.; P. Hood & D. Marsh (2010). *Content and Language Integrated Learning*. Cambridge University Press.

Cross S. & H. Markus (1994). Self-schemas, Possible Selves and Competent Performance. *Journal of Educational Psychology*, Vol. 86, No. 3, pp. 423–438.

Forbes (2016). LeaderBoard: *30 UNDER 30: Pioneering Women*. Online Resource: http://www.forbes.com/sites/kathryndill/2016/06/02/30-under-30-pioneering-women/#11fb20de56dd [Accessed 3 October 2016].

Garcia, A.; F. Seoane & J. Garcia (2015). *Entrepreneurship and the University: how to create entrepreneurs from university institutions*. XXIX AEDEM Annual Meeting San Sebastián / Donostia 2015.

HSBC Amanah Banking (2009). TOUR GUIDE. [Television Commercial]. United Arab Emirates. Online Resource: https://www.coloribus.com/adsarchive/tv-commercials/hsbc-amanah-islamic-banking-tour-guide-12967805/ [Accessed 3 October 2016].

Hoang, H. & J. Gimeno (2015). Entrepreneurial Identity. *Entrepreneurship*. Vol. 3, pp. 1–6.

Ito, T.; T. Kaneta & S. Sundstrom (2015). Does University Entrepreneurship Work in Japan?: A Comparison of Industry-University Research Funding and Technology Transfer Activities Between the UK and Japan. *Journal of Innovation and Entrepreneurship.* Vol. 5, No. 8, pp. 1–21.

Kagami, S. (2015). Innovation and University Entrepreneurship: Challenges Facing Japan Today. S. Oum; P. Intarakumnerd; G. Abonyi & S. Kagami (Eds.) *Innovation, Technology Transfers, Finance, and Internationalization of SMEs' Trade and Investment,* ERIA Research Project Report FY2013, No. 14. Jakarta: ERIA, pp. 97–121.

KickStarter.com (2016). Kickstarter.com.

Markus, H. R. & P. Nurius (1986). Possible selves. *American Psychologist,* Vol. 41, pp. 954–969.

Meara, N.; J. Day; L. Chalk & R. Phelps (1995). Possible selves: applications for career counseling. *Journal of Career Assessment.* Vol. 3, pp. 259–277.

McCasland, P. (2010). Not Just a Commercial: Narrative That Demonstrates Communication Dynamics. In *KOTESOL Proceedings 2009: Pursuing Professional Excellence in ELT,* Korea TESOL. pp. 235–243.

Ministry of Economy, Trade and Industry (METI) (2009). *Survey Report on Entrepreneurship Programs in Japanese Universities.*

Ministry of Economy, Trade and Industry (METI) (2010). *Global Jinzai.*

Ministry of Economy, Trade and Industry (METI) (2013). *Industrial Competitiveness Enhancement Act.* June 14, 2013, Tokyo, Japan.

Ministry of Education, Culture, Sports, Science and Technology (MEXT) (2003). *White Paper on Education, Culture, Sports, Science and Technology.*

Ministry of Education, Culture, Sports, Science and Technology (MEXT) (2008). *2007 White Paper on Education, Culture, Sports, Science and Technology. Comprehensive Promotion of Education Policy/Internationalization of Universities and Their Local Contribution.*

Ministry of Education, Sports, Science and Technology (MEXT). (2010). *Survey of Industry-University Cooperation.* 16 August 2010.

Ministry of Education, Culture, Sports, Science and Technology (MEXT) (2012). *Daigaku kaikaku jikko puran.* June 2012. [The Plan to Change Universities].

Ministry of Education, Culture, Sports, Science and Technology (MEXT) (2013). *Report compiled on the second basic plan for the promotion of education.*

Nakata, Y. (1995). New goals for Japanese learners of English. *The Language Teacher,* Vol. 19, No. 5, pp. 17–20.

Nisen, M. (2013). Business Insider. Here's What Shark Tank Looks Like in Nine Countries. *Business Insider.* Online Resource: http://www.businessinsider.

com/shark-tank-international-versions-2013-11?r=US&IR=T&IR=T [Accessed 3 October 2016].

Nufufu.com (2014). *Why doesn't the business start-up rate in Japan go up?*

Oyserman, D.; D. Bybee & K. Terry (2006). Possible selves and academic out comes: How and when possible selves impel action. *Journal of Personality and Social Psychology*, Vol. 91, pp. 188–204.

Payne, J. (2000). The unbearable lightness of skill: the changing meaning of skill in UK policy discourses and some implications for education and training. *Journal of Educational Policy*. Vol. 15, No. 3, pp. 353–369.

Raposo, M. & A. de Paco (2011). Special issue: entrepreneurship and education links between education and entrepreneurial activity. *Entrepreneur Management Journal*, Vol. 7, No. 2, pp. 143–144.

Shuman, L.; M. Besterfield & J. McGourty (2005). The ABET "Professional Skills" – Can they be taught? Can they be assessed? *Journal of Engineering Education*, Vol. 94, No. 1, pp. 41–55.

Shinato, T.; K. Kamei & L. P. Dana (2013). Entrepreneurship education in Japanese universities– how do we train for risk taking in a culture of risk adverseness? *International Journal of Entrepreneurship and Small Business*. Vol. 20, No. 2, pp. 184–204.

Yashima, T. (2002). Willingness to communicate in a second language: The Japanese EFL context. *Modern Language Journal*, Vol. 86, pp. 54–66.

Yokoyama, K. & S. L. Birchley. (2014). Japanese Women Working on the World Stage: HRM in the UN. *Proceedings of the Women's Leadership and Empowerment Conference, Tomorrow People*, Bangkok Thailand.

Yokoyama, K. (2015). Emerging Japanese Self-initiated Expatriates (SIE) Case Studies from Bangkok and Hong Kong. *Proceedings of The Fifth Workshop in Talent Management by the European Institute for Advanced Studies in Management* (EIASM).

Van Gelderen, M. W.; A. R. Thurik, & N. Bosma (2005). Success and risk factors in the prestartup phase. *Small Business Economics*. Vol. 24, No. 4, pp. 365–380.

Wharton School (2013). The Entrepreneurship Vacuum in Japan: Why it Matters and How to Address It. *Knowledge@Warton*, 2 January, 2013. Online Resource: http://knowledge.wharton.upenn.edu/article/the-entrepreneurship-vacuum-in-japan-why-it-matters-and-how-to-address-it/ [Accessed 3 October 2016].

Chapter 5
The Role of Universities as Catalysts within Entrepreneurial Ecosystems

Hani T. Fadel, Moaz Mojaddidi & Osama M. Ashri

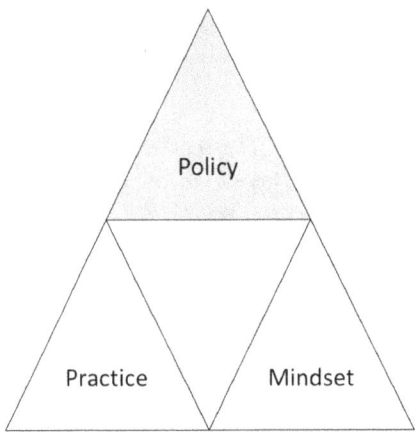

Introduction

Our chapter is an important contribution to this section on policy – and to the book *Teaching and Learning Entrepreneurship in Higher Education* – because we build arguments to answer the question: "Can entrepreneurship really be taught?" And we link our answers to the policies of universities when establishing and maintaining important roles in entrepreneurial ecosystems. Perhaps history provided us with conflicting answers to this apparently simple question. The arguments are directed towards the understanding that entrepreneurship can in fact be taught but only through practice supported by a robust entrepreneurial ecosystem starting at the university level. Following some research, it appears that entrepreneurship in higher education may be looked upon through one of three broad categories: 1) direct teaching of entrepreneurship to students and its incorporation into university courses and/or modules (i.e., curricular activities);

2) establishment of entities that would foster entrepreneurship as a culture among students and graduates (i.e., extracurricular activities); and 3) universities that launch their own enterprises such as holding companies and subsidiaries, buying shares in companies, and building hotels and other investments (i.e., spin-offs) (Robinson & Blenker, 2014). Touching upon the possible instrumental roles that universities may play can motivate policymakers to bring relevant sectors to work in a complementing manner for the better good of the entrepreneurship mindset in a given nation. Table 1 summarises the different terms and definitions we use in our chapter.

Term	Running Definition
Entrepreneurship	The pursuit of opportunity beyond resources controlled (Stevenson, 1985).
Entrepreneur	Someone who perceives an opportunity and creates an organisation that pursues it (Bygrave & Zacharakis, 2011).
Entrepreneurial ecosystem	A system whose domains/components must interact in a coherent way with the purpose of creating an enabling environment where entrepreneurs can thrive and prosper.
Saudi Arabia's *Vision 2030*	Lays out Saudi Arabia's blueprint for achieving the Kingdom's ambitious long-term goals. The vision is based on three main themes: 1) A Vibrant Society; 2) A Thriving Economy; 3) An Ambitious Nation.
Start-ups	Entrepreneurial ventures typically describing newly emerging, fast-growing businesses. Usually refers to a company, a partnership, or an organisation designed to rapidly develop a scalable business model.
Business Incubators	According to the International Business Innovation Association (IBIA), business incubators nurture the development of entrepreneurial companies, helping them survive and grow during the start-up period, when they are most vulnerable. These programmes provide their client companies with business support services and resources tailored to young firms (Business Incubation FAQs, 2016).
Rising universities	Fairly newly established universities, lacking significant infrastructure and human capital.
Established universities	Universities started >30 years ago with reasonable infrastructure, facilities, and human capital.

Table 1: Arbitrary and adopted definitions of terms that will be used throughout the chapter.

Reading our chapter, you will gain the following three insights:
1. what is an entrepreneurial ecosystem, and how does it link to higher education;
2. what are the possible policies of universities in establishing, and maintaining a role in governing entrepreneurial ecosystems; and
3. what are the policies and roles of Taibah University in establishing and maintaining their role in an entrepreneurial ecosystem.

We have structured out chapter in four main sections: In the first section, we recognise the broad description of an entrepreneurial ecosystem. What is it? What are the elements that comprise it? And in what context can it be used? In the second section, we shifts to the national entrepreneurial trends and tendencies in Saudi Arabia. Saudi Arabia is located in the southeastern corner of the Asian continent, with a total population of 31 million, as of 2015. It is a diverse and evolving economy with significant cultural impact, having clear plans for diversifying economic resources and involvement of the coming generations in self-employing and rewarding businesses. An overview of the current entrepreneurial ecosystem in Saudi Arabia is also given. In section three, we move on to discuss how universities fit as catalysts within the entrepreneurial ecosystem. Focus is placed on university roles in the Saudi entrepreneurial ecosystem. Inspiring examples are given from current Saudi entrepreneurial movements. In section four, we display the case of Taibah University – an ambitious, rising university that is making promising steps forward in an attempt to reserve its spot on the entrepreneurial movement map (i.e., the ecosystem of both the Madinah region and of Saudi Arabia at large).

Section 1: The Entrepreneurial Ecosystem

In their summit in Brisbane in 2014, the G20 leaders called for an enhancement in economic growth through promoting competition, entrepreneurship, and innovation (G20 Leaders' Communiqué, 2014). They also advocated the reduction of unemployment, especially amongst younger generations, through encouragement of entrepreneurship (G20 Leaders' Communiqué, 2014).

Historically, the influence of governments and their roles in encouraging entrepreneurship has evolved and changed significantly. Governmental influence ranged between attempts for mere replication of known success stories to the development of major science parks, fostering universities, research and development (R&D) centres, and venture financiers in search for "hot deals" (Mazzarol, 2014). The success of such attempts varied notably, and in light of such variation, establishment of entrepreneurial ecosystems seemed very appealing.

The concept of entrepreneurial ecosystem was used earlier by management writers as an umbrella term for fostering economic development and wealth creation. Figure 1 shows the nine major elements comprising an entrepreneurial ecosystem, where it clearly illustrates the interconnections and the interdependencies between the various elements (Mazzarol, 2014).

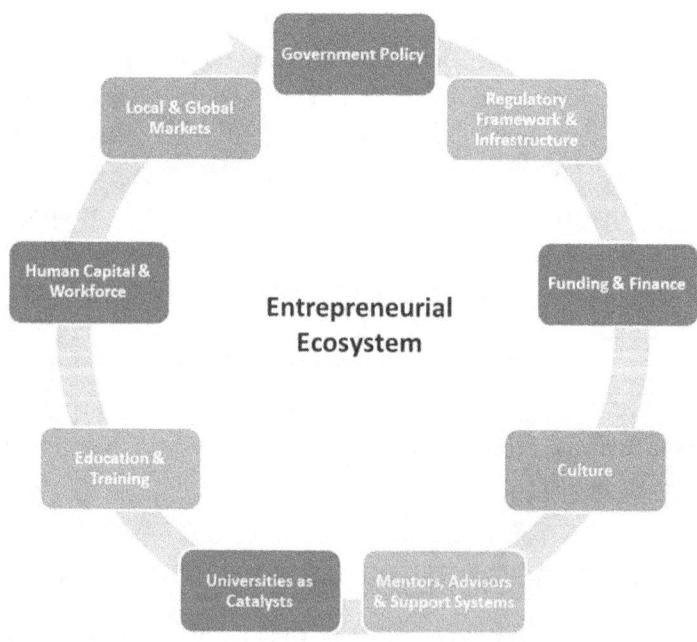

Figure 1: The different elements of the Entrepreneurial Ecosystem as adopted from Mazzarol (2014).

Isenberg (2010) clearly highlighted the importance of governmental policies within the entrepreneurial ecosystem. Governments should be aware that the replication of other models, despite their success, does not necessarily imply a successful transformation, since each model is built in different conditions and under different circumstances. In addition, the government may consider playing an indirect role in facilitating the incorporation of the private sector from the start, rather than playing a direct managerial and restricting role (Isenberg, 2010).

Section 2: The Entrepreneurial Ecosystem in Saudi Arabia

The general direction of the government of Saudi Arabia, one of the G20 leader nations; was to diversify economic resources. This direction is part of Saudi Arabia's *Vision 2030* (VISION 2030, 2016). *Vision 2030* is composed of three key pillars. The first pillar is related to the status of Saudi Arabia as the heart of the Arab and Islamic worlds. The second is the country's determination to become a global investment powerhouse. The last, but not least, is transforming the country's strategic location into a hub connecting three continents: Asia, Europe, and Africa (Figure 2). An example from Saudi Arabia's *Vision 2030* is illustrated in Figure 3, which shows how the Small and Medium-Sized Enterprise (SME) Authority plans to support the movement. This ambitious vision is supported by the *National Transformation Plan* (NTP2020), which is designed to build the institutional capacity and capabilities needed to achieve the goals of *Vision 2030* (VISION 2030, 2016).

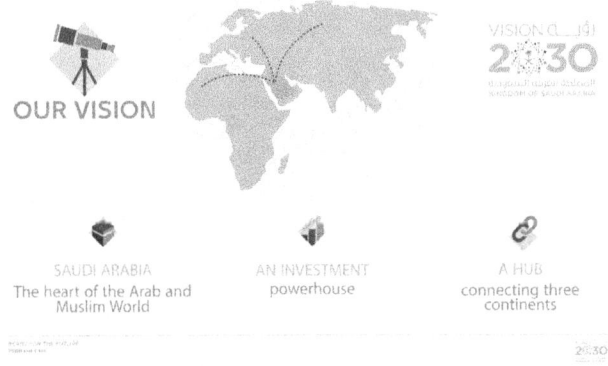

Figure 2: The global importance of Saudi Arabia as foreseen and illustrated by the three key pillars of the Saudi Vision 2030 (VISION 2030, 2016).

Chapter 5

WE WILL FACILITATE
ACCESS TO FUNDING
AND ENCOURAGE
FINANCIAL
INSTITUTIONS TO
ALLOCATE UP TO **20%**
OF OVERALL FUNDING
TO SMES

BY 2030

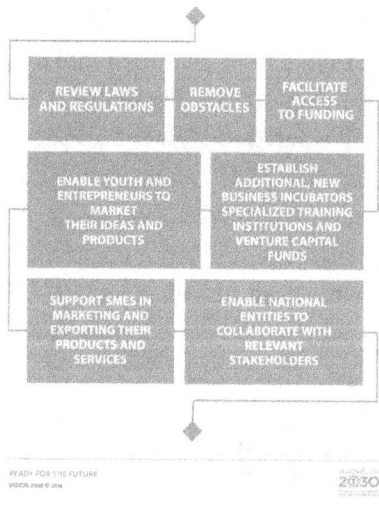

Figure 3: The SME Authority's plan to facilitate and support the entrepreneurship movement as part of the Saudi Arabia's Vision 2030 (VISION 2030, 2016).

Moreover, the central research and grant-providing body in the Kingdom, King Abdulaziz City for Science and Technology (KACST), provided an important game-changing plan along the same transformation line; that is, the National Science, Technology and Innovation Plan (NSTIP).

The NSTIP is meant to direct science research and technology development in Saudi Arabia towards the long-term development goals of the country (Al-Swailem, 2014). In addition, technology-based business incubator programmes (BADIR) were launched by KACST and opened up branches in different parts of the Kingdom, some of which are located in local universities and co-managed by the respective universities and BADIR staff (Khorsheed et al., 2014). Universities are known to play a significant role in achieving national economic priorities, as they contribute to the knowledge and know-how, teach the talent pool needed by employers and develop in students the skills and know-how needed by entrepreneurs.

Section 3: The Role of Universities Within an Entrepreneurial Ecosystem

Universities may generally be involved within an entrepreneurial ecosystem by following one of two models: the bottom-up (community-led) model and the top-down (university-led) model (Graham, 2014). The bottom-up model is operated by the students, alumni, and/or entrepreneurs. It is more or less self-dependent and relies solely on its own efforts to rise within the regional economy. Once successful, a dynamic and inclusive ecosystem results via strong partnerships of trust between the regional entrepreneurial community and the university (Graham, 2014). However, this model may face certain difficulties when attempting to regulate and institutionalise its entrepreneurial profile, since regulating and governing bodies were not involved from the start, although such an aspect should not be of concern if all set requirements are appropriately fulfilled in due course (Graham, 2014).

The top-down or champion model, on the other hand, functions mainly through established university structures and is based on ongoing university research (Graham, 2014). This model accounts for key regulating bodies and stakeholders already from the planning phase, resulting in a robust and fully institutionalised approach (Graham, 2014). One danger facing the model is marginalisation of the students, alumni, and entrepreneurs, which can be minimised with constructive collaborations (Graham, 2014).

Chapter 5

Universities as Entrepreneurial Catalysts

Paul Graham, cofounder of Y Combinator, stated that: "*There are no technology hubs without first rate universities. If you want to make a Silicon Valley, you not only need a university, but one of the top handful in the world.*" Y Combinator is an American seed accelerator started in March 2005 and is arguably considered the world's most powerful start-up incubator. A university can act as a catalyst for entrepreneurship by deepening students' interests to start their own businesses and by providing them with the right environment to pursue such endeavours. To achieve that, universities have to create an energetic environment that sparks and accelerates potential entrepreneurs' action to start their own businesses. A holistic approach is required through building a university-based entrepreneurial ecosystem that includes incubators, mentors, specialised training, and technology commercialisation offices, amongst other elements. The role of such universities as catalysts also extends beyond the boundaries of the campus to engage within the regional entrepreneurial ecosystem, particularly in social entrepreneurship, as illustrated in the case in this chapter.

One celebrated example is the case of Massachusetts Institute of Technology (MIT). According to estimates in a report co-authored by Professor Edward Roberts and Professor Fiona Murray, MIT alumni had launched 30,200 companies as of 2014, employing about 4.6 million people, and generating annual revenues of $1.9 trillion (Aulet *et al.*, 2015). If those MIT-backed companies constituted a country, it would be the 10th largest economy in the world.

Universities and educational bodies would serve as catalysts in the entrepreneurial ecosystem on a national level, providing opportunities for citizens to start up, manage, and successfully implement their own businesses. A notable strategy in this context would be the *Entrepreneurial Thought and Action*®, a unique term – and consequently a school of thought – coined by Babson College, the leading school on entrepreneurship in the US for several consecutive years. The strategy simply focuses on universities' roles of preparing youths to successfully tackle unexpected circumstances in an entrepreneurial way, rather than supplying them with rarely useable factual knowledge (Greenberg *et al.*, 2011).

Universities and colleges may be part of their own entrepreneurial ecosystem (i.e., the higher education entrepreneurial ecosystem), implementing a university-based entrepreneurship ecosystem that gets students more immersed on the practice side of entrepreneurship beyond merely the theories taught in the classroom. This can be achieved by integrating vital resources for fostering an environment where students can sprout and thrive as entrepreneurs. Examples of such resources include:

- entrepreneurship courses/programmes;
- incubator/accelerator programmes;
- technology transfer office/technology commercialisation office;
- start-up grants; and/or
- student-run entrepreneurship clubs/organisations.

In addition, the Ministry of Education (MOE) has a number of initiatives related to entrepreneurship as part of the *NTP2020*, with an estimated cost of SAR 99,900,000. These include the development and deployment of the independent schools model to reach 2,000 schools run by small establishments. Developing an awareness programme on investment and entrepreneurship for high school and university students was also another initiative set by the MOE (Ashri, 2016).

How Do Saudi Universities Act as Catalysts Within an Entrepreneurial Ecosystem?

In Saudi Arabia, universities play a central role in transforming the current oil-based economy into an economy that harvests the assets generated by the knowledge-creating bodies in the Kingdom. In response to the national trend stated earlier, universities started establishing vice presidencies of entrepreneurship and innovation. The mandate of these vice presidencies was to create independent business entities owned by universities and private investors to build trust and private investments to increase the private income for those universities. On the other hand, the government, semi-government bodies, and non-governmental organisations (NGOs) established entities that fund, support, and promote entrepreneurships and small and medium-sized enterprises (SMEs) nationwide, which later on started interacting with key educational organisations such as universities.

When looking into Saudi universities, a clear line demarcates established universities from rising ones. Many of the aforementioned programmes/services still do not exist in the latter. Programmes and services in rising universities are more often filtered down to a few courses/programmes and student-run clubs/organisations. Hence, it is vital that rising universities seek to understand why it is difficult to establish the other elements that are still non-existent in their higher education entrepreneurial ecosystem. This should be followed by devising plans to overcome obstacles and accelerate the establishment of the missing pieces of the ecosystem. According to the Saudi *Vision 2030*, the Saudi economy should boost start-ups and SMEs, where rising universities throughout Saudi Arabia should play their role in revolutionising the country's economy.

One solution that seems strategic in building rising universities' capacity is to team up with existing NGOs that have a mandate to stimulate entrepreneurship spirit among the youth (Ashri, 2013). A good example of such an NGO is Injaz, a non-profit organisation that illustrates the value of touting entrepreneurship outside the traditional classroom. Injaz has programmes that promote business and entrepreneurship education at the primary and higher education levels in Saudi Arabia ("Saudi Injaz", 2014). Injaz seeks to educate youths on entrepreneurship, business, and other work-readiness skills through workshops. The programme works closely with the MOE and engages various stakeholders from the private and public sectors.

Another example is Namaa Al Munawara, which is a non-profit, quasi-government organisation whose mandate is to catalyse the entrepreneurship ecosystem within Madinah or the Almadinah Almunawwara region of Saudi Arabia while contributing to the region's overall socio-economic development (see Figure 4 for an illustration of the 13 different regions of Saudi Arabia, which are in turn comprised of region capitals and governorates). With the right mandate, competence, and motivation, Namaa Al Munawara has succeeded in orchestrating and developing an ecosystem platform for spurring entrepreneurism in the Almadinah Almunawwara region. This ecosystem platform is comprised of the following five essential components: regional competitiveness, risk minimisation, access to market, capacity building, and funding. To address these aforementioned areas, five strategic integrated initiatives were spawned, which are: Almunwara Innovation & Design Labs (for females); Madina Made (a seal for authenticating the origin of products produced in the region); Almunwara Industrial Development and Wahat Almunwara for retail in addition to Almunwara Headquarter spanning an area of more than 6000 m² that will house a wide spectrum of activities and initiatives for fostering the regional entrepreneurial ecosystem (Ashri, 2015).

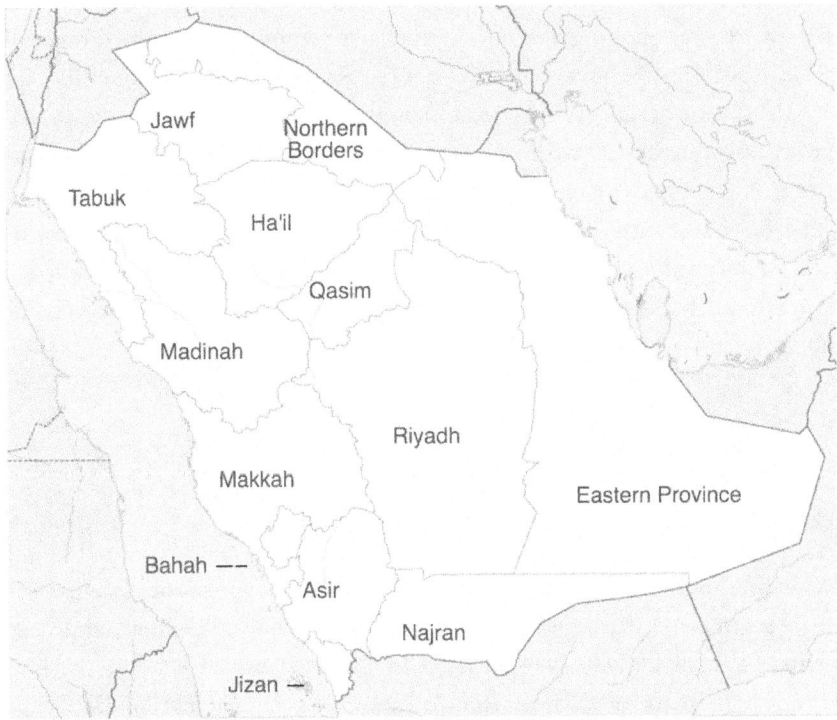

Figure 4: The 13 different regions of Saudi Arabia, each of which is comprised of a region capital and governorates (Source: Wikipedia).

Leading Examples of Educational Organisations within the Entrepreneurial Ecosystem of Saudi Arabia

There are at least a handful of inspiring examples that are currently contributing to the entrepreneurial movements in Saudi Arabia and are in line with the national *Vision 2030*. From the governmental sector, one should mention King Abdullah University for Science and Technology (KAUST), which is a good example – although nonconventional – of a university that harnesses the true power of partnership between large corporations and the academic world to create research that can be translated immediately into industries. However, the biggest endowment for a government university was created and raised funds for by King Saud University (KSU) in Riyadh, the oldest university in the Kingdom. Yet, Umm Al Qura University (UQU), although considered to be a rising university, still demonstrated numerous success stories on different aspects (Ashri, 2013). It is worth mentioning that UQU forms a nice and unusual example of a local bottom-up entrepreneurial model. King Abdullah Economic City (KAEC), another emerging governmental organisation, has recently signed promising agreements with Babson Global in the US to initiate collaborations on a postgraduate level for the improvement of the entrepreneurial experience in Saudi Arabia. Private sector organisations have also contributed significantly in the Saudi entrepreneurial field. These include, but are not limited to, Prince Sultan University, College of Business and Technology (CBT), Hekmat College, and Effat University (Ashri, 2013).

Section 4: Taibah University: A Case of an Ambitious "Top-Down" Catalyst within a Diverse Entrepreneurial Ecosystem

As is the case with any organisation, universities as educational bodies set their strategic plans based on their respective visions, missions, and core values. Taibah University – situated in the holy city of Madinah – had its strategic plan set with a vision of becoming an internationally recognised, comprehensive, Saudi university dedicated to excellence in teaching, research, and community service (Alsarrani *et al.*, 2011). The plan comprised a number of carefully designed projects, aligned with clearly stated goals. More importantly, a number of directed strategies within the formulated plan reflected the clear intention to serve as an important catalyst within the entrepreneurial ecosystem of the country. Among those directed strategies was "diversifying income resources" through identifying new financial resources (Alsarrani *et al.*, 2011). This was thought to be achieved by:

1. activating partnerships with business and industries;
2. expanding consultation services to private, public, and non-governmental organisations;

3. developing endowment resources;
4. increasing the number of academic chairs;
5. expanding parallel and continuing education programmes.

Also, "creating an appealing and inclusive environment" through building an attractive and inclusive campus was another stated directed strategy by the university (Alsarrani et al., 2011). Means of achievement included:

1. complete the campus construction;
2. replace all leased premises with modern buildings owned by Taibah University;
3. ensure that the campus reflects Madinah cultural heritage;
4. build sport facilities;
5. establish banquet halls;
6. construct convention centres.

Sub-Directories: A Focused Approach to Serve as an Effective Catalyst

In order to refine and time the directions of the university's strategic plan, the vice presidency for business and knowledge innovation was established. The vice presidency envisioned, among other things, supporting the developmental role of the university. This is to be achieved through the building of a stimulating environment for innovation, creativity, and entrepreneurship, activating community partnerships for the development of self-university resources, and achieving a knowledgeable society. In other words, the goals of the vice presidency were all aiming at implanting the entrepreneurship culture in the younger generations. All such goals interrelate and connect to core values such as work enjoyment and happiness service, commitment to quality and excellence, self-monitoring and constructive competition, accountability and professional accounting fair value, partnership of solidarity and responsibility, belonging to the agency and loyalty to the university, continuing education and increasing achievement, readiness and proactive, proactive initiative, and creativity and innovation (Taibah University Vice Presidency for Business and

Knowledge Innovation, 2016). As a natural consequence, and to put plans into actions, the Taibah University Center of Entrepreneurship was established. The center was meant to act as a scientific and professional reference for the successive generations of successful entrepreneurs. It aims at (Taibah University Center of Entrepreneurship, 2016):

1. disseminating entrepreneurial culture and building leadership capacity among university students and employees to empower them to establish and lead entrepreneurial enterprises successfully;

2. development of creativity and innovation skills of students to transform them into creative and innovative pioneers;

3. building positive behaviour among the youth towards self-employment and providing them with the necessary knowledge, experience, and skills to compete in the labour market;

4. acquaintance with the concept and application mechanisms of knowledge economies, building a knowledge society, and the requirements for transition into productive applied education.

Areas of Achievement/Progress	
• Collaboration with local companies to provide opportunities and support for entrepreneurs.	• Collaboration with internal and external, local and international companies and bodies to perform a number of programmes/workshops on building entrepreneurial skills.
• Cooperation with charity foundations to take care of building entrepreneurial projects in local orphanage houses.	• Participation in the Saudi International Conference for Associations and Centers for Entrepreneurship and other national and international workshops.
• Preparation of a project for studying job opportunities and established business areas in front of university students in the construction sector.	• Establishment of a number of virtual student business organisations.

Table 2: Examples of accomplishments of the Taibah University Center of Entrepreneurship by the end of 2015.

The center provides key programmes related to the establishment of a culture of self-employment, programmes on building entrepreneurial skills, and programmes related to entrepreneurial projects and virtual institutions. Table 2 shows a number of accomplishments by the center up to 2015.

Rural Economic Development Program

Taibah University Research and Consulting Institute (TURCI) is a frontier through which the university presents much of its commissioned projects to the community. Its service profile includes applied research, consulting projects, supervisory roles, and technical and academic advice. Although not originally created under the structures intended to support the university's pursuit of injecting entrepreneurial spirit into its community of influence, TURCI started to play a catalytic role in the entrepreneurial ecosystem of the Almadinah Almunawwara region. TURCI chose to embark on a series of consulting projects that initially started as community service projects to employ Saudi labour on the payroll of construction companies in activities that develop rural areas. In less than three years, 932 Saudi villagers living in small communities scattered over 43 villages across the governorate of Alula (one of the seven governorates in the Madinah region) became full-time employees under 11 companies. It is worth mentioning that those particular companies have no standing in Alula governorate. Villagers were employed on the basis of wages in return for production of food products, crops, and livestock. Alula governorate was selected due to its foreseen potential as a tourism area that houses one of UNESCO's heritage sites and is targeted by the government to be carefully developed. However, it still has a long way to go to become a world-class tourist attraction.

The Rural Economic Development Program (REDP) is an extension of the ongoing project titled "Nationalization by Development" (NBD), which has been implemented under the supervision of TURCI in Alula and its rural areas. NBD is primarily focused on creating employment opportunities for rural communities through the corporate social responsibility (CSR) funds of different employing companies that have no existence in the Alula governorate. The NBD is designed as such so that employing companies have contracts with TURCI to formulate projects of a developmental nature that hire local villagers in rural areas to set up various types of farms and are paid fixed salaries for obtaining certain output from these farms. Farm products are sold in the local market by the employees, who share a certain percentage of the sale proceeds with the employing company. NBD has little focus on local economic development, as the output targets against the monthly salary are set very low, and there is no regular monitoring from the employing companies' side of the actual situation on the ground.

REDP is designed to move from an employment-centred approach to a more rural economic development focus. Just like NBD, REDP will involve setting up various farming and non-farming subprojects in rural areas, consisting of:

- Moringa tree farms;
- sheep and goat farms;
- women business centres, and others.

However, under REDP, these projects will be designed, implemented, and monitored on more scientific grounds, and private sector investors will be involved from the beginning to move through certain phases (Figure 5).

Basic Production (Phase 1) → Value Additions (Phase 2) → Export (Phase 3)

Figure 5: The REDP project movement phases.

The Gaming Industry and Establishment of Fabrication Laboratories

Another path that rising universities could pursue to "catalyse" entrepreneurship is by focusing on the gaming industry and application development among young generations, where start-ups can be built around online games and applications that provide certain services. The relatively low budget and little need to develop complex business models and logistics may elect this option to be strategic and central to create start-ups for students and new graduates of such disciplines.

Building a fabrication laboratory in rising universities is a third option to facilitate its students joining the "Fab Lab" culture that is spreading fast throughout the world. Here, students are invited to try and fabricate models of the ideas they are developing and working on to create prototypes. However, building the fabrication lab without having a full system in place may have a negative impact on the process. Nevertheless, it has been shown that it is rather easy to harvest creativity and convert intellectual property to possible assets of commercial value. Hence, an intellectual property policy that regulates the relationships of all property rights between stakeholders is a mandatory starting point.

Virtual Student Business Organisations: A Unique University Entrepreneurial Experience

The Center of Entrepreneurship at Taibah University launched a pioneering project by establishing virtual student business organisations. These would ultimately enable students to apply business practices on the basis of professional investment and scientifically solid grounds; be unique in creativity, innovation, and leadership skills; build and run entrepreneurial enterprises successfully; form a positive attitude towards self-employment; and realise the connection between the university outcome and the labour market requirements.

The process starts by submitting a proposal for a project by the students, either from one of the suggested topics by the center, or from the students themselves. Either way, the project is expected to fill in an area that forms a common public and labour market interest. The center and the university, accordingly, cover all legal aspects and signing of contracts with related bodies or second parties, without the need of issuing an official commercial record from the Ministry of Commerce. The university would also provide support in handling the financial part through the formal university accounting system. Such steps would allow the students at this stage to focus on the actual experience without the hassle of preparation and exhaustive legal paperwork and measures. In addition, this positively impacts the university's reputation in the market by assuring that the approved projects are conducted based on certain standards. However, care is taken that the students will not get carried away in these simulation exercises without being aware of the circumstances and obstacles awaiting them in the real world.

Several projects have already been established in areas of translation, food supply, programming, graphics designing and media, all with promising results. Others are still underway in various fields such as tourism, recycling, and automobile care (Abu Bakr, 2014).

Chapter 5

Conclusion

The role of universities as catalysts within the entrepreneurial ecosystem is evident. Their contribution in creating a culture of entrepreneurship is central for economic competitiveness and success as well as in economic sustainability. The presented case is an example of the top-down entrepreneurial model and demonstrates how governmental policy may positively affect the different components of the ecosystem, including the role of universities. Several innovative strategies may lead to achieving the goals set by the interacting elements of the entrepreneurial ecosystem, particularly those involving empowering the younger generations with the necessary confidence and skills to "swim" safely and independently in the market. Despite the statement of strategic plans and clear visions, rising universities still struggle to reach their stated goals, particularly those concerning entrepreneurship, due to deficiencies in various aspects such as financial and human capitals and infrastructure.

Acknowledgement

The authors would like to thank the vice presidency for business and knowledge innovation at Taibah University and its different subdivisions for providing some of the information used in this report.

Disclaimer

The authors report no conflict of interest related to the mentioned information. Data were collected from readily available information from official online resources. The flow of information represents the views of the authors.

About the Authors

Hani T. Fadel is an Assistant Professor of Periodontology with a degree in Medical Education. He currently serves as Academic Vice Dean and supervises the Smile Dental Student Club at Taibah University Dental College and Hospital (TUDCH), Madinah, Saudi Arabia. He can be contacted at this e-mail: hani.fadel@yahoo.com

Moaz Mojaddidi is Assistant Professor of Diabetic Neuropathy at Taibah University College of Medicine. He currently serves as Dean of Research and Consultation Institute at the university. He can be contacted at this e-mail: moaz.manchester@gmail.com

Osama M. Ashri is the Head of Entrepreneurship and SME Development at King Abdullah Economic City. He previously served as VP of Strategy and VP of Industrial Development at Namaa Almunawara. He can be contacted at this e-mail: oashri@gmail.com

Bibliography

Abu Bakr, M. (2014). *The Entrepreneurial System and Its Stimulating Environment.* Paper presented at the Saudi International Conference for Entrepreneurship Associations and Centers, Riyadh, Saudi Arabia.

Al-Swailem, A. M. (2014). Saudi national science, technology and innovation plan towards knowledge based economy. *BMC Genomics*,Vol. 15, No. 2.

Alsarrani, A. Q.; M. A. Alghabban; I. M. Alturk; M. S. Alotaibi; N. S. Al-Qadi; H.H. Noor; S. A.Taher; Z. H. Raddadi; K. Bayomi; M. Alkashef; N. R. Aljabri; H. A. Zaman; M. M. Alsraihi; M. S. Mahroos & A. M. Abdelwahab (2011). *Taibah University 2020 Master Strategic Plan.* Taibah University. T. U. Press.

Ashri, O. M. (2013). *Navigating Saudi Arabia's Entrepreneurial Ecosystem.* Babson College.

Ashri, O. M. (2015). *Concurrent Session 3D: Entrepreneurs Development.* Paper presented at the ATD MENA Conference & Exhibition, Riyadh, Saudi Arabia.

Ashri, O. M. (2016). *Entrepreneurship & SMEs Development: Saudi Arabia's NTP 2020 Relevant Initiatives and Associated Costs.* Online Resource: http://www.slideshare.net/oashri/entrepreneurship-smes-development-saudi-arabias-ntp-2020-relevant-initiatives-and-associated-costs [Accessed 3 October 2016].

Aulet, B.; F. Murray & E. B. Roberts (2015). *Martin Trust Center for MIT Entrepreneurship 2014–2015 Annual Report.* Martin Trust Center for MIT Entrepreneurship. December, 2015.

Business Incubation FAQs (2016). Online Resouce: https://www.inbia.org/resources/business-incubation-faq [Accessed 3 October 2016].

Bygrave, W. D. & A. Zacharakis (2011). *Entrepreneurship.* West Sussex: John Wiley & Sons Ltd.

G20 Leaders' Communiqué (2014). Paper presented at the G20 Leaders' Summit, Brisbane, Australia.

Graham, R. (2014). *MIT Skoltech Initiative: Creating university-based entrepreneurial ecosystems: Evidence from emerging world leaders.* Massachusetts Institute of Technology.

Greenberg, D.; K. McKone-Sweet & H. J. Wilson (2011). *Entrepreneurial Thought and Action: A Methodology for Developing Entrepreneurial Leaders.* Online Resource http://www.babson.edu/executive-education/education-educators/babson-insight/Articles/Pages/entrepreneurial-thought-action-methodology-developing-entrepreneurial-leaders.aspx [Accessed 3 October 2016].

Isenberg, D. (2010). How to Start an Entrepreneurial Revolution. *The big idea.* Online Resource: https://hbr.org/2010/06/the-big-idea-how-to-start-an-entrepreneurial-revolution [Accessed on 3 October 2016].

Khorsheed, M. S.; M. A. Al-Fawzan & A. Al-Hargan (2014). Promoting techno-entrepreneurship through incubation: An overview at BADIR program for technology incubators. *Innovation*, Vol. 16, No. 2, pp. 238–249.

Mazzarol, T. (2014). *6 Ways Governments Can Encourage Entrepreneurship.* Online Resource: https://www.weforum.org/agenda/2014/12/6-ways-governments-can-encourage-entrepreneurship/ [Accessed 3 October 2016].

Robinson, S. & P. Blenker (2014). Tensions between rhetoric and practice in entrepreneurship education; an ethnography from Danish higher education. *European Journal of Higher Education*, Vol. 4, pp. 80–93.

Saudi Injaz. (2014). Online Resource: http://www.injaz-saudi.org/ [Accessed 3 October 2016].

Stevenson, H. H. (1985). *Preserving entrepreneurship as you grow.* Boston, MA: Harvard Business School.

Taibah University Center of Entrepreneurship (2016). Online Resource: https://www.taibahu.edu.sa/Pages/AR/Sector/SectorPage.aspx?ID=6&PageId=36 [Accessed 3 October 2016].

Taibah University Vice Presidency for Business and Knowledge Innovation (2016). Online Resource: https://www.taibahu.edu.sa/Pages/AR/Sector/SectorPage.aspx?ID=6&PageId=217 [Accessed 3 October 2016].

VISION 2030 (2016). *National Ttransformation Program.* Online Resource: http://vision2030.gov.sa/en [Accessed 3 October 2016].

Section 2: Practice

Chapter 6

Integrating Innovation and Entrepreneurship into All Undergraduate Courses: The Case of La Trobe University in Australia

Silvia McCormack & Chris Scanlon

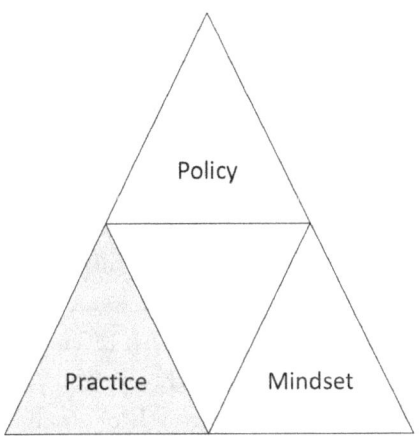

Introduction

Our chapter is an important contribution to this section on practice – and to the book *Teaching and Learning Entrepreneurship in Higher Education* – because we provide a case study of how La Trobe University (LTU) in Melbourne, Australia, has implemented a strategy to enable every undergraduate student to participate in entrepreneurial education as a standard part of the curriculum. We discuss how and why this strategy was implemented into all undergraduate courses. Our ambition to do so, has been driven by the recognition that the skills, knowledge, and attitudes that are integral to entrepreneurship – which we, following

Drucker (2015), define as *"seizing opportunities and managing these effectively to realise their potential"* (La Trobe University, 2015:6) – are increasingly central to the contemporary workplace. This has been driven by a number of interrelated factors: enhancing student employability in a highly competitive labour market, changing patterns of employment, and the demands of national economic competitiveness. The LTU-focus is not to educate students about innovation and entrepreneurship, but rather to develop the knowledge, skills, and mindset needed to be innovative and entrepreneurial, either for themselves in developing a start-up or working for an employer. Entrepreneurial education, as we define it, combines both developing the mindset and skills of an entrepreneur and the practical knowledge needed to establish a business, start-up, or become self-employed (Lackeus, 2015:7, 13). The term *mindset* is interpreted to be a person's attitude or disposition, such as their passion to be entrepreneurial, their level of perseverance to overcome obstacles, or their pro-activeness. Knowledge aspects include aspects such as value creation, while idea generation and skills include aspects such as setting goals and priorities (Lackeus, 2015:13).

Our initiative follows current trends in Australian universities. From reasonably recent origins, entrepreneurial education has grown to become a major part of university curricula. Universities in the US, UK, Europe, and also Australia now offer subjects, and in some case courses at both undergraduate and graduate level, that teach the skills and attributes needed to become an entrepreneur. Typically, these courses are offered by business schools as an outgrowth of small business research and management studies (Landström, 2007). In some contexts, such as the US, such courses have been introduced in response to student demand. In others, European countries for example, they have emerged in response to de-industrialisation and the rise of cyclical unemployment in advanced economies throughout the 1970s and 1980s and changing government policies stressing the need for an entrepreneurial culture (see Landström, 2007:95–126). In that respect, our chapter can be said to bridge the sections on policy and mindset. In reading our chapter, you will gain the following three insights:

1. arguments for why entrepreneurial education should be a core part of the undergraduate curriculum;

2. through practical examples you will be shown how entrepreneurial education can be incorporated into a range of disciplines; and

3. get to know best practices and ways to anticipate challenges in developing an all-of-university approach to entrepreneurial education.

Our chapter has four main sections. First, we outline the scope and meanings of entrepreneurial education. Second, we examine the broader Australian context and drivers that have placed entrepreneurship at the forefront of education. Third, we focus on the specific practices of entrepreneurial education and present the case study of LTU and how it has been integrated across the curriculum. Fourth, we conclude with some reflections on the challenges and lessons learned in extending entrepreneurial education beyond the business school.

Section I: What Is Entrepreneurial Education?

Entrepreneurship within the academy is plagued by the notion that it cannot be taught. Contrary to this, and following Drucker, we suggest that entrepreneurship is a behaviour rather than personality trait. Gibb (2005:31) further states that given that entrepreneurship is a human endeavour, it is shaped by a person's attitudes, behaviours, capabilities and skills, *"the need for which is contingent upon levels of uncertainty and complexity in the task environment facing individuals and organisations"*. There is sufficient evidence that not only can entrepreneurship be taught, but that it should be taught (Gibb, 2005; Kinner, 2015; Lackeus, 2015).

Nevertheless, entrepreneurial education is a developing field with a range of opinions about how to teach it, what to teach, how to assess it, and even how to define it. Shane & Venkataraman (2000:218) define the academic field of entrepreneurship as the *"scholarly examination of how, by whom, and with what effects, opportunities to create future goods and services are discovered, evaluated, and exploited"*.

Entrepreneurship within the academy goes beyond scholarly examination (see also Johnsson *et al.* in this volume). It can be further refined by the concepts *"enterprise education"*, which focuses on *"developing a mindset, skills and abilities"*, and *"entrepreneurship education"*, which focuses more on the *"setting up a business' or start-up"* and *"becoming self-employed"* (Lackeus, 2015:7). Following Erkkilä (2000), Lackeus adopts the unifying term "entrepreneurial education" as encompassing both enterprise and entrepreneurship education (Lackeus, 2015). Lackeus argues that the common thread linking enterprise and entrepreneurship education is the creation of value.

For the purposes of this chapter, we conceive the term *value* broadly to include both monetary value, processes, and social networks that indirectly create the conditions for the generation of monetary value. This latter notion of entrepreneurship is sometimes called "social entrepreneurship". Social entrepreneurship gained traction in the late 1990s and early 2000s and was closely, although not exclusively, associated with attempts to renew social democratic politics in countries such as the UK and Australia under the banner of a "third way" in government (Giddens, 1998:83–84). Social entrepreneurs draw together people and underutilised resources from the private, public, and community sectors to develop practical solutions to pressing social ills (Leadbeater, 1997:8; Latham, 2001:23–24). Researchers have since refined the concept of social entrepreneurship further to refer to businesses that seek to utilise profits for a social good and the work of community workers and activists who, by virtue of their social position and ability to connect people and resources, and create and sustain social value (Puredo & Mclean, 2006).

Section 2: The Key Reasons for Expanding Entrepreneurial Education: The Australian Context

The key reasons for expanding entrepreneurial education beyond business education has been driven by interrelated factors: globalisation and concerns around national economic competiveness; enhancing student employability; and changing employment patterns and trajectories. Whilst these factors are experienced globally, in this chapter we focus on the Australian context.

Globalisation and National Economic Competitiveness

The development of entrepreneurial education in universities is a response to processes of globalisation (Gibb, 2005). In particular, the growth and pervasiveness of communications technologies such as the Internet and mobile communication devices since the 1980s has enhanced the processing and exchange of information. Technological advances have *"compressed social time-space"* (first coined by Harvey, 1989) by increasing the mobility of people and the ease of transportation of goods. At the same time, these tools usher in what Giddens (1990:14; 1998:21–24) refers to as *"time-space distanciation"*, whereby social, economic, and cultural interactions between geographically distant and culturally disparate locales become more common to everyday experience and start to influence the shape and structures that govern social and economic life. At the same time, technology and *"expert systems"* (Giddens, 1990:112–114) — bodies of knowledge that can be abstracted from particular places and time — become central to economic growth and employment across industries.

Since at least the end of World War II, and accelerating in the 1980s, these processes have helped to make universities increasingly central to achieving and enhancing national economic competitiveness (Australian Government, 2012; Ernst and Young, 2012; Schramm, 2006; The World Bank Group, 2007; Universities Australia,13 April 2013). To compete effectively in a global *"knowledge economy"* (OECD, 1996), countries such as Australia require a highly skilled workforce where a culture of innovation and entrepreneurship is actively cultivated and pervasive.

In December 2015, for example, the Australian Prime Minister launched the Government's *National Innovation and Science Agenda* (NISA) (Commonwealth of Australia, 2015). The Australian Federal Government plans to spend almost $1.1 billion over four years to promote business-based research, development, and innovation (Turnbull, 2015). NISA funding will benefit universities by providing incentives for industry-research collaboration to commercialise ideas and solve problems; to develop science, technology, engineering, and mathematics (STEM) skills in high school; to attract talent and skills; to train Australian students for the jobs of the future; and to bring innovative talent to Australia (Turnbull, 2015).

Universities have responded to such policies by adapting teaching and research budgets and resources accordingly. In 2016, Universities Australia (UA), the peak body of Australian universities, released the *Keep it Clever* policy statement, urging Australian universities to educate for innovation and entrepreneurialism at an early stage of undergraduate programmes to ensure that the skills of university graduates support

Australia to remain competitive (Universities Australia, 2016). It also urges universities to collaborate with industry to create products and services to generate new sources of income.

Enhancing Student Employability

The linkages between universities and national economic priorities have had — and will continue to have — an effect on teaching and learning. Since the early 2000s, graduate capabilities such as communication, teamwork, critical thinking, and problem-solving skills have been integrated into course and subject learning outcomes (Litchfield *et al.*, 2010). These capabilities are highly valued by employers (Norton, 2012).

Most universities around the globe also have explicit statements about employability. In part, this has been driven by the demands of a highly competitive job market, but it also reflects the university's mission to prepare graduates for lifelong learning rather than transmitting a reasonably stable body of knowledge. As the Australian Council of Deans of Education (ACDE) puts it: "*The new learning is less about imparting defined knowledge and skills and more about shaping a kind of person: somebody who knows what they don't know; knows how to learn what they need to know; knows how to create knowledge through problem solving; knows how to create knowledge by drawing on informational and human resources around them; knows how to make knowledge collaboratively; knows how to nurture, mentor, and teach others; and knows how to document and pass on personal knowledge*" (ACDE, 2004:21–22).

Such traits map seamlessly onto entrepreneurs who have developed the knowledge, skills, and mindset to engage with levels of complexity in the task environment; treat failure as an opportunity to learn; and collaborate to co-create new approaches to problem solving to derive innovative solutions that create value. Lackeus' (2015:13) description of entrepreneurial competencies supports the claim. Lackeus groups entrepreneurial competencies into cognitive and non-cognitive competencies. It is the non-cognitive competencies that align well to the ACDE proposed traits.

The cognitive competencies include:
- knowledge (e.g., value creation, idea generation, how to get things done without resources); and

- skills (e.g., conducting market research, creating a business plan, managing people and setting priorities).

The non-cognitive competencies include:
- attitudes (e.g., self-efficacy, strength of entrepreneurial identity, being comfortable with uncertainty and ambiguity, being creative, and the ability to overcome adverse circumstances).

Changing Employment Patterns and Trajectories

Ten years ago, Gibb & Hannon (2006:4) wrote that a university degree is an *"entry ticket to the world of work"*, not a *"voucher for a job for life"*. Today's students are repeatedly confronted with news that the jobs that they are being trained for today may be automated, moved off-shore, or no longer exist in the next 10 years (StartupAUS, 2016). Furthermore, it is estimated that 40 percent of existing jobs are likely to disappear in the next 10–15 years (Durrant-Whyte et al., 2015:48), and it is predicted that today's young people will hold *"as many as 17 different jobs, in five different careers, over the course of their working lives"* (Commonwealth of Australia, 2015:12).

These changes affect even those jobs that have in the past been regarded as safe from automation. Developments in machine learning and sophisticated algorithms are predicted to either de-skill or do away with many of these jobs. Ford (2015) suggests that some of the professions at risk of such changes include accounting, pharmacy, and computer programming. By contrast, the jobs that will be *"least affected"* by these changes are *"those that involve high levels of human creativity or social intelligence"* (StartupAUS, 2016:7).

Whether these predictions prove accurate or not, today's job ads already call for graduates with an entrepreneurial mindset and with a focus on networking and risk-taking. A recent job advertisement for an account manager, for example, asked for applicants with an *"innovative and entrepreneurial mindset to grow client portfolio as if it were your own business"* (SEEK, 2015). Entrepreneurial knowledge, skills, and mindset are not only relevant to people interested in start-ups and self-employment but are increasingly sought in a range of professional contexts (Neck et al., 2014). Graduate preparation should adapt accordingly.

Chapter 6

Section 3: Entrepreneurial Education in Australia: Current State of Play

Entrepreneurial education in Australian universities is a relatively recent development (Kinner, 2015). The field grew out of research into small businesses and, for much of the post-war era, struggled for research funding and academic legitimacy (Landström, 2005:121). Matters began to change in the early to mid-1990s with Deakin University being the first university to offer small business in an MBA programme, while the University of New England offered subjects related to entrepreneurship at graduate and master levels (Landström, 2005). Courses and subjects continued to grow rapidly throughout the 1990s and 2000s. A 2014 review on entrepreneurship education programmes found that over 95% of Australian universities teach it at undergraduate level and 95% at postgraduate level (cited in Kinner, 2015:18).

Whilst this appears to be a wide coverage, it is uneven. Firstly, most of this teaching occurs in business schools (Kinner, 2015:18). Kinner adds that due to their siloed nature in business schools, entrepreneurship programmes generally have low enrolments and therefore attract limited investment from the university for employing high-quality external lecturers with experience in entrepreneurship.

Secondly, there seem to be widely divergent approaches about what to teach and how to teach it (Maritz et al., 2015). Furthermore, there is little information available about the type of entrepreneurial programmes and their learning outcomes and assessment tasks (Maritz et al., 2015). The study by Maritz et al. (2015), which involved all of Australia's 43 accredited universities, revealed that entrepreneurial education pedagogies and content lag behind other countries, such as the USA. The biggest drawback was cultural: many universities and academics do not regard producing entrepreneurs as their role (Maritz et al., 2015). Kinner (2015) reports that no formal evaluation has been conducted in Australia related to the maturity of the entrepreneurial education programmes and their economic impact. The outcomes of the programmes have been inconclusive and research into entrepreneurial education in Australian universities needs to be undertaken (Colette, 2013).

The remainder of this chapter outlines how LTU has sought to expand entrepreneurial education beyond the business school to be an integral part of the undergraduate curriculum. The intention has been to provide opportunities for students to develop entrepreneurial knowledge, skills, and mindset while respecting the integrity and mores of disciplines and academics.

Section 4: Innovation and Entrepreneurship at LTU

LTU was established in 1964 as a teaching and research university. The university is a multi-campus university with the main campus in the northern metropolitan area of Melbourne and four regional campuses located in country Victoria. In the Australian higher education system, LTU is considered a mid-size university in terms of student numbers and is organised into two colleges divided along the social sciences and commerce and the sciences and engineering (La Trobe University, 2012). In 2012, LTU initiated a number of changes to teaching and learning, including the introduction of *"Three Essentials"* to be integrated into every undergraduate degree. These Essentials are:

- Innovation and Entrepreneurship (I&E);
- Global Citizenship; and
- Sustainability Thinking.

These are part of a broader strategy to differentiate LTU's degrees and are intended to:

- *"equip students to think and respond beyond conventional boundaries;*
- *foster adaptable thinking;*
- [develop] *the capacity to apply knowledge and skills in a future as yet unknown to us"* (La Trobe University, 2015:6).

While there are significant overlaps between the three different areas covered by the Essentials, only I&E will be discussed in this chapter to keep to the theme of the anthology. Pittaway & Edwards (2012) developed a typology of entrepreneurship education to describe four programme types. These are:

1. Education *about* entrepreneurship, where the aim is to develop awareness about setting up and running a business;

2. Education *for* entrepreneurship, where students undertake experiential, inquiry tasks or projects that develop key knowledge and skills to set up and run a future entrepreneurial endeavour. This includes new enterprise formation, self-employment, or economic self-sufficiency;

3. Educating *through* or *in* entrepreneurship, which entails learning through doing in a controlled environment. An example is students running a real consultancy within an entrepreneurial context; and *Embedded* practice, in which entrepreneurship is taught through disciplines or subjects. An example here is biochemistry students learning about intellectual property. This provides students with an awareness and experiences of entrepreneurship (adapted from Pittaway & Edwards, 2012:780–782).

Using this typology, LTU has sought to adopt an approach that aligns to "*for*", "*through*", or "*embedded*" programme types. The LTU focus is to develop students to be innovative and entrepreneurial, either for themselves in developing a start-up or working for a future employer (see also Parkes and Lamb in this volume). Importantly, this is to take entrepreneurial education beyond the traditional boundaries of the business school, to create opportunities across the curriculum.

Students at LTU who enrol in subjects in which I&E is integrated will develop:

+ *"understanding and experiencing the dynamics of change;*

+ *the generation and effective management of new ideas;*

+ *the ability to network, forge partnerships, collaborate and effectively communicate;*

+ *flexibility and creativity in developing ideas, and in resolving complex problems;*

+ *the capacity to apply theory, locate and synthesise knowledge resources, prioritise action and manage associated risks"* (La Trobe University, 2015:6).

Biggs' (2003a, 2003b) Constructive Alignment (CA) is applied to curriculum development at LTU. A CA process ensures that all the curriculum components work towards the same purpose, which is to achieve the learning outcomes (see also Parkes and Lamb in this volume). The key elements of I&E are integrated in a subject's learning outcomes, student learning activities, and assessment tasks. Informed by Biggs' work on curriculum alignment and the importance of assessment tasks driving student learning, the LTU policy on Essentials states that there must be one major assessment task of 25 percent or more drawing on the content of the Essential in each subject. Students who pass the subject with the integrated Essential will automatically meet the requirement for the Essential (La Trobe University, 2015). Despite the overlaps in the Essentials, no more than one Essential can be covered in one subject. This requirement is driven by practical considerations, ensuring that the teaching and learning around the single Essential remains a substantial focus of the subject.

Typically, the Essential is integrated in a core (compulsory) subject in the first, second, or third year of study. In most majors, students have access to subjects that address the Essential at least once in their degree programme. All majors must either include subjects with an Essential integrated or space must be available within the degree for students to take relevant electives from other areas that have an Essential integrated in their curriculum (La Trobe University, 2016). It is envisaged that most students will focus on one Essential each year and have the opportunity to complete all three by the time they graduate. There is no preferred order of completion.

The next section describes three case studies in which I&E is integrated into the curriculum and the variation of ways of achieving it.

Case Studies: I&E at LTU

Three undergraduate subjects were selected as the cases, including first- and third-year core humanities subjects and a second-year elective management subject. The aim was twofold: firstly, to gain a narrative description of each of the three cases, and secondly, to make explicit the implicit knowledge of how I&E has been integrated into each subject.

One key person teaching each of the three subjects was interviewed using open-ended, semi-structured questions. The interviews were audio recorded, transcribed, and analysed using a thematic approach. Each theme is informed by the literature discussed in the previous sections. Subject information, documents, and policy guidelines were collected, analysed, and interpreted. Each case is now described and key common themes reported.

Case 1: A Third-Year Compulsory or Elective Humanities Subject

The first case study is a subject in the Public Relations (PR) degree. Students enrolled in the subject run a PR agency that works for external clients. Academic staff in the PR programme run and oversee the agency, sourcing clients and coordinating students and the workflow. Around 45 students are enrolled in the subject, most of whom are completing the third year of their Communications degree. Some students enrolled in other degrees take the subject as an elective. Students participate in a four-hour seminar every week over two semesters or a 24-week period and can extend the study over a third semester as an elective. The subject is offered at the metropolitan campus and at one regional campus.

The subject is an example of educating students *"through"* entrepreneurship (Pittaway & Edwards, 2012). Students get close to the lived experience of an innovative communications professional and entrepreneur, selecting the project they would like to work on and then pitching to the subject coordinator by outlining the value they can add to the client's project. Projects are then allocated to teams based on their pitch and choice. In teams, the students apply their knowledge, skills, and mindset to a unique real-world communication problem or task and enact solutions that drive value for the client.

Activities that aim to develop entrepreneurial knowledge and skills and an entrepreneurial mindset

Some projects are routine communications briefs, whereas others lack clearly defined parameters or outcomes. More complex projects enable students to learn the value of research, as it assists them in generating new ideas and making decisions. It also allows them to identify and accurately scope project components to enable them to better manage their time and workflow to develop solutions to a professional standard. In a fast-paced environment, students may discover that their knowledge and skills are not sufficient and that they may need to undertake "just-in-time learning" on the job. They also learn client liaison, organising activities in the form of project management including implementing and marketing the project.

The subject is designed to create multiple opportunities for students to think about themselves as entrepreneurs — as agents, rather than as compliant employees — working in collaboration with others. Assessment activities are scaffolded, team-based tasks, with one task leading into the subsequent task. There is ongoing feedback from peers, lecturer, or clients.

The subject incorporates time and project management software which records the efforts of students as measured against set project role expectations. Effort is weighted at 20 percent of the total assessment. This includes weekly meetings, briefings, and scheduling of work. A second task involves students in client liaison, organising project activities, contributing to the effectiveness of the agency, and completing time records. This task is also weighted at 20 percent. The bulk of the assessment — 60 percent — involves the implementation and marketing of the project. Students are assessed more on the process and their effort rather than on the final product, which varies between student groups and projects allocated.

These tasks are designed to provide a framework for students to break new ground and develop their knowledge and skills beyond the formal curriculum, effectively becoming subject matter experts in new and emerging areas of public relations. Teaching staff act more as mentors and coaches rather than "founts of wisdom". As the subject coordinator put it, "*it's a student-run agency and I keep saying* [to the students] *your job is to make me redundant*".

The subject has had some success in realising this aspiration. For example, one 23-year-old student has developed social media campaigns for fashion houses. As the subject coordinator freely admitted, the student's knowledge and skills of this area of public relations far outstrip his own.

Professional communications is an area where innovative and entrepreneurial thinking are imperatives rather than optional add-ons. The disruptions caused by the proliferation of new digital tools and platforms require practitioners to continually adapt to new formats and protocols of professional behaviour. The approach taken in this subject is to embed I&E as an explicit part of the curriculum. As the subject coordinator said: "*If we don't embed I&E, what have we taught them? I don't think there is a choice. The question is how quickly can we get it into the curriculum.*"

Case 2: A Second-Year Elective Business Degree Subject

The second case study is a second-year elective subject offered by its business school and available to all students at all five LTU campuses. In this subject, students work in teams to design and pitch a social enterprise. A social enterprise is defined as a business that produces socially useful goods or services, is not reliant on donations, charities, or government funding, and generates paid work for groups often marginalised or shut out of traditional forms of employment (The Big Idea, 2015). The subject is linked to the Big Idea competition organised and coordinated by the *The Big Issue* magazine, and its mission is to develop *"solutions to help homeless, marginalised and disadvantaged people positively change their lives"* (The Big Idea, 2016:1).

The subject is an example of educating students *"for"* entrepreneurship. Students are encouraged to engage with their local community to develop research-driven, commercially, environmentally, and socially sustainable solutions to pressing social needs. Therefore, students who go on to implement the business plan also engage in education *"through"* entrepreneurship (see Pittaway & Edwards, 2012) by realising a working social enterprise.

The subject content is delivered via a combination of lectures, webinars, tutorials, and self-organised group/team sessions over a 12-week period. The content is taught by staff who have achieved entrepreneurial and social entrepreneurial success. Students also engage with business leaders and social entrepreneurs across a variety of business sectors outside the university throughout the judging process (The Big Idea, 2016).

Activities that aim to develop entrepreneurial knowledge and skills and an entrepreneurial mindset

Over the 12 weeks, students are guided through a process for generating, developing, and refining their ideas for a social enterprise. Each learning activity is aligned with the submission requirements of the competition. The learning activities include an innovation workshop facilitated across all campuses simultaneously by LTU staff. The focus here is on generating good ideas by guiding the students through a problem-solution thinking process. This is followed by an entrepreneurship workshop where they are shown a business model canvas (see Clark *et al.*, 2012). The business model canvas is a one-page communication tool that captures the core elements or drivers of a business model and forms 15 percent of the overall assessment. Students also participate in workshops on developing group work skills, including self-awareness and good communication, and are provided with coaching and assistance through external partners such as the Victorian social enterprise training organisation Groupwork Institute of Australia.

The bulk of the assessment tasks focus on the development of the business plan (30 percent) and the pitch (15 percent), which is presented and submitted by video. Students start working on their business plan and video pitch early in the semester and are given feedback and support from the academics, the regional campus coordinators, and a dedicated project manager. These personnel act as project advisors. The top student teams are invited to present at a special one-day pitch event that is judged by LTU staff and successful social entrepreneurs. The highest scoring team is then invited — and supported — to enter the national competition run by *The Big Issue*.

In 2015, 78 students enrolled in the subject. Student teams are generally made up of 3–4 students with diverse discipline backgrounds. For example, the student team that won the 2013 *The Big Idea* national competition included students studying business, agricultural science, and international development. Each student brought their own special knowledge to design a social enterprise that would employ disadvantaged young people in a business creating decorative flower and plant boxes made from recyclable materials for hotels and restaurants.

Moreover, students have taken their knowledge and skills beyond the subject and competition. One of the students in the successful 2013 team approached a community centre to seek their interest in implementing the plan to develop the green wall project. The student began volunteering at the centre and soon moved into a part-time paid role. She applied what she had learnt through *The Big Idea* programme to help secure a significant grant from the Lord Mayor's Charitable Trust in Melbourne. This grant enabled the centre to successfully establish a social enterprise coffee shop in the neighbouring medical centre. Similarly, the 2015 winning team have continued to develop their plans for events, organising a company to plan and develop events to engage young people in rural and regional centres. Another student has found work with an international youth organisation after pitching some of the ideas he developed through the subject. These examples suggest that the learning experiences are authentic and transferrable beyond the context of the subject (see also Johnsson et al. in this volume).

Case 3: A First-Year Core or Elective Humanities Subject

The third case study is of a first-year core subject in the three-year Bachelor of Arts degree. Students in other degrees can also take the subject as an elective. Over 750 students are enrolled and it is delivered at all five of LTU's Victorian campuses over a 12-week period. Fourteen staff teach the subject in weekly two-hour seminars attended by up to 30 students.

I&E has recently been integrated into the subject and has not as yet been taught. Drawing on Pittaway & Edwards' (2012) typology, we suggest that this is an example of educating students "*for*" entrepreneurship, as it encourages students to engage in activities that develop knowledge, skills, and the mindset of social entrepreneurs.

The subject is an interdisciplinary exploration of some of the most influential ideas in the history of the Western world, including freedom, imperialism, secularisation, and the individual. The subject traces the origins of these ideas and examines their manifestation in 21st century Australia. Students discover how these ideas have changed over time and develop an understanding of the dynamics of change. Through inquiry research, they identify and critically evaluate the central ideas underpinning public discussion on a range of political and cultural issues.

Activities that aim to develop entrepreneurial knowledge and skills and an entrepreneurial mindset

The core I&E assessment task requires students to identify a challenge to freedom in contemporary Australia that is relevant to them, someone they know, or their community and take measures to change it. Students work in groups to develop an outcome or a solution that addresses the problem. The group distils a complicated and multifaceted idea into a set of problems that can be addressed with evidence-based solutions.

Through research and analysis, students discuss strategies from a range of potential options to devise a solution to the problem. The solution is underpinned with supporting information gained through the group's research. This informs the group's pitch to a "panel of stakeholders", who they need to convince as to why their new idea or plan would add value to the issue being addressed. The panel members are the group's peers, who play the roles of experts making decisions to back or not back the plan.

The students are then shown how to write up their issue and solution in the form of a formal letter to someone who could affect change. An example might be writing a letter to a member of parliament, newspaper editor, or campaign site. Students decide whether they choose to send the letter and use their work for real-world change. If students act on this letter, it could be life changing. They could become part of grassroots change and/or activism, and this could shape their future direction. This enables students to understand concepts of freedom and provides them with skills to change, for example, a value by bringing the issue to the attention of the government and lawmakers.

Students watch interviews with local campaigners who have effected grassroots changes in their communities. For example, one speaker documents a grassroots campaign to have same-sex parents recognised on their children's birth certificates in Victoria. This shows students that grassroots campaigns can be successful through rallying other people and influencing key decision makers.

The teaching team of this subject see this as a way to teach social entrepreneurship, demonstrating to students that an arts degree can have practical applications, not just in a vocational context but in a life-changing context that is meaningful to the students' lives and the lives of those in their community. They wanted to excite students and show them that they are learning to be articulate and critical as well as having the skills to advocate for their community.

Key Commonalities of Best Practices

The three case studies show that I&E can be taught in a number of different ways across a range of degrees *"for"* or *"through"* entrepreneurship and that it is an experiential process. Whilst Cases 1 and 2 have relatively small classes of 45–78 students, I&E is being infused in a group project of over 750 students in Case 3.

The key commonalities of the cases are, first, that teaching and learning occurs primarily through seminars, workshops, team meetings, and meetings with industry or community stakeholders. Students work collaboratively in interdisciplinary teams.

Second, these examples highlight the value of diverse skills and knowledge. In all of these case studies, particularly 2 and 3, interdisciplinary knowledge is welcome because it offers enhanced possibilities for I&E.

Third, in all of the case studies, teaching staff assume the roles of mentor/coach rather than as experts who direct students. Students develop and apply their ideas to resolve complex problems. The teachers guide the students when necessary, and their role is no longer that of the subject expert but a guide or coach. Students are enabled to develop their knowledge and skills to become the experts for their project and teach others (see Thomassen, in this volume).

Fourth, the projects enable students to learn the value of research by drawing on informational and human resources around them, as this assists them in generating new ideas, resolving complex problems, and in making decisions. It also allows them to identify and accurately scope project components to better manage their team's workflow and to develop solutions to an expected professional standard. It enables students to engage in just-in-time learning and learn what they need to know as they encounter problems that require speedy resolution (see Parkes & Lamb, in this volume).

Fifth, the assessment tasks are in the form of real-world projects, they are diverse, and they fit with students' interests (see Johnsson et al., in this volume). They allow students to collaborate, apply theory, consolidate their skills and knowledge, to deal with uncertainty, and to engage with the kinds of complex problems described by Gibb (2005) and ACDE (2004). Furthermore, feedback is delivered through a range of different channels, including teachers, peers, and stakeholders. The frequent feedback enables students to be pro-active to overcome adverse circumstances and re-adjust their solution without fear of failure. The student assessment for the subject is weighted more toward student effort, perseverance, and the actions that students take than the final product.

Sixth, opportunities are created for students to interact with and learn from successful, practicing entrepreneurs or activists who model ways to connect people and resources to create and sustain social or financial value (Pruedo & Mclean, 2006). This form of learning demystifies I&E and shows students that I&E can be achieved by teams of students in arts and humanities as well as in business and shapes their entrepreneurial identity.

Seventh, students meet industry and community stakeholders with whom they collaborate, network, and forge partnerships, and to whom they pitch their ideas. Students develop a range of transferable capabilities which are keenly sought by employers. Importantly, students learn to think about other forms of employment open to them other than the traditional forms (see Thomassen, in this volume; Parkes & Lamb, in this volume). The key components necessary for setting up classroom learning environments that promote entrepreneurial education are summarised in Table 1. These key aspects were synthesised from the case studies.

Entrepreneurial learning environments	
What the teacher does	**What the students do**
Provides students with knowledge of the basics of entrepreneurship/activism, such as generation of novel ideas, effective management of ideas, value creation, development of a business model.	Interdisciplinary team members with different knowledge domains interact to share, integrate, synthesise, and condense knowledge to: • resolve complex problems or technical challenges, • create new perspectives and/or new knowledge, • identify what they need to know to achieve project goals and engage in just-in-time learning by drawing on informational and human resources around them.
Sets up student workshops on developing group work skills, including, for example, self-awareness, leadership, and effective communication skills.	
Allocates students into interdisciplinary project teams.	Knowledge is co-created by student teams through seminars/workshops/team meetings/meetings with industry or community stakeholders/entrepreneurs or activists. This has the potential to lead to novel and creative solutions and new ways of thinking by students.
Facilitates seminars, workshops, team meetings, meetings with industry or community stakeholders.	
Co-teaches with entrepreneurs or sets up learning opportunities such as workshops with entrepreneurs or activists.	Students focus on creating value and benefits for a wider community.

Entrepreneurial learning environments	
What the teacher does	**What the students do**
Sets interdisciplinary teams to work on real-to-life projects that create value for the outside world (either monetary or social) in a controlled and supportive environment. The projects are diverse and fit with student interests.	The team collaborates in making key project-related decisions to develop the new idea/creations by scoping the project components, managing their team's workflow, prioritising and sustaining action, and managing associated project risks. Each team member's input and effort is important to the project's success. Student teams are in control in achieving their objectives.
Sets and expects professional standards being applied by student teams.	
Allows students to use their creativity to develop new solutions to projects but remains vigilant and available for students as a coach or "guide at the side". Recognises areas of need and guides students to success.	The consequences of the decisions that the team members make are evaluated by the team and, in this way, students engage in reflection and peer feedback. This sets up the conditions for significant further learning. Further learning also occurs through teaching and mentoring each other or by drawing on further informational or human resources. In this way, the students become the experts of their projects.
Sets up a process for frequent feedback through a range of different channels, including themselves, peers, and stakeholders.	
Judges student success by the generation of student effort, activities in which they engage, and the processes students use to achieve an outcome and not solely on the final outcome.	Students seek frequent feedback about their actions through varied channels, including teachers, peers, and stakeholders. The feedback enables students to re-adjust their solution without fearing failure.
Assists in developing more entrepreneurial graduates who have the potential to contribute to Australia's economic benefits.	Students learn to network, forge partnerships, collaborate, and communicate with stakeholders, entrepreneurs, or activists. Through this interaction, students experience how an entrepreneur or activist thinks and acts. This may develop the student's own entrepreneurial/activist passion, identity, and mindset.
	The experience allows students an insight into entrepreneurialism as a potential work role other than traditional employment.

Table 1: Entrepreneurial learning environments – what the teacher does and what the students do.

In concluding this best practice discussion, it is useful to think of the curriculum as a system that exists and functions in an environment interconnected with other systems, as shown in Figure 1. This framework depicts global forces, the Australian economic context, and the higher education context, as described earlier, as having an impact on the curriculum system by driving the system to enhance graduate employability and, as described in this study, through I&E.

Global Forces →
- Globalisation
- Economic competitiveness
- Pervasiveness of technologies

↓

Australian Economic Context →
- National economic competitiveness requires a highly skilled workforce
- Technologies are changing employment patterns
- I&E is seen as important to economic and job growth
- National Innovation and Science Agenda (NISA) is launched by the prime minister

↓

Higher Education →
- Linked to the economic growth of the nation
- Changing patterns in graduate employability
- Universities Australia launches *Keep It Clever Policy* promoting the integration of I&E

↓

La Trobe University →
- Directed by policy levers from higher education and by the government
- Needs to enhance its graduate employability rate
- Has embedded graduate capabilities and the Three Essentials, including I&E, into all disciplines in the undergraduate curriculum

↓

Curriculum design (system) focused on innovation and entrepreneurship

Input (1)	Process (2)	Output (3)
Learning outcomes have discipline knowledge, innovative and entrepreneurial knowledge, skills, and attitudes embedded. Students learn from academics, entrepreneurs/activists, community stakeholders, and from each other. Learning occurs in seminars, workshops, team meetings, meetings with industry or community stakeholders.	Students work in interdisciplinary teams and are engaged in real-world projects that fit student interests and create value to stakeholders. Students connect and collaborate with the outside world. Frequent feedback on the development of the project deliverables by peers, teachers, entrepreneurs, and stakeholders. Students use this input to re-adjust their solution. Assessment is weighted more towards student effort, action, and process than the final product.	Graduates who think and respond beyond conventional boundaries, adaptable thinkers who have the capacity to apply their knowledge in an as yet unknown future. The transferable skills acquired are keenly sought by employers. Graduates who have experienced I&E as a potential alternative to traditional employment.

Figure 1: Framework of the forces that impact on the curriculum system.

Conclusion

Ten years ago, it was questioned whether entrepreneurship could be taught (Gibb, 2005). Today's question is how can we give all university students the tools and ability to innovate and become entrepreneurial to create economic and/or social value. This chapter has explored why entrepreneurial education should be a core part of the undergraduate curriculum. It has provided practical examples of how entrepreneurial education can be integrated into a range of disciplines as an all-of-university approach to entrepreneurial education.

This process has not been without challenges. Some staff have expressed scepticism about the value of the Essentials. In particular, some staff are concerned that the minimum 25 percent assessment task devoted to the Essential will crowd out core disciplinary content. Others are concerned that I&E reframes education as a commercial activity which conflicts with the core values of disciplines and the University (Lopez, 2016). Alternatively, it is regarded as imposed from above; as one of our interviewees put it, the Essential was implemented because *"we were told to"*. The Essentials were also introduced in the context of a major restructuring that saw five faculties reorganised into two colleges and around 350 staff made redundant to better position LTU for the future (ABC, 2014).

Despite these challenges, aligning the curriculum with entrepreneurial education is gaining traction. By mid-2015, the University structure had been embedded sufficiently and the new colleges were given the role of implementing the Essentials. The college in which these case studies are set implemented I&E into at least one core subject of every major. With greater communication about the scope of what I&E means to incorporate social enterprises and social entrepreneurship, some of the early obstacles are steadily being overcome.

If nothing else, the decision to make entrepreneurial education a central part of all degrees has sparked rich conversations about I&E that otherwise would not have occurred. In particular, the LTU definition of I&E has had a positive impact in developing quality I&E subjects, such as those in Case 1, 2, and 3. These show that the learning can be deep, meaningful, and long-lasting and that students would be prepared for a future by, in the words of LTU's Essential, being equipped *"to think and respond beyond conventional boundaries, to foster adaptable thinking and the capacity to apply knowledge and skills in a future as yet unknown to us"* (La Trobe University, 2015:6).

About the Authors

Dr Silvia McCormack is the Academic Coordinator (Coursework) in the College of Arts, Social Sciences and Commerce at La Trobe University, Melbourne Australia. She can be contacted at this e-mail: s.mccormack@latrobe.edu.au

Dr Chris Scanlon is Associate Professor and Chair, Learning and Teaching in the College of Arts, Social Sciences and Commerce at La Trobe University, Melbourne Australia. He can be contacted at this e-mail: c.scanlon@latrobe.edu.au

Bibliography

Australian Broadcast Commission (ABC) (2014). *La Trobe University confirms it is cutting 350 jobs as part of a restructure.* Online Resource: http://www.abc.net.au/news/ [Accessed on 3 October 2016].

Australian Council of Deans of Education (ACDE) (2004). *New teaching, new learning: A vision for Australian education.* Canberra: Australian Council of Deans of Education.

Australian Government (2012). Budget 2012–2013. *Budget Overview.* Canberra: Government of Australia.

Biggs, J. (2003a). *Teaching for quality learning at university: What the student does.* Buckingham: Society for Research into Higher Education & Open University Press.

Biggs, J. (2003b). Aligning teaching and assessing the course objectives. Paper presented at the *Teaching and Learning in Higher Education: new trends and innovations conference*: University of Aveiro, 13–17 April 2003.

Clark, T.; A. Ostwalder & Y. Pigneur (2012). *Business model you: a one-page method for reinventing your career.* John Wiley & Sons.

Colette, H. (2013). Entrepreneurship education in HE: are policy makers expecting too much? *Education + Training,* Vol. 55, No. 8/9, pp. 836–848.

Commonwealth of Australia (2015). *National Innovation and Science Agenda.* Canberra: Commonwealth of Australia.

Drucker, P. F. (2015). *Innovation and entrepreneurship: Practice and principle.* New York: Routledge.

Durrant-Whyte; H. F.; I. McCalman; S. O'Callaghan; A. Reid & D. Steinberg (2015). *The impact of computerisation and automation on future employment.* Melbourne: Committee for Economic Development of Australia.

Erkkilä, K. (2000). *Entrepreneurial Education: mapping the debates in the United States, the United Kingdom and Finland.* Abingdon: Taylor & Francis.

Ernst and Young (2012). *University of the future.* London, UK: Ernst and Young Global Limited.

Ford, M. (2015). *Rise of the robots technology and the threat of a jobless future.* New York: Basic Books.

Gibb, A. (2005). *Towards the entrepreneurial university: Entrepreneurship education as a lever for change.* University of Durham National Council for Graduate Entrepreneurship.

Gibb, A. & P. Hannon (2006). *Towards the entrepreneurial university?* Durham: University of Durham.

Giddens, A. (1990). *The consequences of modernity.* London: Polity Press.

Giddens, A. (1998). *The Third Way: The renewal of social democracy*, London: Polity Press.

Harvey, D. (1989). *The condition of postmodernity: an enquiry into the origins of cultural change*. New York: Blackwell.

Kinner, C. (2015). *Boosting high-impact entrepreneurship in Australia – A role for universities*. Canberra: Government of Australia.

La Trobe University (2012). *Future Ready: Strategic Plan 2013-2017*. Online resource: http://www.latrobe.edu.au [Accessed on 3 October 2016].

La Trobe University (2015). *La Trobe essentials procedure policy*. Online resource: http://www.latrobe.edu.au [Accessed on 3 October 2016].

La Trobe University (2016). *Essentials quick guide for innovation and entrepreneurship*. Online resource: http://www.latrobe.edu.au [Accessed on 3 October 2016].

Lackeus, M. (2015). Entrepreneurship in education: What, why, when, how, Organisation for Economic Co-operation and Development (OECD). Paris: OECD.

Landström, H. (2007). *Pioneers in entrepreneurship and small business research. Springer Science & Business Media*, Vol. 8, pp. 3–10.

Leadbeater C. (1997). *The Rise of the Social Entrepreneur*. London: Demos.

Litchfield, A.; J. Frawley & S. Nettleton (2010). Contextualising and integrating into the curriculum the learning and teaching of work-ready professional graduate attributes. *Higher Education Research & Development*, Vol. 29, No. 5, pp. 519–534.

Latham, M. (2001). The New Economy and the new politics. *The enabling state: People before bureaucracy*, pp. 23–24.

Lopez, D. (2016). La Trobe: be the difference (and be fired), Red Flag, 4 June. Online Resource: https://redflag.org.au [Accessed on 3 October 2016].

Maritz, A.; C. Jones & C. Shwetzer (2015). The status of entrepreneurship education in Australian universities. *Education + Training*, Vol.57, No. 8/9, pp. 1020–1035.

Neck, M.; G. Greene & G. Bush (2014). Teaching entrepreneurship. A practice based approach. MA, USA: Edwards Elgar.

Norton, A. (2012). Mapping Australian higher education. *Grattan Institute Report*. Melbourne: Grattan Institute.

OECD (1996). *The knowledge-based economy*. Paris: OECD

Pittaway, L. & C. Edwards (2012). Assessment: examining practice in entrepreneurship education. *Education + Training*, Vol. 54, No. 8/9, pp. 778–800.

Puredo, A. M. & M. Mclean (2006). Social entrepreneurship: A critical review of the concept. *Journal of World Business*, Vol. 41, No. 1, pp. 56–65.

Schramm, C. J. (2006). *The entrepreneurial imperative: How America's economic miracle will reshape the world (and change your life)*. New York: HarperCollins.

SEEK. (2015). SEEK Job Search Account Manager. Online Resource: https://www.seek.com.au/jobdetails/30134660/apply [Accessed on 3 October 2016].

Shane, S. & S. Venkataraman (2000). Academy of Management. *The Academy of Management Review*, Vol. 25, No. 1, pp. 217–226.

Shepard, L. A. (2013). The role of assessment in a learning culture. *Educational Researcher*, Vol. 29, No .7, pp. 4–14.

StartupAUS (2016). Economy-in-transition-discussion paper: startups, innovation and a workforce for the future. Online Resource: Startupaus.org [Accessed on 3 October 2016].

The Big Idea on Vimeo (2015). Online Resource: https://vimeo.com/126461476 [Accessed on 3 October 2016].

The Big Idea (2016). Online Resource: http://thebigidea.org.au/ [Accessed on 3 October 2016].

The Big Issue (2016). Online Resource: http://www.thebigissue.org.au/ [Accessed on 3 October 2016].

The World Bank Group (2007). Education for the knowledge economy: Tertiary education. The World Bank Group.

Turnbull, M. (2015). National Innovation and Science Agenda. *Media release*. Canberra: Government of Australia.

Universities Australia (13 April 2013). Multi-billion dollar university budget hit the biggest since 1990. *Media release No 17/13*. Canberra: Universities Australia.

Universities Australia (2016). Keep it clever policy statement 2016. Canberra: Universities Australia.

Chapter 7

Planning to Teach Entrepreneurship: Our Rough Guide to Research-Informed, Practice-Based Curriculum Design at Aston University, UK

Julian Lamb & Geoff Parkes

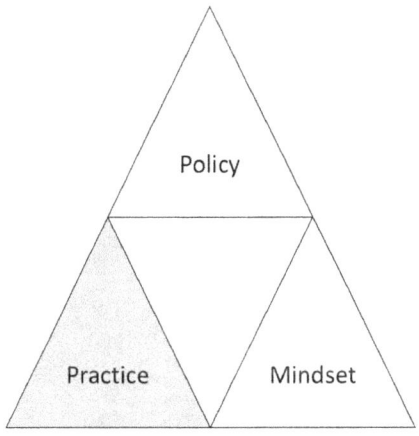

Introduction

Our chapter is an important contribution to this section on practice – and to the book *Teaching and Learning Entrepreneurship in Higher Education* – because we recount our experience developing a new research-led entrepreneurship module at Aston Business School – part of Aston University in Birmingham, UK. The module is a taught undergraduate module with the title "Marketing and the Entrepreneurial Firm" (MEF) which was developed for a final-year undergraduate class in the BSc Marketing stream. We find it important to start our chapter with a discussion about what we mean by entrepreneurship. There are many different perspectives on what it means; and indeed, there are those who seek to differentiate entrepreneurship, with its focus on ownership of a firm, from *intrapreneurship*, with its focus on being an employee of a firm (Maier & Zenovia, 2011). By "entrepreneurship" we mean the skills of those who are key change-agents in an enterprise, irrespective of whether they are the owners of that enterprise or not: and our research found that entrepreneurs are skilled in four main areas: *seeking advice, problem-solving, communicating,* and *collaborating.*

We believe it is important to "nail our colours to the mast" at an early point in this chapter: being explicit about our stance will enable the reader to understand both the manner by which we have engaged with curriculum design and our fundamental philosophical standpoints regarding entrepreneurship that informed the design. In terms of the module design process, it also informs the "programme philosophy", which is akin to the mission statement and stands as a reference point by which the design can be checked and benchmarked. We discuss the programme philosophy in more detail towards the end of the chapter. Our stance towards entrepreneurship can be summarised as:

- Entrepreneurship is "something" that can be taught;

- Entrepreneurship is not confined to the arena of profit-maximisation in society;

- Entrepreneurship is not a subject that can be left to declarative lecturing styles;

- Entrepreneurship is not solely equated with "big business".

Entrepreneurship is "something" that can be taught; and teaching is taken in the widest sense to include coaching, mentoring, facilitating, and so forth. This stance is a fundamental and robust critique of those who seek to convince others that entrepreneurship cannot be taught and that it is an innate quality that somehow pre-exists in some people but not others (Thomassen, in this volume). We observe that many modern-day narratives about successful entrepreneurs are located in biographies that are non-academic, perhaps even anti-academic. For example, Farndale's recent interview with eminent British entrepreneur Lord Sugar reveals a clear subtext that university education might be a waste of time for successful entrepreneurs (Farnedale, 2011). *Our stance is emancipatory*:

we assert that anyone can be entrepreneurial – it is not confined to an elite few.

Entrepreneurship is not confined to the arena of profit-maximisation in society; instead, we take a political stance that profit maximisation is just one lens, among many, that an entrepreneur might adopt to clarify his or her objectives for a successful enterprise. We extend the notion of entrepreneurship to not-for-profit, social enterprise, and even educational development: we, the authors of this chapter, consider ourselves to be entrepreneurs in educational development (Hørsted & Nygaard, in this volume). Above all, *our stance is emancipatory*: we assert that profit generation should not dominate what successful entrepreneurs do, it is just one agenda amongst many.

Entrepreneurship is not a subject that can be left to "drift in the doldrums" of declarative lecturing styles by self-proclaimed experts in the field. As noted above, our basic proposition is that entrepreneurship can be taught; however, the pedagogical underpinnings of such teaching need to be unpacked, researched, and explained with care and rigour. We take heed of Freire's (1970) caution that teachers can, and do, hold great power in relation to the transmission of ideologies about entrepreneurship. In this respect, we see that *the pedagogy of entrepreneurship is an emancipatory concept*; where the design of learning ought to enable participants to explore their own view about what drives *their* entrepreneurial life and not merely mimic what experts say.

Entrepreneurship is not solely equated with "big business". Universities are often keen to associate themselves with high-value corporate brands and personalities. This is an understandable approach: higher education is a service industry that relies upon reputation and brand association; however, we embrace the importance of small firms within the economic engine. To put this into perspective, the UK has over four million enterprises of all sizes, roughly three million firms have no employees, and one million firms employ less than ten people. Only 200,000 firms employ between 10 and 249 people, and there are only around 8,000 firms that employ over 250 people (Frazer, 2014). If economic resilience is considered, this distribution is "risky business" in the face of global economic stress (Lamb & Leach, 2008).

In light of this, we feel that entrepreneurship should not necessarily aspire to "big business" but should also focus on the development of our localised "living" economies. Napoleon is often misquoted as saying that the UK is a nation of "shopkeepers"; whether he said it or not, the truth is that the engine of the UK's market economy is indeed located within the majority of small to medium-sized enterprises (i.e., those with less than 250 employees). This makes the context of SMEs highly germane to the research and design of entrepreneurship teaching; and from a programme design perspective emancipates students from the dominant ideology that "big business" is the only real measure of success.

Reading our chapter, you will gain the following three insights:

1. learn about how we practice our "research and design" approach to teaching entrepreneurship at Aston University;

2. get our account of the research that was commissioned in the context of entrepreneur-stakeholder engagement for the module's design; and finally,

3. get a "rough guide" to curriculum design for other teachers of entrepreneurship.

We have structured our chapter with four main sections. First, we present the two distinct types of "curriculum design principle" at Aston University, and the recent Aston guidelines for module design. This gives an overview of the approach to curriculum design in our university and help you understand our design of the MEF-module. Second, we introduce a longer section on the research which led to our specific design of the MEF-module. We did extensive research with 60 entrepreneurs and got to understand what drives their business. Third, we present out taught MEF-module in much more detail. And fourth, we sum it all up by presenting a rough guide to anyone who wish to design an entrepreneurship curriculum.

Section 1: The Aston Approach to Curriculum Design

Aston University has taken great strides in the promotion of a design approach to curriculum development, and MEF is offered as a "showcase" of the Aston approach. The design of this module did not occur in a vacuum and it is important to explain the national and institutional setting in which our entrepreneurship module was created. The body that governs the quality of learning in teaching in the UK is the Quality Assurance Agency (QAA). The QAA defines a programme as "an approved course of study that provides a coherent learning experience and normally leads to a qualification"; any programme leading to an award falls within the QAA Framework for Higher Education Qualifications (www.qaa.ac.uk). Within the context of the QAA framework, Aston's design approval process aims to evaluate proposals against a range of reference points: key of all are that academic standards are appropriate to the award level and students' experience of the programme will be such that it enables the achievement of the award. In addition, Aston identifies further key reference points in the design of curricula that include:

- Statutory requirements, such as those relating to special educational needs, disability, equal opportunities and diversity, and health and safety (www.opsi.gov.uk);

- The UK Quality Code for Higher Education and relevant subject benchmark statements (www.qaa.ac.uk/assuring-standards-and-quality/the-quality-code);

- Professional body requirements.

A key innovation in the new approach to curriculum design at Aston is the role of the Design Navigator. The Design Navigator acts as both consultant and facilitator in the process of design to ensure that the principles are enacted, or if not, that a rationale for any variance is given. The Design Navigator also ensures programme-level coherence and addresses a number of "design challenges". Examples of "design challenges" include (but are not limited to) employability, student engagement, globalisation, and sustainability. A Design Navigator is a relative expert in teaching and learning, curriculum design, and academic quality. Each Design Navigator is a volunteer, trained for the role by Aston's Centre for Learning Innovation and Professional Practice. There are two distinct types of "curriculum design principle" at Aston: these relate to *process* and *product*.

We will first look at the design "process" that, amongst other considerations, requires curriculum designers to embrace stakeholder engagement and provide evidence of how stakeholders have contributed to the design of the programme. Stakeholders may include teachers, central services (such as careers and employability teams), students, employers; and of course, for our module, local entrepreneurs. Later in this chapter, we will explore in detail how we engaged with local entrepreneurs using a bespoke research project to inform the design of the entrepreneurship module. Next, looking at the design "product", Aston provides a set of benchmarks which should be the starting point for the design of all new modules. This intention behind these criteria is to enhance comparability across the university such that a module in the Business School should, for example, be the same "weight and assessment load" as a module in the School of Engineering. This does not prevent the design of curricula beyond the benchmark, but if a variance is proposed, a design-centric rationale is required in order to gain approval.

The new Aston guidelines for module design include:

- Modules will not have more than four learning outcomes.
- Modules will not have more than two items of assessment (independent of the size of the module).
- Assessment load per module will not exceed 2,000 words per 10cr (or equivalent) independent of the academic level of the module.
- Each module specification presented for approval should be accompanied by a summary assessment-briefing document, complete with associated outline assessment criteria.
- Programme Teams will evidence a programme-level approach to assessment design and assessment staging at the points of programme approval and review.

Table 1: Programme product design principles: www.aston.ac.uk.

Section 2: Designing an Entrepreneurship Module at Aston – Engaging with Entrepreneurs to Find out What They Actually Do

During the early programme philosophy design phase, it was decided that local entrepreneurs are a key stakeholder group for teaching entrepreneurship; and it was argued that it is essential to underpin teaching with current and practice-based views regarding what entrepreneurs *actually do*. With this in mind, rather than creating a syllabus and then asking entrepreneurs to comment, a comprehensive research project was undertaken to inform the syllabus. The research was conducted across sixty small firms with the specific intention of establishing what entrepreneurs actually "do" in the pursuit of successful business outcomes.

Many of the early studies in entrepreneurship took a personality trait perspective and were focused on what makes an entrepreneur (McClelland, 1961; Sandberg & Hoffer, 1987; Brockhaus, 2004; Baum & Locke, 2004; Ciaveralla, 2004; Rauch & Frese, 2007). For example, risk-taking was one characteristic, with the inference being that if an individual was not born with this trait, then a career as an entrepreneur was unlikely. Though extensive, we believe that trait-centred research lacks any definitive conclusions in the search for an entreprenuerial gene; and in line with our emancipatory stance that anyone can become an entrepreneur, it was decided to use behaviour rather than trait as the key in our stakeholder research phase (see Johnsson et al. in this volume). Underpinning our approach, we also observed a growing call to take a behavioural perspective to discover "what do entrepreneurs actually do", and as such our research fits within a growing and compelling body of literature (Mueller, 2013; Bird et al., 2012).

In the context of our research-led module design, managerial behaviour has also been described as "*a missing field of research within the small business literature*" (O'Gorman et al., 2005:2), and Bird et al. (2012) have highlighted the need for reliable measures. Other authors have called for an alternative paradigm (Bygrave, 1992), involving more field studies and longitudinal research, and embracing the use of multi-dimensional approaches linked to the real working situation of the owner-manager (e.g., Caird, 1993; Gibb & Davies, 1990). The research-led curriculum design therefore provided the opportunity to make a contribution to entrepreneurship research, identify behavioural characteristics of entrepreneurs, and concomitantly use the results to design a module that develops real and authentic skills in undergraduates.

In developing the content, the aim was also to demonstrate good understanding of curriculum design with a clear rationale, aims, and appropriate learning outcomes, including specifically linking to research. There was also a clear need to focus on the student rather than on the teacher and to reduce the amount of declarative "information transfer" in contact time with the student. The so-called "flipped classroom" approach was therefore employed. The goal was to encourage an "action" research, or an active-learning approach where the learning encounter becomes the focus. The aims of the module and the focus on behaviour of the student needed to be clear, concise statements (Petty, 2003:392). Intended learning outcomes were to be written and underpinned by the concept of "constructive alignment" (Biggs & Tang, 2007:55). As such, the learning outcomes were designed in parallel with the assessment and delivery methods: each driving the other and each connecting with the other like a finely crafted "dovetail joint"; in other words, nothing missing and nothing extra in the curriculum than that which is explicit in the learning outcomes. This was especially important because of the potentially nebulous nature of "entrepreneurship" where there could have been shadowy learning outcomes: that is, those that the teacher expects the student to know or be able to do in the assessment but which are not articulated in the learning outcomes or the explicit prior learning.

Feedback was also considered particularly crucial, because for most students this process would likely be their first exposure to the entrepreneurial environment (Nicol & McFarlane-Dick, 2006). This feedback would therefore help students clarify what good performance is (goals, criteria, standards), and how to self-assess and encourage motivational beliefs and self-esteem (Rust, 2002). A key objective of the research was therefore to provide a foundation for the design of effective learning outcomes of the entrepreneurial module; and these were aligned to "students understanding and developing entrepreneurial behaviour".

Research-For-Design: So, What Do Entrepreneurs Actually Do?

The module's research was undertaken with 60 entrepreneurs to identify behavioural competences. The study used behavioural competence as a lens through which to examine the different views between entrepreneurs. In order to minimise the effect of situational conditions, the study focused on a single sector, "creative industries", thus controlling for proximal explanations (Magnusson & Endler, 1977) in a sector growing at twice the rate of the economy. Specifically, the objectives of the research were to:

1. Present a behavioural competency profile for a sample group of entrepreneurs and identify the differences between individuals;

2. Explore the use of psychometric testing in explaining and predicting how individual entrepreneurs drive the firm;

3. Develop a methodology for students to identify their own competences;

4. Provide students the opportunity to identify their own competences, and to develop these in an action learning context.

A convenience sample (Bryman, 2008) of 60 entrepreneurs was recruited. In order to participate, the entrepreneur had to evidence:

- A desire to grow coupled with an increase in employment by 20% in at least one year in the last five years;
- The raising of funds or the intention to raise funds in the future (financial sustainability was seen as common for all lenses of entrepreneurship);
- Active trading (indicated in year of incorporation);
- A minimum of one employee in addition to the entrepreneur.

A profile of the sample is summarised as follows:

Turnover (£000's)				Employees (No.)		Year Incorporated		
<£100	100–500	500–1000	+1000	<10	10+	1995–2000	2000–2005	2005–2011
27	20	6	7	46	14	3	14	43

Table 2: Panel profile of entrepreneurs.

Competency data on each entrepreneur was collected using Aston Business Assessments (ABA, 2011), a personality inventory assessment that measures nine behavioural competences on a scale of 0 to 10. The nine competencies together with research propositions are detailed in Table 3.

The ABS test is grounded in the Big Five Model of personality (Goldberg, 1990) and Bartram's Great Eight Competency Model (Bartram, 2005). Semi-structured interviews were recorded, taking between thirty minutes and one hour with each entrepreneur annually over three years. The questionnaires were designed in order to evidence entrepreneurial behaviour, defined as "the concrete enactment by individuals (or teams) of tasks or activities" within a funding context (Bird, 2012:890). Using an analytic induction methodology (Znaniecki, 1934), the research question is examined using propositions with the goal of most accurately representing the reality of the situation. These propositions are noted in Table 3.

Trait Competency and Proposition:	References:
P1: Working with Others: Being able to work with others provides opportunities to access finance.	Granovetter (1982).
P2: Communicating, Meeting, and Presenting: Being a good communicator can facilitate access to finance.	Baum & Locke (2004); Collins & Porras (1994); Rauch & Frese (2007).
P3: Innovating and Creating.	Rauch et al. (2014); Schumpeter (1934).
P4: Problem Solving.	Sarasvathy (2004); Dew et al. (2008); Rauch (2009); Sarasvathy et al. (2001).
P5: Planning and Organising.	Black (1998); Shapero (1975); Ciavarella (2004); Ajzen (1991).
P6: Driving for Results.	Delmar & Wiklund (2008); Locke & Latham (1990).
P7: Working with Customers.	Granovetter (1982).
P8: Leading Others.	Collins & Porras (1994); Rauch (2009).
P9: Coping with Pressure.	Sarasvathy (2009); Dew et al. (2008); Rauch (2009).

Table 3: Research propositions.

In addition to the statistical results, qualitative, semi-structured interviews explored the activities of the entrepreneur; these being the process through which they try and raise funds, for example, and what evidence there is of using behavioural competences in order to achieve their funding objectives. Interviews were recorded, transcribed, and coded directly using NVivo 10 qualitative research software, seeking to avoid the weaknesses highlighted by Bazeley (2007:132).

Results

The mean data for the Behavioural Competency Score (BCS), 0–10 scale for all 60 of the entrepreneurs (T1-T60), is presented as follows:

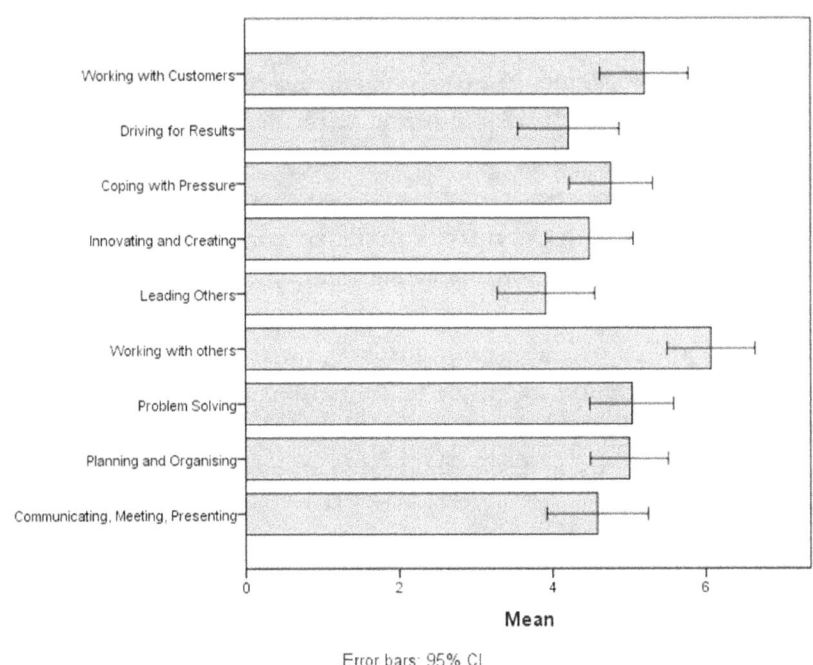

Error bars: 95% CI

Table 4: Mean BCS scores – 60 entrepreneurs (scale 0 to 10).

The results from this research indicate a tendency for higher competences in collaborative behaviours, along with business planning and problem solving. Working with Others (6.07) and Working with Customers (5.2) are the highest scores. Leading Others (3.92) and Driving for Results (4.22) have the lowest behavioural competency scores. These results are in line with more recent studies (Zhao, 2010) that the clichéd view of the swashbuckling entrepreneur emphasising leadership (Brockhaus, 1982) and locus of control (Begley & Boyd, 1987), for example, are at odds with reality.

Cluster analysis, using Ward's method, was then performed to identify groups (clusters) within the 60 cases of entrepreneurs; that is, those entrepreneurs who share similar characteristics across the nine behavioural competences. For ease of clarity of subsequent analysis, each group is given a name and the mean scores for each group are noted in Figure 1 and presented as follows:

The Capables group has the highest competence scores in all groups; again, Working with Others is the strongest (7.14), followed by Communicating, Meeting and Presenting (6.68), Working with Customers (6.61), and Driving for Results (6.14). Although the remaining competencies have lower scores, they are still higher than the other two groups. On balance, this group is the closest to the traditional view of entrepreneurs.

The Collaborators group has a focus on co-operation with high competency in Working with Others (6.67) and Working with Customers (5.4), followed by lower scores for Innovating and Creating (5.53) and Problem Solving (5.2).

The Low Competences group displays low scores across all competences; Planning and Organising (4.29) is the strongest competency in this group. The group is the most introverted; less interested in others, with few social skills, and is methodical in approach.

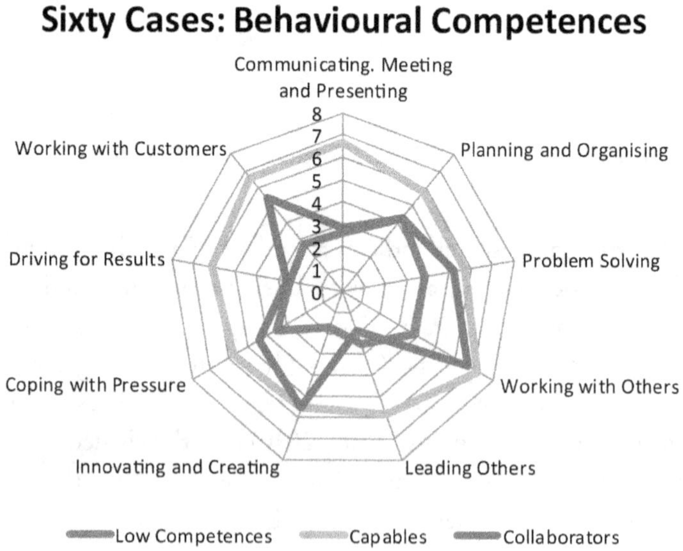

Sixty Cases: Behavioural Competences

Figure 1: The distinctive differences between the three clusters.

Drilling Down: Success in Gaining Finance

Having gained an overall view of "what entrepreneurs do", the research then drilled down to focus on behaviour in one theme: successful access to finance. The aim behind this is to explore and understand the behaviour of entrepreneurs in a specific skill set: that is, securing finance, where finance can be for either profit or not-for-profit enterprises. Table 5 details the number of entrepreneurs in each cluster, and among them the number of entrepreneurs making successful, unsuccessful, and non-applications (didn't apply) in each of the three years of data collection. Interviews were carried out between September 2011 and August 2014 and as much as possible at 12-month intervals. Four cases dropped out of the programme after Year 1; 56 cases were analysed in Years 2 and 3.

Twenty-eight entrepreneurs in the Capables cluster took part in the study in Year 1. This reduced to 26 who agreed to continue their participation in the study in Years 2 and 3. The Capables cluster was consistently more successful in funding applications over the periods; 11 entrepreneurs (39%) in this cluster made successful applications in Year 1, thirteen (50%) in Year 2, and 13 (50%) in Year 3. This group also had the fewest unsuccessful applications; only three over the three-year period. The number of Capables choosing not to apply for finance was also fairly stable over the period. Fifteen Collaborators participated in the study throughout the three-year period. Collaborators had mixed results.

The highest proportion of this cluster making successful applications was in Year 2 with seven (47% of Collaborators); this group had four unsuccessful applications over the three-year period and also had the highest proportion of non-applications (67%, 40%, and 66%, respectively). Seventeen Low Competence entrepreneurs embarked on the study and this reduced to 15 for Year 2 and 3. The Low Competence group had the lowest level of success; 13 unsuccessful applications over the period with a success rate below 27%. Non-applications were also high at 64%, 33%, and 60%, respectively.

Year 1 Finance Applications	Capables	%	Collaborators	%	Low competence	%
Applied and Successful	11	39%	4	27%	2	12%
Applied and Unsuccessful	1	4%	1	7%	4	24%
Didn't Apply	16	57%	10	66%	11	64%

Year 2 Finance Applications	Capables	%	Collaborators	%	Low competence	%
Applied and Successful	12	50%	7	47%	4	27%
Applied and Unsuccessful	1	4%	2	13%	6	40%
Didn't Apply	12	46%	6	40%	5	33%

Year 3 Finance Applications	Capables	%	Collaborators	%	Low competence	%
Applied and Successful	13	50%	4	27%	3	20%
Applied and Unsuccessful	1	4%	1	7%	3	20%
Didn't Apply	12	46%	10	66%	9	60%

Table 5: Applications v clusters.

Using the BCS scores, the study also analysed Behavioural Competency by funding outcome, and these are illustrated in Figure 2. Unsuccessful applications had lower levels of competencies compared with entrepreneurs, who either chose not to apply or made successful applications. Successful cases were stronger in Communicating, Meeting, Presenting, Leading Others, Coping with Pressure, and Driving for Results. Didn't Apply cases were stronger in Planning and Organising, Problem Solving, Working with Others, Innovating and Creating, and Working with Customers.

Funding Outcome by Cluster: Significance Test

Collecting three tranches of data produced a sufficient sample to make further statistical analysis appropriate. Analysing all applications over the three-year period, a chi-squared test was performed and confirmed the significance of the relationship between cluster membership and application outcome ($\chi2$ (1, n=172)=21.488, p<.000). This shows that cluster membership is an indicator of funding outcomes.

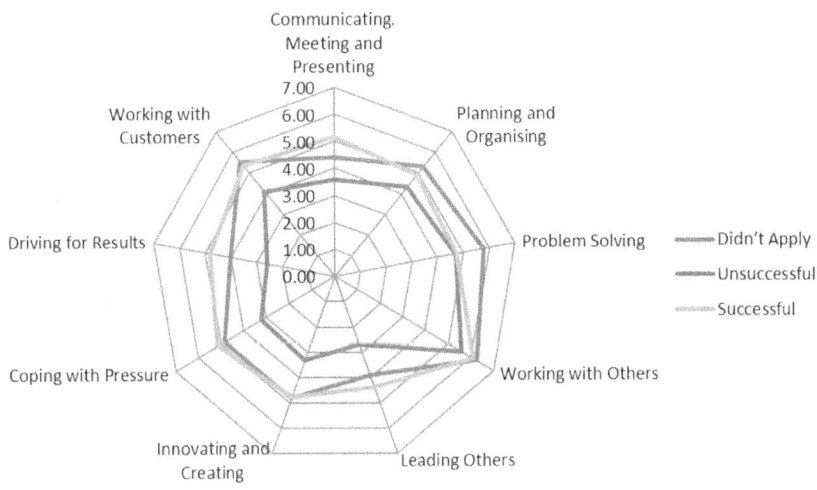

Figure 2: Successful v Unsuccessful v Didn't Apply.

Using Advisors

To provide increased insight into the degree to which entrepreneurs work with others, each entrepreneur was asked in every phase of the study to confirm if advisors had been used to assist decision-making in relation to funding. Table 6 analyses this by cluster. In the study, 77% of Capables reported using advisors in each year of the study. Also, 60% of Collaborators made use of advisors. Conversely, only 25% of the Low Competences cluster had appointed advisors during the period.

Chapter 7

Clusters v Use of Advisors	Capables	Collaborators	Low competence
Use of Advisors	77%	60%	25%
No Use of Advisors	23%	40%	75%

Table 6: Advisors v clusters.

Table 7 indicates the relationship between the use of advisors and applications outcomes:

Use of Advisors	Yes	No
Applied and Successful	47%	19%
Applied and Unsuccessful	2%	24%
Didn't Apply	52%	57%

Table 7: Applications v advisors.

In the study, 47% of cases with advisors reported successful applications, in contrast with 19% of non-advised entrepreneurs. When analysed with the Behavioural Competency scores, this group also outperforms non-advisors across all competences:

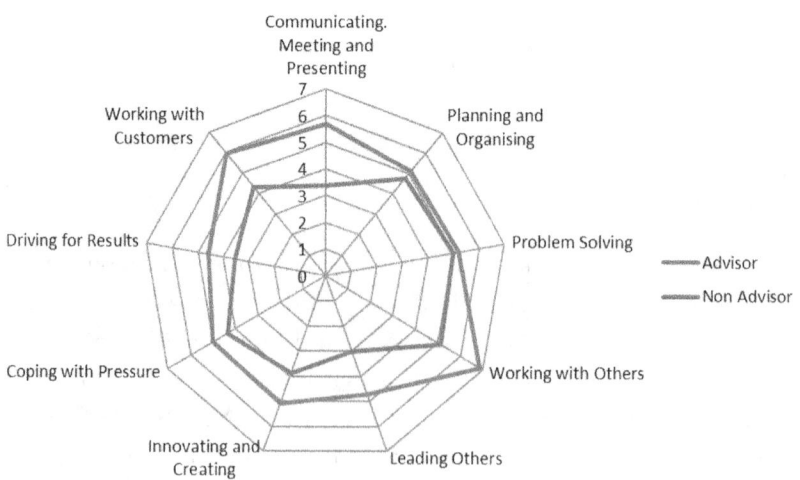

Figure 3: Advisors v non-advisors.

Advisors by Cluster: Significance Test

Analysing the use of advisors over the three-year period, a chi-squared test was performed and confirmed that the relationship between cluster membership and use of advisors was significant ($\chi2$ (1, n=172)=32.974, p<.000). A chi-squared test was performed and confirmed that the relationship between using advisors and application outcome was significant ($\chi2$ (1, n=172)=27.462, p<.000). This would indicate the use of advisors results in more successful funding applications.

Qualitative Interviews

The nine behavioural competences were used as a guide to frame the semi-structured interviews and explore what the entrepreneur actually "did" in order to fund the firm. In addition, a tenth code was developed – Behavioural Difficulties – in order to explore how each cluster reacted to problems in the funding process. Making up each of the Behavioural Competence Codes are a number of coded themes which emerged during the course of the interviews; descriptions for these are in Appendix 1.

Year 1 Coded Interviews

Working with Others was the strongest theme in Year 1. An example of this was the emerging theme of Serial Networking. The business was established in 2010 and the entrepreneur used private equity and angel finance to fund the business. He talks about how he used his network (coded to Serial Networking) to source funding: *"I am an LBS alumni... one of my ex-classmates runs an offshore angel group... cooperating with her on the Isle of Man to pitch in front of high net worth individuals..."*

Planning and Organising, Communicating and Presenting, and Innovating and Creating were also strong interview themes. For example, T9 used a government-backed bank loan to start and develop the business and plans to use private equity to expand in the future. He describes how he has developed a method of managing capacity in order to estimate the investment required for the business: *"I have detailed capacity planning (Capacity Planning) translated into a spreadsheet which gives us a dynamic target to hit each month..."*

Equally, Low Competency entrepreneurs had a significantly higher density (55%) of codes, indicating difficulties associated with sourcing finance. For example, T13 explained: "Your (plan) P&L to a degree goes (Bad Planning) out the window... all very unpredictable. So it's guesswork..."

Year 2 Interviews

Working with Others; Communicating, Meeting and Presenting; Innovating and Creating; and Problem Solving continued to be strong themes in the interviews and together make up. Working with Others is particularly strong for Capables and those entrepreneurs making successful applications; for example, T45 expanded into the US and talks enthusiastically about the use of advisors: "This year we brought in advisors from the West Coast... Head of Mobile at Winga... she is a new investor one we have brought in (this year)."

Compared with Year 1 interviews, Collaborators, in particular, were keener to give examples of problem-solving competences. For example, T29 made changes through a new model which included a revenue share with a partner: "Now more focus on smaller amounts... get teamed up with global marketing partner... revenue share with them (Developing a New Business Model)... when we are bigger will go back to Bruno Mars...".

Communicating, Meeting and Presenting was also again discussed in successful cases. T45 (a Capable) approached a number of new private investors: "Did pitches... clearly... looked at... angels who want to invest and make a social impact... (Approaching Investors)... we did a pitch there and ended up getting £90K from that group... got introduced to them in order to give a reference for someone else and they ended up being interested in the business..."

Again, Low Competences accounted for the largest number of behavioural difficulties, accounting for 75% of the themes that were coded.

Year 3 Coded Interview Analysis

Working with Others was again the strongest theme, in particular with Capables and Collaborators. Compared with Year 2, Innovating and Creating was also a stronger theme, particularly amongst those that were successful in funding applications. T08 (a Capable) successfully applied for a grant in the year and described the support he received from the SME Educational Programme: "*Yeah, it was unbelievable, the training, the coaching, the people that came to the presentation, the follow-up stuff... I can just pick up the phone and speak to people, they're there to basically find someone or find a way.*"

A closer examination of the data also indicated that Driving for Results, along with Communicating, Meeting and Presenting and Planning and Organising, were strong themes amongst successful entrepreneurs. Innovating and Creating was a strong theme, particularly amongst self-funded entrepreneurs. Problem Solving was a strong competency in the non-applying group of entrepreneurs, indicating a propensity to develop alternative strategies to solve funding availability.

Research Conclusions

Analysing the results of the quantitative study and the behavioural competency score, together with the qualitative interviews, it was clear that a number of the research propositions described earlier could be confirmed. In particular, and relevant to the MEF module, competency was in a number of areas key to successful outcomes. For example, Working with Others has been a strong theme through all three phases of the interviews, particularly with Capables and Collaborators. Key themes emerging from the three-year study included networking, using advisors, and investigating joint ventures. It is also the strongest competence in this group of entrepreneurs and is the strongest competence amongst successfully applying entrepreneurs. Communicating, Meeting and Presenting is associated with having social confidence in meeting and speaking, as well as communicating clearly and persuasively. Business angels have become an important source of equity finance to SMEs, and business angel activity and communication skills are key in presenting investment propositions.

Themes emerging in the study included presenting to potential international investors, and there was evidence of social boldness, the confidence to interact with strangers (Zhang & Souitaris *et al.*, 2008) and entrepreneurs attempting to send signals to prospective investors (Spence, 1973) at pitching events, for example. In this study, Communicating, Meeting and Presenting was a strong competency amongst Capables and amongst successful applications.

Section 3: Designing a Research-Led Entrepreneurship Module

From the research, four key themes emerged which had a significant contribution to the design of the MEF entrepreneurship module:

1. *The significance of collaborative behaviour in the context of resource acquisition for successful entrepreneurs.* It was clear that some business owners were predisposed with this behavioural competence, but some would require personal development in order to improve capability;

2. *The importance of communication skills and the ability to "sell the story" around a business proposition.* The essence of marketing, the ability to tell a compelling story, was reported to be key to being an entrepreneur;

3. *The need to seek and use advice.* Even relatively nascent entrepreneurs utilised a team of advisors in order to provide guidance for business decisions. Some of these formally through the appointment of non-executive positions, but not always. The research found that advisors played a key role with entrepreneurs;

4. *The ability to be able to problem solve.* Small firm owners are faced with a variety of problems requiring a range of skills and competences. The research provided clear evidence that those entrepreneurs with these skills were more successful.

The design approach for the MEF entrepreneurship module was *parti pris* in relation to these four findings. The stages of design proceeded from aims; level descriptors, learning outcomes, delivery style, and assessment. It is important to note that this was not a sequential, one-way process from aims to assessment: the design process is iterative. At each stage, the design could flow in any direction such that, for example, when the assessment is reviewed it is possible to return to the learning outcomes and redesign accordingly. This is the testing process where the constructive alignment of the design is modelled and tested.

Research-Informed Constructive Alignment: Designing the Fine Detail of the Module

The findings of our research: "what do entrepreneurs do", can been summarised as: *collaborate; communicate; seek advice; problem solve*. These key research findings were embedded in the module learning outcomes. By the end of the module, the student would be able to:

1. Demonstrate a detailed understanding of entrepreneurial competences and the role these play in marketing the small firm;

2. Explain the complexity of the competitive environment and its implications for small firms;

3. Review the challenges facing marketing decision-makers in a small business and, through working with others and seeking advice, maximise opportunity for resource acquisition;

4. Select appropriately from a toolkit of marketing concepts and analytical tools in order to apply these and communicate to relevant stakeholders.

Learning Outcome/Entrepreneurial Behaviour	Collaborate	Communicate	Seek Advice	Problem Solve
Demonstrate a detailed understanding of entrepreneurial competences and the role these play in marketing the small firm.	✓	✓	✓	✓
Explain the complexity of the competitive environment and its implications for small firms.		✓		
Review the challenges facing marketing decision-makers in a small business and, through working with others and seeking advice, maximise opportunity for resource acquisition.	✓		✓	
Select appropriately from a toolkit of marketing concepts and analytical tools in order to apply these and communicate to relevant stakeholders.		✓		✓

Table 8: Mapping of learning outcomes to entrepreneurial behaviour.

These outcomes were also constructed in a Kolbian (1984) framework to both stimulate and simulate students' reflective practice such that actual experience of the firm and reflection on the salient issues is followed by:

- Abstract conceptualisation of the subject (theories, concepts, and models of marketing); then
- Active experimentation (developing strategies for marketing); then
- Communication and dissemination (collaborative skills).

From the outset, the module was designed to provide students with the opportunity to engage directly with the external environment using technology-enhanced participation in the active learning process. This builds on the research outcomes, allowing students the opportunity to develop real life skills that are aligned constructively with the learning outcomes, learning activities, and assessment. The use of technology-enhanced learning was adopted using established, proven approaches that have already been used and tested at Aston; these include, for example, BlackBoard VLE, Panopto (Aston Replay), and other non-consecutive seminar approaches. Students at Aston are familiar with these technology-enhanced approaches and therefore the risk in the application of these is reduced.

Assessment and Feedback, Including Formative Feedback

The assessment for the module is aligned to both the learning outcomes and the entrepreneurial behaviour.

1. Group Report addressing marketing issues for a real, small firm;
2. Client Presentation. With the "client's" agreement, students will formally present back to the client on the results of their work and the client will be asked to provide informal feedback;
3. Reflective Diary. Students will complete an online reflective diary on their project, including their observations on the firm and the problem they are investigating. This will assist in their completion of the group report personal assessment. This will encourage students to consider how marketing strategy is considered in a real firm;
4. Individual concept analysis under examination conditions.

Learning Outcome/ Entrepreneurial behaviour	Collaborate	Communicate	Seek Advice	Problem Solve	Assessment Task
Demonstrate a detailed understanding of entrepreneurial competences and the role these play in marketing the small firm.	✓	✓	✓	✓	Group report
Explain the complexity of the competitive environment and its implications for small firms.		✓			Client presentation
Review the challenges facing marketing decision-makers in a small business and, through working with others and seeking advice, maximise opportunity for resource acquisition.	✓		✓		Reflective diary
Select appropriately from a toolkit of marketing concepts and analytical tools in order to apply these and communicate to relevant stakeholders.		✓		✓	Concept analysis

Table 9: Mapping of learning outcomes to entrepreneurial behaviour.

Working with an entrepreneur gave students the opportunity to observe competences in action and, through the group report, address a specific problem faced by the firm. This problem related specifically to the reality of the current competitive environment, for example, through new product launches. Through the reflective diary, and the online support of "Water Cooler" and "Ask the Advisor", students were encouraged to reflect on challenges facing marketing decision-makers by actually working with others and seeking advice themselves. The concept test provided an opportunity to demonstrate an understanding of marketing concepts and analytical tools.

Section 4: A Rough Guide to Entrepreneurship Curriculum Design

This chapter describes and explores the design of an entrepreneurship module at Aston University that was informed by bespoke, prior research into "what entrepreneurs do". This research formed part of a key stakeholder engagement strategy in our module's design. The aim was to design a module that reflected, if not simulated, the skills and competencies (rather than traits) of actual local entrepreneurs. The research found that "what entrepreneurs do" is to: *collaborate; communicate; seek advice; problem solve*. Drawing on our experiences, we have developed a rough guide to designing entrepreneurship modules:

- Programme (or curriculum) philosophy;
- Stakeholder engagement and the design navigator;
- Evaluation, review, and dissemination.

Programme (or Curriculum) Philosophy

This is akin to the mission statement and provides a clear set of benchmarks for the design team. We differentiate *curriculum* from *programme* for the simple purpose of indicating when the philosophy relates to a distinct programme of studies (such as a degree) or a more loosely defined learning journey (i.e., curriculum) such as an option path within a degree or a stand-alone module that does not, in itself, constitute a complete programme. There needs to be genuine buy-in to the philosophy by the founding members of the design team. As such, there is a pre-phase in which the programme philosophy is discussed and agreed. We recommend that "nominal group technique" is used to find consensus within the design team; it is proven in our practice of programme design, and in the wider literature, to be an effective method for consensus building in curriculum (O'Neil & Jackson, 2006). We recommend that the creation of the programme philosophy does not involve wider stakeholders beyond the founding members. Some might find this surprising, but we hold that is it for *educators* to establish the pedagogical and philosophical brief for a new programme within which stakeholders can then be engaged to co-create the design. To exclude some stakeholders at this stage may be seen as a contentious proposal, hypocritical perhaps, but from our experience we believe that education is a political venture and our politics are orientated towards critical pedagogy (Freire, 1970). Once we have set our pedagogical manifesto, we can engage with the wider entrepreneurial community.

As an illustration of this rough guide, and building on our philosophical declarations given at the beginning of this chapter, the curriculum philosophy would be: *"Teaching on the FME module is designed from the perspective that learning is a social activity best undertaken within a multi-disciplinary community. We see learning as a product of discussion, debate, and the co-creation of knowledge. Using conceptual modules and theoretical perspectives of entrepreneurship, we engage students in debate and critical reflection upon the tacit ideologies about professionalism and success for those who aspire to be entrepreneurs. We uphold diversity of identities within an anti-oppressive and anti-discriminatory context that holds that anyone can be an entrepreneur."*

Stakeholder Engagement and the Design Navigator

From our curriculum philosophy, it is clear to see that our keystone concept of stakeholder engagement flows from inclusivity and the co-creation of both knowledge and curriculum design. Much has been written about stakeholder engagement, including (but not limited to) students, teachers, careers advisors, employers, professional bodies, course administrators, alumni, and so forth. However, for the purpose of our rough guide, we add one recommendation: that stakeholder engagement can be facilitated through bespoke research. Earlier in this chapter, we discussed our research with entrepreneurs into "what they do", and it was found that one key skill of an entrepreneur is the ability to "sell an idea". In view of this, we suggest that stakeholder engagement with entrepreneurs can be enacted through bespoke research that provides the reference points to ensure an authentic syllabus; we do not believe that it is essential to bring entrepreneurs into the programme design studio where their views might shadow those who are less empowered to engage or sell their ideas.

We also recommend the use of a design navigator, as is the case at Aston University. The design navigator acts as both consultant and facilitator in both the process of design and, more specifically, as a pilot to the design team as they navigate through the context-situated "design challenges" of a programme. A design navigator ought to be a relative expert in learning, teaching, curriculum design, and academic quality; and importantly, the role of design navigator ought to be recognised by the university so that those in the role have an appropriate institutional mandate to engage.

Evaluation, Review, and Dissemination

Whilst we have not explored the evaluation, review, and dissemination in the body of our chapter (due to limitations of space), we recommend that the design of entrepreneurship teaching and learning is part of a regular iterative cycle in a Kolbian manner (Kolb, 1982). In addition to the quality enhancement benefits, which are noted widely in the literature, it enables curriculum designers to ensure that social, economic, and political changes remain current within the syllabus.

Conclusion

Our chapter provides an important contribution to this anthology through recounting how a new entrepreneurship module was created according to a research-led approach within the new guidelines for curriculum design at Aston University in the UK. Whilst we hope that the research recounted in the chapter is of value to those who have an interest in what entrepreneurs do, we believe that details of our module's design and the accompanying rough guide provide a framework for those who are about to engage in the creation of an entrepreneurship module.

In summary, we recommend that:
- Design commences with the co-creation by educators, not entrepreneurs, of a curriculum/programme philosophy;

- The curriculum/programme philosophy is the mission statement that encapsulates the pedagogy (and any other key orientations) of the proposed learning and teaching experience. It also acts as a central reference point when design challenges are encountered;

- Stakeholder engagement is central to design, but engagement does not necessarily require face-to-face participation in design activities. We found that bespoke research with entrepreneurs (as stakeholders) has the benefit of providing the voice of entrepreneurs whilst redressing the power for those who may otherwise find themselves shadowed by the strong voice of entrepreneurs;

- A design navigator is central to effective and productive design, but only if the higher education institution provides a clear mandate to the design navigator to facilitate and intervene.

About the Authors

Dr Julian Lamb leads the HEA-accredited PGCert Learning and Teaching in Higher Education at Aston University. He can be contacted at this e-mail: j.lamb1@aston.ac.uk

Geoff Parkes is Senior Teaching Fellow, Head of the Marketing and Strategy Group, and Associate Dean International at Aston Business School. He can be contacted at this e-mail: parkesgs@aston.ac.uk

Bibliography

Ajzen, I. (1991). The Theory of Planned Behavior. *Organizational Behavior & Human Decision Processes*, Vol. 50, No. 2, pp. 179–201.

Bartram, D. (2005). The Great Eight Competences: A Criterion-Centric Approach to Validation. *Journal of Applied Psychology*, Vol. 90, No. 6, pp. 1185–1203.

Baum, J. R. & E. A. Locke (2004). The Relationship of Entrepreneurial Traits, Skill, and Motivation to Subsequent Venture Growth. *Journal of Applied Psychology*, Vol. 89, No. 4, pp. 587–598.

Bazeley, P. (2007). *Qualitative Data Analysis with NVivo*. Sage.

Begley, T. M. & D. P. Boyd (1987). Psychological Characteristics Associated with Performance in Entrepreneurial Firms and Smaller Businesses. *Journal of Business Venturing*, Vol. 2, No. 1, pp. 79–93.

Bird, B. & L. Schjoedt (2009). Entrepreneurial behavior: Its nature, scope, recent research, and agenda for future research. In Carsrud, A. & M. Brannback (eds.) *Understanding the entrepreneurial mind*. New York: Springer, pp. 327–358.

Bird, B.; L. Schjoedt & J. R. Baum (2012). Entrepreneurs Behavior: Elucidation and Measurement Introduction. *Entrepreneurship: Theory & Practice*, Vol. 36, No. 5, pp. 889–913.

Black, J. (1998). Entrepreneur or entrepreneurs? Justification for a range of definitions. *Journal of Business and Entrepreneurship*, Vol. 10, No. 1, pp. 45–65.

Brockhaus, R. H. (1982). *I-E Locus of Control Scores as Predictors of Entrepreneurial Intensions*. Academy of Management.

Bryman, A. (2008). *Social research methods*. New York: Oxford University Press

Bygrave, W. & J. Timmons (1992). *Venture Capital at the Cross Roads*. Boston: Harvard Business School Press.

Caird, S. P. (1993). What do Psychological Tests Suggest about Entepreneurs? *Journal of Managerial Psychology*, Vol. 8, No. 6, pp. 11–20.

Ciavarella, M. (2004). The Big Five and venture survival: Is there a linkage? *Journal of Business Venturing*, Vol. 19, No. 4, pp. 465–483.

Ciavarella, M.; A. Buchholtz; C. Riordan; R. Gatewood & G. Stokes (2004). Big Five and venture survival: Is there a linkage? *Journal of Business Venturing*, Vol. 19, pp. 465–483.

Collins, J. & J. Porras (1994). *Built to Last: Successful habits of visionary companies*. New York: Harper.

Delmar, F. & J. Wiklund (2008). The Effect of Small Business Managers Growth Motivation on Firm Growth: A Longitudinal Study. *Entrepreneurship: Theory & Practice*, Vol. 32, No. 3, pp. 437–457.

Dew, N.; S. Read; S.D. Sarasvathy & R. Wiltbank (2008). Outlines of a behavioral theory of the entrepreneurial firm. *Journal of Economic Behavior & Organization*, Vol. 66, No. 1, pp. 37–59.

Farndale (2011). *Lord Sugar: University is a waste of time*. Online Resource: http://www.telegraph.co.uk/culture/tvandradio/the-apprentice/8480671/Lord-Sugar-University-is-a-waste-of-time-Apprentice-interview.html [Accessed on 23 August 2016].

Fraser, S. (2014). *'Back to Borrowing? Perspectives on the 'Arc of Discouragement.'* Enterprise Research Centre, White Paper No. 8.

Freire, P. (1970). *Pedagogy of the Oppressed*, 30th Anniversary ed. New York: Continuum, 2006.

Gartner, W. B. (1989). Some Suggestions for Research on Entrepreneurial Traits and Characteristics. *Entrepreneurship: Theory & Practice*, Vol. 14, No. 1, pp. 27–37.

Gartner, W. B.; B. J. Bird & J. A. Starr (1992). Acting As If: Differentiating Entrepreneurial From Organizational Behavior. *Entrepreneurship: Theory & Practice*, Vol. 16, No. 3, pp. 13–31.

Gibb, A. & L. Davies (1990). In pursuit of frameworks for the development of growth models of the small business. *International Small Business Journal*, Vol. 9, No. 1, pp. 15–31.

Goldberg, L. R. (1990). An alternative 'Description of personality – The Big Five factor structure. *Journal of Personality and Social Psychology*, Vol. 59, pp. 1216–1229.

Granovetter, M. (1973). The Strength or Weak Ties. *American Journal of Sociology*, Vol. 78, pp. 1360–1380.

Lock, E. & G. Latham (1990). *A Theory of Goal Setting and Task Performance*. New York: Prentice Hall.

McClelland, D. C. (1961). *The Achieving Society*. Princeton.

Maier, V. & C.P. Zenovia (2011). Entrepreneurship versus Intrapreneurship. *Review of International Comparative Management*, Vol. 12, No. 5, pp. 971–976.

Mueller, S.; T. Volery & B. von Siemens (2012). What Do Entrepreneurs Actually Do? An Observational Study of Entrepreneurs' Everyday Behavior in the Start-Up and Growth Stages. *Entrepreneurial Theory and Practice*, Vol. 36, No. 5, pp. 995–1017.

O'Neil, M. J. & L. Jackson (1983). Nominal Group Technique: A process for initiating curriculum development in higher education. *Studies in Higher Education*, Vol. 8, No. 2, pp. 129–138.

O'Gorman, C.; S. Bourke & J. A. Murray (2005). The Nature of Managerial Work in Small Growth-Orientated Businesses. *Small Business Economics*, Vol. 25, No. 1, pp. 1–16.

Rauch, A. & M. Frese (2007). Let's put the person back into entrepreneurship research: A meta-analysis on the relationship between business owners' personality traits, business creation, and success. *European Journal of Work & Organizational Psychology*, Vol. 16, No. 4, pp. 353–385.

Rauch, R.; R. van Doorn & W. Hulsink (2014). A Qualitative Approch to Evidence-Based Entrepreneurship: Theoretical Considerations and an Example Involviong Business Clusters. *Entrepreneurial Theory and Practice*, Vol. 38. No. 2, pp. 333–368.

Sandberg, W. R. & C. W. Hofer (1987). Improving New Venture Performance: The Role of Strategy, Industry Structure, and the Entrepreneur. *Journal of Business Venturing*, Vol. 2, No. 1, p. 5.

Sarasvathy, S. D. (2004). Making It Happen: Beyond Theories of the Firm to Theories of Firm Design. *Entrepreneurship Theory and Practice*, Vol. 28, No. 6, pp. 243–263.

Schumpeter, J. (1934). *The Theory of Economic Development*. Cambridge, Mass.: Harvard University Press.

Shapero, A. & L. Sokol (1982). The social dimensions of entrepreneurship. In C. Kent; D. Sexton & K. Vesper (Eds.), *Encyclopaedia of entrepreneurship*, pp. 72–90.

Spence, M. (1973). Job market signalling. *Journal of Quarterly Economics*, Vol. 87, No. 3, pp. 355–379.

QAA (2016). *QAA Framework*. Online Resource: http://www.qaa.ac.uk/en/Publications//Documents/qualifiications_frameworkpdf [Accessed on 23 August 2016].

Zhang, J.; V. Souitaris; P.-h. Soh & P.-k. Wong (2008). A Contingent Model of Network Utilization in Early Financing of Technology Ventures. *Entrepreneurship: Theory & Practice*, Vol. 32, No. 4, pp. 593–613.

Znaniecki, F. (1934). *The Method of Sociology*. New York: Farrar & Rinehart.

Chapter 8

Developing Student-Practitioners: Two Localised Methods for Teaching and Learning Entrepreneurship

Nathan Rauh-Bieri

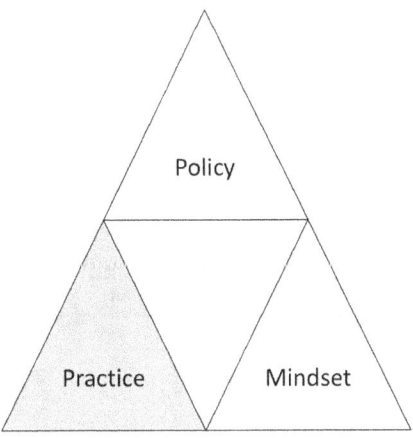

Introduction

My chapter is an important contribution to this section on practice – and to the book *Teaching and Learning Entrepreneurship in Higher Education* – because I introduce two localised methods for teaching and learning entrepreneurship in higher education: 1) the professional education workshop (PEW); and 2) the multidisciplinary action project (MAP). Both take place outside of the typical formal classroom setting. To ground my chapter, I draw on the experience and research of the William Davidson Institute (WDI) at the University of Michigan. Reading the chapter, you will gain the following insights:

1. Entrepreneurial development benefits from a localised approach: one which is applied, contextually relevant, and experiential;

2. Localised pedagogical methods effectively integrate theory and practice;

3. The teaching and learning outcomes of these methods are knowledge, skills, and abilities, which together make up *entrepreneurial acumen*;

4. When the above are realised, student-practitioners are developed.

I have structured the chapter into four main sections. First, I answer the obvious question: "Why This Approach?". Here I argue for the need for teaching and learning entrepreneurship in higher education. Second, I examine the professional education workshop in detail and discuss pedagogical implications of using it. Third, I move to the second localised method for teaching and learning entrepreneurship, the multidisciplinary action project, and present it in detail and discuss its pedagogical implications. In the fourth and final section, after examining each method in turn and highlighting its best practices, I then identify some of the common lessons and practices that emerge. These lessons and practices deepen our understanding of learning and teaching entrepreneurship in higher education, since each develops formal students and working practitioners alike into student-practitioners who possess entrepreneurial acumen.

Section I: Why This Approach?

When it comes to education today, change is in the air. The online education sector is expanding. Employer-provided on-the-job training is increasing, as is the number of employees finding their own learning opportunities through massive online open courses (MOOCs). Demands for competency-based forms of education are rising. Executive education remains a sizeable global industry. New visions for pedagogy abound. Teaching and learning is no longer formally tied to the business school (if it ever was).

In response to these changes, there is an increased recognition that developing entrepreneurs in their local context requires more applied approaches than have traditionally been employed within higher education. The methods of teaching and learning entrepreneurship explored below are two of many possible responses. I argue that their strength lies in that they apply across learning contexts; their practices translate academic resources into concrete, actionable forms for practitioners in local entrepreneurial ecosystems (for more on entrepreneurial ecosystems, see Fadel et al., in this volume). These methods for equipping active entrepreneurs in context need not compete with the kinds of training provided within the traditional business school environment; rather, they can expand and deepen higher education's ability to develop student-practitioners who gain the knowledge, skills, and attitudes – in short, acumen – to succeed in the long-term, beyond the formal classroom.

My purpose in exploring these methods is to commend their key advantages to others in higher education – whether specifically focused on entrepreneurship or not. Between these methods, I argue that educators can glean insight into effectively developing students and practitioners in a way that holds together theory and practice and develops in them knowledge, skills, and attitudes needed for long-term practice. Even though the scope of this chapter does not include prescriptions for replicating these models in other settings, I nonetheless hope it will provide you with insights that are applicable to your own educational context.

Guiding Framework

Having introduced the theme of this chapter, I will now provide the framework which guides this chapter: its context, terms, and overarching model. After this, I will explore the two methods in detail.

Context

This chapter is based on the experience of the William Davidson Institute at the University of Michigan (WDI). As an independent research institute at the University of Michigan, WDI brings a singular perspective on teaching and learning entrepreneurship to the present volume. As a non-profit provider of short-term, professional workshops with a research-based approach and a contextual focus on emerging markets, WDI is neither a traditional university nor an executive education company. At the same time, its affiliation with the University of Michigan and partnership with the Ross School of Business enables it to train MBA students through action-based learning projects and access leading thought-resources on management education. Through involvement in these entrepreneurial development activities, and with a focus on emerging economies, WDI occupies a unique perspective on developing entrepreneurs. Although WDI focuses its entrepreneurship efforts within emerging economies, as mentioned, I aim to demonstrate how these methods apply to teaching and learning across geographical and socio-economic contexts. Moreover, I intend for educators working in a variety of roles, disciplines, and contexts to find something useful for their own practice in the model, methods, and practices discussed below.

Terms

Entrepreneurship has been defined in various ways. For the purposes of this chapter, I define *entrepreneurship* as the practices by which one generates economic activity. In light of WDI's mission to support economic development within emerging economies, these methods primarily focus on entrepreneurship in the context of business. It is well-noted, however, that entrepreneurship education is increasingly not restricted to business (for an interdisciplinary approach to entrepreneurship education, see McCormack & Scanlon's chapter in this volume). I define entrepreneurship *development* as the process of preparing the whole person for entrepreneurial practice. This, I argue, requires the participant to become a *student-practitioner*: a continuous learner whose learning is enacted in active practice. Developing entrepreneurs engages the learner in multiple levels of Bloom's taxonomy (Bloom *et al.*, 1956); it entails the learner's holistic formation as an entrepreneur.

In what follows, I name the main outputs of entrepreneurial development as *knowledge*, *skills*, and *attitudes* (KSAs). Although KSAs often stand for "knowledge, skills, and *abilities*", for present purposes I argue that skills and abilities are indistinguishable in practice. Furthermore, by merging "abilities" with "skills" and adding "attitudes", I follow the insight of an exceptional student MAP team – Team A – whose unpublished work with entrepreneurs in India found that *attitudes* better rounds out the desired outputs of entrepreneurial development. In this chapter's unique use of KSAs, then, *knowledge* includes the "remember" and "understand" levels of Bloom's taxonomy; *skills* include technical know-how as

Developing Student-Practitioners

well as the "apply" level of Bloom's taxonomy; and *attitudes* is related to one's mental habits as they are directed toward entrepreneurial practice.

One note on *attitudes*: WDI's close work with diverse local partners has confirmed that when it comes to the practice of entrepreneurship, one's mindset plays a significant role in achieving entrepreneurial success (for more on entrepreneurial mindset, see Johnsson et al.'s chapter in this volume). Like more traditional training topics (e.g., operations, accounting), mindset can be addressed in workshops with the desired goal of inculcating entrepreneurial attitudes. *Attitudes*, then, join *knowledge* and *skills* as the outputs of entrepreneurship development (more on this below).

These three outputs (KSAs) comprise the ultimate outcome of entrepreneurship development, which is *entrepreneurial acumen*. Acumen is when KSAs are translated into entrepreneurial behaviours; when a learner performs entrepreneurial acumen, KSAs have taken root. Acumen shows itself by one's ability to make good judgments in the domain of entrepreneurship; the Cambridge English Dictionary defines it as *"the ability to make correct judgments"*. Entrepreneurial acumen is both practical and informed by theory (one's own and published), cutting across academic and practical categories. It is neither practiced into being only nor transmitted conceptually only; it must be developed. Difficult to codify, it takes years of practice (Clyde, 2015). At best, each method discussed below instils several levels of Bloom's taxonomy. In each, the learner gains the overall ability to exercise good entrepreneurial judgment in practice, or to behave with entrepreneurial acumen. In its own way, each method develops entrepreneurial acumen in the learner, or student-practitioner. The student-practitioner is a person who has successfully learned not only how to learn but also how to apply this learning in the context of her particular ecosystem; in other words, she has been developed to perform entrepreneurial activities with acumen.

A Model for Developing Entrepreneurs

To understand the overall relationship between the above terms, one can visualise a funnel-shaped diagram (see Figure 1, below), beginning at the top with the wide range of potential suitable methods and curricula for developing entrepreneurs (including training, topics, tools), distilled

Chapter 8

down to the main outputs of KSAs, and then finally distilled down to the overall outcome of entrepreneurial acumen.

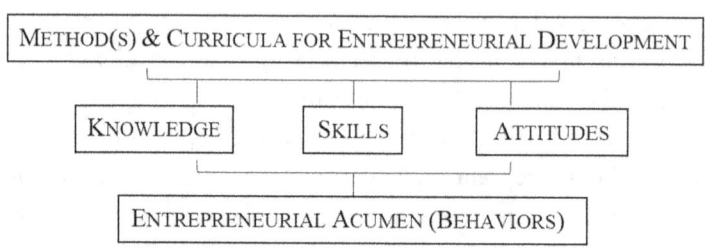

Figure 1: Entrepreneurial development model.

Having provided a guiding framework for this chapter, let me now examine in depth the two concrete methods that will anchor it: the professional education workshop (PEW) and the multidisciplinary action project (MAP).

Section 2: Professional Education Workshop (PEW)

WDI designs and delivers on-the-ground workshops for entrepreneurial practitioners (primarily SME owner/managers in emerging economies). Participants attend these workshops for two days up to two weeks to focus on a variety of basic management topics. To support these offerings, WDI's research focuses on best practices for developing active entrepreneurs in emerging markets. This research draws on university resources for teaching business essentials. Yet WDI's education efforts begin with assessing local needs, collaborating with a local partner, and together, designing a contextually relevant curriculum and delivering it within the partner's locale.

In most cases, the site of the PEW is markedly different from the formal MBA classroom. As such, it requires concerted attention to pedagogy and learning outcomes. For example, what teaching practices must be employed in a course on "Financing a New Business" when the students are not MBAs but rather Rwandan small business owners with little formal business knowledge and often steep cultural barriers to accessing bank loans (Brown, 2016)? Such considerations inform PEW design and delivery.

Pedagogical Advantages

From its experience assessing PEW outcomes, successes, and challenges, WDI observes that the following insights support effective teaching and learning:

1. When the majority of a PEW's participants have not previously received formal business training, their learning is best served by focusing on business planning and assessment skills, using the Business Model Canvas and other tools. Planning a business introduces learners to a range of business topics but tethers these subjects to the learner's own (business) objectives. This exercise is thus concrete, applied, and learner-centred from the outset;

2. Learning retention is heightened because learners already have their own businesses (or significant responsibility in one); they can immediately translate and apply learning to their job;

3. The expectation is set from the beginning that the PEW will be active and interactive. Participants should be primed to expect not lecture-based passive engagement but an interactive environment which employs Dougan's (2016) best practices in andragogy, or the theory of adult learning: (1) Design as a "cooperative effort between facilitator and learner"; (2) Recognition that "adults are most energized about material that has immediate relevance for their jobs or personal lives"; (3) A "problem-centred rather than subject centred" process (e.g., "How do I access capital?" rather than "Bank Loans 101"); (4) Evoking and incorporating learners' valuable prior experiences. These points align with Knowles' (1998) best practices in andragogy;

4. PEWs are consistently most successful when they feature *clear, concrete* – which is to say, applied, rather than cognitive or descriptive – and *concise* learning objectives at the start of the programme,

which are consistently referenced throughout. As busy people who are spending valuable time away from work and family, practitioners need to see the PEW's immediate relevance to their goals. The question closest to the mind of the active entrepreneur is: "How will this benefit my organisation?"

To support learning objectives, one WDI instructor intentionally incorporates three distinct learning elements into each PEW session:

a. *Learn.* This includes descriptive, fact-based *knowledge*: theories, concepts, models, and frameworks for participants to collect and test. This recognises that facts are required before skills and experiences can be absorbed and applied. This matches how people usually learn, moving from basic mental skills (remembering) to more complex ones (analysing, synthesizing, evaluating, creating);

b. *Practice.* Exercises can take a number of forms (cases, group projects, games, etc.), but the main idea is action-based learning – using concepts, theories, frameworks, models to proactively solve real-world business problems (which build *skills*). Exercises are most effective when they fit into learning objectives and are contextualised to the participants' region, sector, or market;

c. *Reflect.* Reflection asks participants to make connections to their own situations after they have undergone other types of thinking and have toolkits ready for the reflective task (Schön, 1987). As Cope & Watts (2000) observe, most adults learn most effectively from first doing and then reflecting. While reflection can take a number of forms, one instructor habitually devotes five minutes at the end of every session to ask three questions: 1) What did you learn? 2) How does it apply to your organisation (or why not)? 3) What will you do when back at your workplace? This element is directed outward toward the business problem to be solved, but reflection can lead participants to identify and confront mental mindsets holding them back and can cultivate new *attitudes*.

5. Whether participants are postgraduates (with prior classroom experience), SME owner/managers (who are responsible for daily operations), or both, an overly theoretical approach will not stand; the PEW must connect at every point to the practitioner's real business needs. Furthermore, since the PEW is a cohort of peers who weigh teaching against their own and one another's experiences, it counters any drift into abstractions;

6. A learner-centred PEW is inductive rather than deductive; it is guided by learning outcomes rather than driven by a set of propositions;

7. Teaching practitioners improves pedagogical practice: instructors who teach active entrepreneurs typically find their learning-facilitation skills sharpened by the participants' demand for actionable takeaways, and this in turn informs their practice when they return to teaching in degree programmes.

In this overview of the pedagogical practices employed in WDI's professional education workshops, it becomes clear that the most successful entrepreneurship instructors employ a learner-centred teaching model: one that begins with understanding where the participants are coming from, engages them with a variety of cases and action-based learning tools, and structures the content to encourage workplace application.

Section 3: Multidisciplinary Action Project (MAP)

In addition to designing and delivering PEWs, WDI supports MAP projects. MAP projects are field-based action-learning projects conducted by student teams outside the formal classroom. The MAP programme originated at the University of Michigan's Ross School of Business, where it has been developed over the past 25 years. As it is now practiced, a MAP team features four first-year MBA students who travel internationally and work full-time for up to seven weeks on a project hosted by a corporate, educational, or non-profit organisation to identify challenges and opportunities the organisation faces in its particular context. WDI partners with the MAP programme to deploy teams from Michigan,

USA, to field-based projects within emerging economies (some recent examples include Morocco, Kosovo, Georgia, and India). On projects supported by WDI, MAP teams primarily serve organisations aimed at developing entrepreneurs – and thereby the local economy.

Tasked with solving real business challenges or exploring growth opportunities on the ground, MAP teams utilise critical thinking, multidisciplinary connections, and real-world applications to provide recommendations and innovative solutions to their host organisations. The host plays an active role in guiding the students' learning and directing their outputs. A balanced team brings diverse skillsets, backgrounds, and work experiences, along with enthusiasm, faculty oversight and guidance, and training resources (including MAP-specific training on a range of topics – e.g., field research, interview methods, and cultural sensitivity). A MAP project provokes the kind of learning only a field-based, team-based, out-of-classroom, intercultural experience can: applied, contextually relevant, and experiential.

In a sense, the MAP project functions as a living case study, affording the pedagogical benefits Broido & Shiloh (2014) observe in learning via narrative, such as featured in the use of the case study. The main difference is that the team and its individual members are themselves *inside* the narrative via the on-site research and consulting process. It might not be their own case – inasmuch as they are consultants making recommendations, rather than managers implementing them – but the MAP presents dimensions of a learning scenario which the case study cannot. Through the methodologies of appreciative inquiry, design thinking, interviews, focus groups, and guided reflection, this method of learning instils not only cognitive but also affective, intuitive, and embodied knowledge (Peet, 2015).

At the conclusion of a successful MAP project, an exchange has taken place: the host organisation is left with the benefits of consulting, and the students come away with valuable, field-based experience in understanding entrepreneurship, organisational strategy, methods of field research, and collaborative skills. Based on the testimony of students, at its best a MAP project provides mutual benefit to both the host and the student team alike. Educational in essence, it transcends a transactional model by forging relationships between the team, supervisor, and other stakeholders.

At its best, the MAP programme's training instils in its teams a healthy "guest" or "learner" mindset, rather than an "expert" or "fixer" mindset for entering an unfamiliar cultural context or organisational culture. Because students enter a context from the outside to identify and solve problems, power dynamics need to be navigated carefully. But when a team of learners approaches their project with the posture of inquisitive guests, recognising their displaced-ness, a significant learning exchange can occur: MAP students learn how to understand their host culture while meaningfully contributing to their host organisation's capacity to create local economic change.

The Case of "Team A"

For brevity's sake, I will focus on the experiences and findings of one exemplary MAP team ("Team A") to demonstrate MAP projects' high potential for developing MBA students' entrepreneurial KSAs (even as they support the KSAs of local entrepreneurs in their host ecosystem). Team A travelled to support an entrepreneur development organisation in a small Indian city for several weeks. Based on the US students' in-country work, their exploration of the entrepreneurship ecosystem using interviews and academic frameworks, and the guidance of professors at the University of Michigan and their local host supervisor, the team reported the conditions they found and proposed recommendations based on the host organisation's stated needs. Team A's experience demonstrates that when a project is done well, students gain extensive knowledge about the conditions in which the entrepreneur is situated – knowledge that is useful in their own careers and for supporting others' careers.

MAP project pedagogy begins with the team's pre-deployment preparation in field research methods, scenario planning, and intercultural competency. Through immersion in a local context, team members learn to engage cross-culturally and read a new market environment. Teams utilise interviews and focus groups to learn about client and stakeholder needs and assess prevailing conditions; they also learn to read entrepreneurial ecosystems. Ecosystems, the hundreds of factors contributing to enterprises' successes or failures, can fit into six domains: culture, policies and leadership, finances, human capital, markets, and infrastructural supports (Isenberg, 2011). Entrepreneurial development programmes intervene in the human capital domain. Partly, this involves teaching entrepreneurs to read their wider entrepreneurial ecosystems. In the case of Team A, this involved dozens of interviews with local entrepreneurs across industries. They then constructed an entrepreneurial typology, mapping the factors at work in the local ecosystem.

Interviewing many entrepreneurs in a short amount of time benefitted host and students alike. The interviews provided the host organisation new insight into how to effectively meet its trainees' needs, but it also offered the MAP students a view into what entrepreneurship is all about – and this developed their own career interests. *"It felt like an intense study in what their challenges were, what made them successful, what they thought was success"*, one team member reported. *"I am interested in entrepreneurship as a career path, and this project gave me more confidence in that."* A teammate agreed: *"This gives me incredible new perspective on what it means to be an entrepreneur."* In this way, Team A's assignment trained its members to see the world as entrepreneurs – even if they are, for the moment, MBA students rather than business owners.

The MAP project instils management practices that translate to students' future careers. For example, Team A utilised the following practices of *design thinking* to great effect: 1) discovery, 2) interpretation, 3) ideation, 4) experimentation, and 5) evolution. Design thinking requires a combination of the cognitive, attitudinal, and interpersonal aspects of problem solving (Brown, 2009). Design thinking draws heavily on two of the main practices that Neck *et al.* (2014) identify as integral to the practice of entrepreneurship: empathy and experimentation. Design thinking provides students with powerful tools to understand client needs, a truly translatable skillset (Seidel & Fixson, 2013).

Even as MAP students study how entrepreneurs effectively develop KSAs, they themselves are developing entrepreneurial KSAs. For example, even as the team assessed how to introduce more holistic learning and training resources, they were required to draw from varied resources. As one Team A member put it, *"We referenced things from our core curriculum, our prior careers, we learned from each other – it truly was multidisciplinary."* Another said, *"To learn in an environment that's totally different from what you're used to – I won't have any greater experience in my life to learn in so many ways at the same time."*

The MAP project epitomises the possibilities experiential learning offers formal business students who are interested in entrepreneurship. It provides what Kolb (1984) sees as the main ingredients of experiential learning: the experience, feedback or interaction with others in the experience, and self-reflection on the experience. Experiential learning requires the learner's active involvement, ability to reflect, analytical skills for processing the experience, and decision-making and problem-solving skills in order to integrate the experience. Experiential learning follows a cycle of concrete experience, reflective observation, abstract conceptualisation, and active experimentation (Kolb, 1984). Mason & Arshed (2013) distil experiential learning's outcomes to: 1) students' improved ability to understand classroom concepts, and 2) students' encounters with learning situations irreproducible in a classroom. As an action-reflection model, the MAP project incorporates all these components. It is experiential learning *par excellence* for MBA students.

As a method of developing entrepreneurs, MAP projects benefit both partners in the exchange. Not only do students aid the host organisations' strategic efforts, but in the process, they learn entrepreneurship itself – as it is performed in local contexts, with MBA classroom frameworks and academic resources in mind to apply, test, and refine. MAP students learn which services meet entrepreneurs' needs and how entrepreneurs learn best. As Team A testifies, this active learning shapes MBA students' career paths, whether as entrepreneurs, within an education sector, or within an emerging market.

Team A's increased ability to work contextually and collaboratively, make recommendations that support local organisations, and create positive social impact exemplifies what the MAP project method of developing entrepreneurs can provide formal MBA students. For active entrepreneurs, the MAP's format (multi-week, immersive, unpaid project) would not be practical; for degree-seeking students, however, it is one of the best ways to understand the challenges and opportunities faced by entrepreneurs in emerging markets and cultivate in themselves entrepreneurial knowledge, skills, and attitudes. It is a strong method for spurring their development as student-practitioners who act with entrepreneurial acumen.

Pedagogical Advantages

To summarise the main advantages of the MAP pedagogical method:

1. MAP projects bridge learning contexts (from academia to entrepreneurial ecosystems); faculty and host supervisors' oversight effectively facilitates students' connecting, comparing, and contrasting classroom frameworks with on-the-ground findings;

2. The main components of a MAP project – teamwork, field research, interviewing, analysing, evaluating, reporting – encompass multiple levels of Bloom's taxonomy, stimulating different types of learning and facilitating complex learning;

3. MAP projects improve global cultural competency (an ever-pertinent skill);

4. For students without prior entrepreneurial experience, the MAP project familiarises them with the kinds of challenges entrepreneurs face and the resources that empower them. In short, the MAP project provides first-hand insight into the nature of entrepreneurship itself;

5. MAP projects' experiential learning develops in formal students the kinds of entrepreneurial knowledge, skills, and attitudes that they would not have been able to access from the business school classroom alone.

Section 4: Implications for Teaching and Learning

I have examined two methods for cultivating in participants' entrepreneurial knowledge, skills, and attitudes (in short, developing entrepreneurs): the professional education workshop (PEW) and the multidisciplinary action project (MAP project). These are but two of many possible approaches to developing entrepreneurs. They will not suit the needs or goals of everyone who works in entrepreneurship education, but they provide insight into pedagogical practices which effectively develop entrepreneurs. Having surveyed each method and reflected on its individual contributions to teaching and learning entrepreneurship, it is time to identify some shared implications:

1. *A practice-based approach replaces a trait-based one.* In contrast to an era of scholarship that attempted to identify certain characteristics differentiating entrepreneurs from non-entrepreneurs (also known as a trait-based understanding of entrepreneurship, as exemplified by McClelland (1961)), recent scholarship suggests there is no one, given, or specific entrepreneurial psychology (e.g., Shane, 2008). Entrepreneurs do not share in common what Little (2014:53) calls *"fixed"* traits; rather, they take up whatever *"free traits"* help them accomplish their entrepreneurial goals. This is perhaps especially true in economic contexts where limited resources drive entrepreneurship out of necessity. Most of the entrepreneurs WDI supports in emerging economies, while certainly bringing their innate, fixed traits to bear on their work, often become entrepreneurs out of economic motive, in pursuit of opportunity, and through grit: entrepreneurship is what is required to make a living. In other words, they become entrepreneurs as they practice it. This aligns with Peter Drucker's (1985:143) insight that *"entrepreneurship is not magic, it is not mysterious and it has nothing to do with genes. It is a discipline. And, like any discipline, it can be learned"*. Following this point, Neck et al. (2014:13) opt for a method-based approach, which views entrepreneurship as a non-linear and fairly messy process requiring an array of tools and practices rather than either the right innate traits or the right research steps. The tools and practices they commend work together to engender *"thinking and acting entrepreneurially"*. The process of learning entrepreneurship is a set of practices that develops learners to *think* as entrepreneurs, which in turn develops them to *act* as entrepreneurs – with entrepreneurial acumen;

2. *Learning entrepreneurship means "learning to learn."* Adaptive learning is integral to a practice-based approach. Based on his experience training several hundred entrepreneurs in Rwanda (most of whom had no prior formal business training), WDI's Brown (2016) concludes that what makes an entrepreneur is cultivating what Dweck (2006:7) calls a *"growth mindset"*: viewing new

experiences and sources as opportunities to learn from rather than merely performances to deliver. This is also, incidentally, what MAP projects intentionally cultivate in their student consulting teams. For Brown, the work of business is ultimately about learning. Whether the learners are MBA students or Rwandan business owners, successfully practicing entrepreneurship requires continual, adaptive learning;

3. *"Displaced" learning leads to fresh learning.* During MAP projects and training programmes, MBAs and entrepreneurs alike are outside of their normal learning environment: the former is in a new cultural context and out of the classroom; the latter is out of the office, likely in a different city, and likely with new people. In both cases, the disorientation can stimulate new thinking; stepping back provides space for fresh insight. As Nygaard & Holtham (2008:14) argue: *"Learning is a process affected by the social position of the learner."* Where you are affects what and how you learn;

4. *Mindset is vital to entrepreneurial development.* Recent research suggests that how entrepreneurs view the world and how they learn – in other words, their mindset – is paramount to helping them succeed (Neck *et.al.*, 2014). Discarding the fixed trait theory allows us to see just how critical mindset is to success in every other area. As a result, entrepreneurship curricula increasingly feature sessions devoted to mindset and personal development alongside more traditional management topics. Harrison *et al.* (2007:333) suggest why: *"Management education … is more about shaping and honing perceptions, mentalities, and dispositions rather than the systematic dissemination of professionalized knowledge."* Teaching mindset varies based on a learner's culture and subject-position within that culture. As examples: having a business fail in the US is often deemed a sign of experience but can be a source of shame in other cultural contexts; and in strongly patriarchal cultures, there are often psychological, as well as social and economic, barriers to women pursuing entrepreneurship. This said, some common mindsets to address include:

   a. *Fear of failure.* Fear of failure is so common an obstacle to entrepreneurial development, entrepreneurial acumen is gained only through engaging it. According to Schlesinger *et.al.* (2012), those who embrace failure's possibility create a future, rather than trying to predict it;

   b. *Facing ambiguity.* Because entrepreneurial ecosystems are often chaotic, unpredictable, and ambiguous, it is educators' roles to prepare learners to excel in highly uncertain environments (Neck, 2011). One instructor who trains many entrepreneurs says: *"The most important skill for entrepreneurs is handling ambiguity."* The same could be said for MAP students: handling ambiguity is honed in the field but serves them long-term in any entrepreneurship-influenced career.

5. *Openness to experimentation.* Experimentation is one of the five core practices that Neck et al. (2014:71) claim leads to *"acquiring knowledge of the concepts and techniques that can be applied in entrepreneurial situations".* This kind of knowledge is specifically afforded in the MAP project setting, where there are supports and sounding boards in place for one to make the kinds of judgments required by external consultants – and entrepreneurs. While no "safe" laboratory exists for practitioners who take time from their jobs to attend a PEW – whose learning and decisions have immediate import for their businesses – a PEW's focus on application, as well as on learning from peers' experiences and cases, serves to offer additional management experience by proxy. If entrepreneurship is learned by practice, as this chapter claims, so too is experimentation;

6. *"Learn, practice, and reflect" is a useful pedagogical pattern.* This teaching sequence proves effective during each session of an intensive training course. It also works well when patterned in the macro learning process of the MAP project: students receive classroom frameworks, test them in a localised consulting context, and then report on their findings;

7. *Foster a facilitative, learner-centred learning environment.* As Neck et al. (2014:1) put it, the role of educators is to *"unleash the entrepreneurial spirit of our students, cultivate a mindset of practice, and build environments in which practice can occur".* The MAP project,

conducted outside of the familiar classroom paradigm, readily accomplishes these educational goals. Similarly to the MAP project, when done well, the PEW unleashes this spirit, deepens a practice mindset, and builds a practice-based environment through custom business planning, cases, group exercises, and structured reflection;

8. *Theory and practice are integrated.* If management education in general and entrepreneurship education in particular has been in a pendulum swing between theory and practice since its modern emergence as a discrete discipline, as Harrison *et.al* (2007) claim, the MAP project and the PEW bridge these poles. The MAP retains the value of frameworks, represented by the famous insight of Kurt Lewin (the father of action research): *"There is nothing so practical as a good theory"* (1951:169). On the other hand, the MAP project heeds Aristotle's words: *"For the things we have to learn before we can do them, we learn by doing them."* By employing practices such as design thinking, for instance, MAP students are able to learn in holistic personal relation to the situation, and yet employ sources for understanding the kinds of knowledge they access during their MAP. Similarly, professional programmes make use of participants' limited out-of-workplace time to provide both job-specific troubleshooting (skills) and serviceable frameworks (knowledge) for use on the job after the programme ends. As Tushman *et al.* (2007) argue, such programmes pair research *rigor* with managerial *relevance*. Both methods thus result in what Neck *et al.* (2011:9) call *"actionable theory"*. Truly localised methods integrate theory and practice.

Conclusion

Entrepreneurship development benefits from more localised methods than have traditionally been employed in the formal classroom. In this chapter, I have presented two localised methods for teaching and learning entrepreneurship: 1) the professional education workshop (PEW), and 2) the multidisciplinary action project (MAP). Based on the experience of the William Davidson Institute at the University of Michigan

(WDI), I have shown how each method develops the knowledge, skills, and attitudes of degree students and practitioners alike. On the one hand, practitioners who attend a PEW are equipped with the resources to continually learn and apply what they learn to their businesses' and contexts' challenges and opportunities. Similarly, in the MAP project, business students become consultants who are immersed in the everyday realities of the practitioner, surveying the ecosystem's opportunities and constraints. Each of these methods of teaching and learning entrepreneurship purposefully integrate theory and practice. Each in its own way develops student-practitioners whose learning is localised – applied, contextually relevant, and experiential – and whose acting is grounded in ongoing learning and reflection. Each method develops student-practitioners with entrepreneurial acumen who actively develop and apply their knowledge, skills, and attitudes within the context of a localised entrepreneurial ecosystem. In short, each method develops *entrepreneurs*.

About the Author

Nathan Rauh Bieri is programme coordinator of Education at the William Davidson Institute at the University of Michigan. He can be contacted at this e-mail: njrb@umich.edu

Bibliography

Bloom, B. (Ed.) (1956). *Taxonomy of Educational Objectives: Handbook 1 Cognitive Domain*. Longman: New York.

Broido, M. & I. Shiloh (2014). The Case for Narrative: Stories as Gateways to Academic Texts. In J. Branch; P. Bartholomew & C. Nygaard (Eds.), *Case-Based Learning in Higher Education*. Oxfordshire: Libri Publishing, pp. 77–90.

Brown, M. V. (2016). *Teaching and Learning with Rwandan Women Entrepreneurs*. WDI Education Initiative. Online Resource: http://wdi.umich.edu/wp-content/uploads/Education-Article-Matt-BrownRwanda.pdf [Accessed 6 August 2016].

Brown, T. (2009). *Change by Design: How Design Thinking Transforms Organizations and Inspires Innovation*. New York: HarperBusiness.

Clyde, P. (2015). Information Flow Analysis and the Theory of the Firm. *Managerial and Decision Economics*, Vol. No. 1, pp. 384–400.

Cope, J. & G. Watts (2000). Learning by Doing: An Exploration of Experience, Critical Incidents and Reflection in Entrepreneurial Learning. *International Journal of Entrepreneurial Behavior and Research*, Vol. 6. No. 3, pp. 104–24.

Dougan, W. L. (2016). *A Guide for Developing and Managing a Good Professional Development Workshop*. Academy of Management Annual Meeting. Online Resource: http://aom.org/uploadedFiles/Meetings/annualmeeting/program/GoodPDWGuide.pdf [Accessed 1 August 2016].

Drucker, P. (1985). *Innovation and Entrepreneurship*. New York: Harper & Row.

Dweck, C. (2006). *Mindset: The New Psychology of Success*. New York: Ballatine.

Harrison, R.; C. M. Leitch & R. Chia (2007). Developing Paradigmatic Awareness in University Business Schools: The Challenge for Executive Education. *Academy of Management Learning and Education*, Vol. 6, No. 3, pp. 333–343.

Isenberg, D. (2011). Introducing the Entrepreneurship Ecosystem: Four Defining Characteristics. Forbes. Online Resource: http://www.forbes.com/sites/danisenberg/2011/05/25/introducing-the-entrepreneurship-ecosystem-four-defining-characteristics/#523fa94f38c4 [Accessed on 1 August 2016].

Knowles, M. (1998). *The Adult Learner: The Definitive Classic in Adult Education and Human Resource Development*. Houston: Gulf.

Kolb, D. (1984). *Experiential Learning: Experience as the Source of Learning and Development*. Englewood Cliffs, NJ.: Prentice-Hall.

Lewin, K. (1951). *Field Theory in Social Science: Selected Theoretical Papers*. D. Cartwright (Ed.). New York: Harper & Row.

Little, B. R. (2014). *Me, Myself and Us: The Science of Personality and the Art of Well-Being*. New York: PublicAffairs.

Mason, C. & N. Arshed (2013). Teaching Entrepreneurship to University Students Through Experiential Learning. *Industry & Higher Education*, Vol. 27 No. 6, pp. 449–463.

McClelland, D. C. (1961). *The Achieving Society*. Princeton, Van Nostrand.

Neck, H.; P. Greene & C. G. Brush (2014). *Teaching Entrepreneurship: A Practice-based Approach*. Cheltenham (UK): Edward Elgar.

Nygaard, C. & C. Holtham (2008). The Need for Learning-Centred Higher Education. In C. Nygaard & C. Holtham (Eds.), *Understanding Learning-Centred Higher Education*, Copenhagen: Copenhagen Business School Press, pp. 11-29.

Peet, M. (2015). *Action Learning in Business Education: Creating Goals for Action Learning*. Michigan Ross Action Learning Conference. Online Resource: http://michiganross.umich.edu/AL-Conference [Accessed 18 May 2016].

Schlesinger, L.; C. Kiefer & P. Brown (2012). *Just Start: Take Action, Embrace Uncertainty, and Create the Future.* Cambridge, MA: Harvard Business School Press.

Schön, D. (1987). *Educating the Reflective Practitioner.* London: Jossey-Bass.

Seidel, V. P. & S. K. Fixson (2013). Adopting "Design Thinking" in Novice Multidisciplinary Teams: The Application and Limits of Design Methods and Reflexive Practices. *Journal of Product Innovation Management,* Vol. 30, No. S1, pp. 19–33.

Shane, S. A. (2008). *The Illusions of Entrepreneurship: The Costly Myths that Entrepreneurs, Investors, and Policy-makers Live By.* New Haven: Yale.

Tushman, M. L.; C. A. O'Reilly; A. Fenollosa; A. M. Kleinbaum & D. McGrath (2007). Relevance and Rigor: Executive Education as a Lever in Shaping Practice and Research. *Academy of Management Learning & Education,* Vol. 6, No. 3, pp. 345–362.

Chapter 9
Promoting Entrepreneurship in Social Services and Healthcare

Sirkka-Liisa Kolehmainen

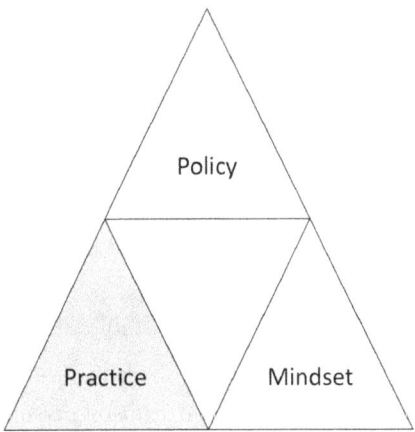

Introduction

My chapter is an important contribution to this section on practice – and to the book *Teaching and Learning Entrepreneurship in Higher Education* – because I show how we have worked to implement entrepreneurship education at the Metropolia University of Applied Sciences (Metropolia UAS) in Helsinki, Finland. We developed a European Social Fund (ESF) project named HYRRÄT – Promoting Entrepreneurship in Well-Being Services – which was carried out between February 2013 and March 2015. The project involved all disciplines within social services and healthcare (what we called "Well-Being Services"), 18 training programmes, about 4,500 students, and about 300 teachers (Metropolia UAS, 2012, 2014). The project had five interrelated aims:

1. to improve students' entrepreneurship skills and encourage students to become entrepreneurs delivering Well-Being Services;

2. to improve teachers' skills so they can develop teaching methods

and materials to use when teaching entrepreneurship education aimed at Well-Being Services;

3. to develop the business environment of companies delivering Well-Being Services;

4. to produce support-material for different life-stages of companies delivering Well-Being Services;

5. to create a foundation for policy-driven structural change and networking in Metropolia UAS.

We used Well-Being Services as our concept, which we defined as a broad umbrella- concept which included education, leisure, entertainment, and social and health-related activities (Kainlauri, 2007). Social services and healthcare entrepreneurship are seen as one part of the wide spectrum of well-being entrepreneurship (Oske, 2008). Reading my chapter, you will gain these three insights:

1. arguments for why we need to teach and learn entrepreneurship in universities;

2. knowledge of how we developed and designed HYRRÄT, which will hopefully inspire you to try similar endeavour at your own university;

3. a discussion of how a project like ours can be a foundation for policy-driven structural changes and networking at universities.

I have structured the chapter in five main sections. First, I address the needs for teaching and learning entrepreneurship. Second, I introduce HYRRÄT and show in more detail what we did. Third, I discuss the importance of the results, what was learned from the project, how the results of the project can be utilised in the future, and what kind of further development-work is required. Fourth, I address how a project like ours can be a foundation for policy-driven structural changes and networking at universities. Fifth, I sum up with a discussion of entrepreneurship education and reflect on our learning points.

Section 1: Why Teaching and Learning Entrepreneurship?

Global trends, such as internationalisation, digitalisation, the rise in people's level of education, service diversification, the aging of the population, and economic pressures are increasing the need for new Well-Being Services. At the same time these trends also increase the pressure to create more efficient, more economical, and more individual Well-Being Services. In addition to the publicly funded Well-Being Services, private and third sector services and networked collaboration are needed to an increasing extent. Within the education sector for Well-Being Services, the need for developing and reinforcing positive attitudes towards entrepreneurship and development of business skills has increased. Due to the changes in the operating environment in the sector for Well-Being Services, entrepreneurs require support from the initial start-up of the company until the change of ownership. I define the changes of ownership as a business transfer. A business transfer *"is understood as a transfer of ownership of the enterprise to another person or enterprise that assures the continuous existence and commercial activity of the enterprise. This can take place within the family, through management buy-outs (sales to non-family management/employees) and sales to outsider persons or existing companies, including takeovers and mergers"* (European Commission, 2002:6; 2012a:9).

Increasing entrepreneurship has been suggested as a means for surviving the Western economic crisis. This increase could be achieved by improving the business environment for small and medium-sized enterprises, introducing measures to encourage changes of ownership, as well as through education, research, innovation, and development targeting these areas (European Commission, 2003, 2010; the Commission of the European Communities, 2008). According to the Nordic Nord Region Report review, Finland is among the leading Nordic countries in terms of innovation, but in terms of entrepreneurship we are clearly lagging behind Europe and the Nordic countries, especially in the emergence of entrepreneurship (Roto et al., 2014; European Commission, 2012b) (see irchley & McCasland, in this volume, for a similar discussion on Japan).

In Finland, small and medium-sized companies play a key role in the creation of new jobs and economic growth. According to the statistics of the Finnish Business Register (2013), 93.3% of a total of 283,000 companies are micro-companies with 1–9 employees. 5.5% are small companies (10 to 49 people). The employment effect of these companies should also be noted. In Finland, aging also applies to the entrepreneurial base. Over the next 10 years, more than 70,000 companies that employ well over 200,000 people will face business transfer. Municipal tax paid by these companies is approximately 1.2 billion euros and state tax revenue is 300 million euros. The universities of applied sciences have a special opportunity to help find successors for these companies (Ahmaniemi et al., 2015).

This development is also reflected in the companies delivering Well-Being Services. According to Statistics Finland, in 2012 Finland had 20,345 delivering Well-Being Service companies, employing about 62,000 people. This was about 6% of the total number of companies (Statistics Finland, 2014.) According to Kainlauri (2007), the average age of entrepreneurs in the social and healthcare sector was 48 years in 2007. It is estimated that as a result of aging, about 4,500 companies delivering Well-Being Services face the change of ownership over the next 10 years. The Finnish education system has identified the need as well as the importance of entrepreneurship education.

Due to a number of development projects, a continuum of entrepreneurship education from early childhood to universities has been achieved in Finland. In universities, especially in applied science and science universities, the following is encouraged: 1) strengthening of student entrepreneurial attitude, 2) supporting entrepreneurial motivation, 3) turning higher education knowledge and innovation into a business venture, and 4) developing and strengthening research and development knowledge into a business stream (Ministry of Education, 2009).

The aim of the Rectors' Conference, ARENE, in 2011 was that *"all bachelor's graduates have embraced intrapreneurship (individual and organizational entrepreneurial mind set and actions) and 15% of bachelor's graduates start an entrepreneurial career within 10 years of the completion of the degree"* (Arene, 2011). At the moment, about 5% of UAS students work as entrepreneurs at the time of graduation (Laitinen-Väänänen et al., 2013; Ahmaniemi et al., 2015), so the goal is still not fulfilled.

Entrepreneurship is not a profession or a career but rather a way of thinking, acting, and dealing with work and life in general. It may therefore occur in detecting opportunities, as innovative and proactive activity, risk taking and managing change and uncertainty in any area of life considering ethics, corporate social responsibility and sustainable development, and thus take different forms depending on the context (Heinonen & Vento-Vierikko, 2002; Ruohotie & Dog, 2001; Rae, 2010; Peltonen, 2014). Training programmes are expected to provide students with the skills and entrepreneurial spirit to strengthen their views on the environment and to develop business skills (Jussila et al., 2005). Entrepreneurship education should not only aim to learn about entrepreneurship and for entrepreneurship, but, above all, it should consist of entrepreneurial learning and learning in an entrepreneurial environment (Cabin & Gorman, 2004; Kyrö & Ripatti, 2006; Paasio et al., 2005). Therefore, entrepreneurship should be seen more holistically, considering the dimensions from intrapreneurship to entrepreneurship.

The process of becoming an entrepreneur is found to be affected by many factors. Recent entrepreneurial research has brought clarity on how the student's attitude towards a career in business, the immediate environment support, self-efficacy beliefs, and entrepreneurial abilities affect the entrepreneurial intentions that can create entrepreneurship. Of these, the support of the immediate environment, attitudes towards entrepreneurial careers, and self-efficacy beliefs appear as the most relevant factors for entrepreneurial intentions (Joensuu et al., 2014). According to Kivelä (2002) and Koiranen (1993) the journey of becoming an entrepreneur may be a long one and take years.

At Metropolia UAS in Helsinki, we became aware of the need to put more focus on teaching and learning entrepreneurship in 2013, when we surveyed the elements of entrepreneurship education in our curricula documents. It showed us that our students had very different experiences across our university. All healthcare degree programmes included a 3 ECTS course, Management, Society and Entrepreneurship (ECTS = European Credit Transfer and Accumulation System). In the curricula of the Faculty of Well-Being and Human Functioning, the amount of entrepreneurship courses varied from 3 to 9 ECTS. In addition, there were 3 ECTS in the curriculum of leadership and quality management studies. In relation to this survey, we also found that entrepreneurship studies were carried out by entrepreneurship teachers, mostly as classroom teaching, not closely linked to the business community. We therefore initiated the HYRRÄT program to increase entrepreneurship across the programmes at Metropolia UAS.

Section 2: The HYRRÄT project

The HYRRÄT project was designed for a two-year term for 2013 to 2015. The project target groups were students, teachers, and entrepreneurs delivering Well-Being Services. Our aim was to promote entrepreneurship by bringing together prospective entrepreneurs, existing entrepreneurs, companies facing ownership transfer, as well as students and teachers within Well-Being Services. We did so by forming a network which should support the companies. Meetings and events were organised as part of the project and they took place in the greater metropolitan region of Helsinki. Common goal-oriented work was supported at events and meetings. Examples of these are the Hyrrät 10, which contained: 1) an intensive business education day for students; 2) pedagogical entrepreneurship development programme for teachers, 3) entrepreneurship fairs; 4) foresight workshops; 5) networking workshops; 6) service design; and 7) ownership transfer workshops.

The project produced a website called *"Reittejä hyvinvointialan yrittäjyyteen"* (Routes to entrepreneurship in Well-Being Services) for the development of entrepreneurship education, teaching methods and materials. The website includes the material produced during the project, such as operating models and tool boxes, and a review on the role of gender in well-being entrepreneurship (available online: http://hyrrat.metropolia.fi).

The materials on the website are classified under the following headings: 1) entrepreneurship in the Well-Being sector; 2) entrepreneurial skills; 3) Start-Up of the company; 4) succeeding in the market; 5) high-quality services; 6) business transfer; and 7) entrepreneurship during education. The materials are intended for use by entrepreneurs-to-be, professionals delivering Well-Being Services, students, teachers, organisations, and business advisory organisations.

Students have assessed the benefits and usability of the website as part of various assignments. We have received a lot of useful feedback for developing the platform, and the aim is to update the platform in the future. The pages will be updated by the Well-Being Department's entrepreneurship teachers and students.

Institutional Organisation of HYRRÄT

Initially a project steering group was formed. The representatives included students, entrepreneurs, as well as representatives from the promoting parties in the Metropolitan area and from the Well-Being business sector. The steering group met four times a year through the entire project period.

Project evaluation was carried out at every meeting, and therefore any shortcomings could be addressed immediately. The project team met about once a month, and the project was managed co-operatively by dividing the responsibilities of the different areas of the project between the team members.

The labour to run the program was hired at the beginning of the semester, so it was difficult for the project workers to contribute fully to the project. There were initial teaching problems for the project relating to fixed-term staff completing their fixed term at the end of the first year of the project, and a new project manager also needed to be re-appointed in summer of 2014. This is expected of an intensive program like this.

For 2014, additional funding was received for the project to model and to develop measures for promoting ownership transfer. This contributed to the fact that the project came in under the estimated budget. Fortunately, it was possible to use the money to disseminate the results of the project.

Initial surveys were conducted among students and teachers. The survey was intended to help us further develop the project activities. The chosen project activities were: 1) courses; 2) workshops; 3) Well-Being entrepreneurship fairs; 4) ownership transfer theme day; and 5) the creation of Well-Being entrepreneurship web pages for presenting the results of the project instead of a printed brochure. These activities are shown on the timeline in Figure 1. These project activities were also evaluated using a survey at the end of the project to measure outcome.

	Spring 2013	Autumn 2013	Spring 2014	Autumn 2014	Spring 2015 Dissemination
Students	Innovation Projects; The Initial Survey.	Innovation Projects; Well-Being Entrepreneurship Education HYRRÄT 10 1 ECTS Credit.	Entrepreneurship Fair; Business Transfer Workshops.	The Final Survey Workshop; Business Transfer Day and Visits.	Entrepreneurship Education for 212 Students; Curricula Design in Master Degree Program.
Teachers	Teachers' Meeting; The Initial Survey.	Teachers Meeting; Pedagogical Entrepreneurship Workshop.	Teachers Meeting; Entrepreneurship Fair; Benchmarking with Lahti UAS; Pedagogical Entrepreneurship Workshop; International Workshop; Entrepreneurship Education Workshop.	Teachers Meeting; The Final Survey; Service Design and Well-Being Entrepreneurship Workshop.	Implementing the new HYRRÄT 10 Website.
Entrepreneurs		Foresight Workshops.	Entrepreneurship Fair; Networking workshops; Business transfer workshops.	Service Design Workshops; Business transfer; Day and Business Visits.	
Networking	The Project Steering Group.	The Project Steering Group 2 x.	The Project Steering Group.	The Project Steering Group 2 x.	The Project Steering Group 2 x.
Publications			Räsänen & Kolehmainen (2014): Role of Gender in Well-Being Entrepreneurship and EE. Haapa-aho (2014): Entrepreneurship in the Well-Being Sector. Views on the Future.	A Website: Routes to Entrepreneurship in Well-Being Services.	Kolehmainen (2015): Well-Being Teachers and Students Survey. Huotari (2015): Model for Service Design Training for Well-Being Entrepreneurs. The final project report

Figure 1: HYRRÄT – project implementation.

Next, I will tell in more detail what kind of results were achieved in the project.

Section 3: Results of the HYRRÄT project

In this section, I will describe the results of the HYRRÄT project. I have divided the main section into subsections. In the first subsection, I describe how we developed the students' entrepreneurial skills, and how we worked to encourage entrepreneurship. In the second subsection, I describe, how we developed the teachers' entrepreneurship education competence. In the third subsection, I then go on to describe how we developed Entrepreneurs' Competences and Guidance to Business Transfer.

Well-Being entrepreneurs, business know-how, we developed a networking, foresight and business transfer issues. In addition, I will tell you how we launched the project outputs, what we learned in the project, and how we can develop entrepreneurship education structures in Metropolia UAS.

Increasing Entrepreneurial Skills and Encouraging Entrepreneurship among Students of Well-Being Services

The initial and final survey measuring entrepreneurial skills was administered during the project. In addition to background knowledge and experience, the interest and attitudes towards entrepreneurship and the willingness to participate in entrepreneurship courses organised by Metropolia UAS was evaluated as well as the entrepreneurial skills acquired in the degree programme.

The number of respondents in the surveys was low, and the respondents were from different degree programmes in the initial and final surveys. The initial survey was answered by 0.2% (N = 35) of the 4,500 students in Well-Being Services and the final survey by 2% (N = 89). In the initial survey, the respondents were mostly students from the degree programme of the Well-Being and Human Functioning Faculty (24/35), while in the final survey most of the respondents were Healthcare and Nursing students (63/89).

The respondents had experience of being employed in a company and of entrepreneurship, and in some cases, the experience was long-term.

Also, the respondents reported having family members or close relatives who work as entrepreneurs, and in the final survey, 45% of the students reported having a member of the family or close relatives working as an entrepreneur in the sector for Well-Being Services. In the final survey, 26 students indicated that they intend to continue in the company of their family or close relatives within 1–5 years.

In both of the surveys, answers to questions concerning interest and attitudes were quite similar. The interest was moderate. The students felt that entrepreneurship requires realistic thinking and a positive attitude, and believed that entrepreneurship requires much more work compared to paid work. Students expressed least interest in participating in Metropolia UAS' entrepreneurship courses.

The survey revealed that interest in entrepreneurship is still quite low, but that there is potential in utilising the entrepreneurial experience in the students' family and relatives, for example. Ownership transfer training is also something that should be invested in in the future. In this survey, only three students participated in the events organised by the project, so the effects of the project on entrepreneurial skills could not be evaluated.

The areas that the students felt least competent in were business law, financial management, and corporate communications. These subjects are not included in the curricula of the Well-Being Services degree programmes. Entrepreneurship in the field of Well-Being Services is highly regulated and knowledge of these subjects would be needed. Increasing co-operation with the business degree programmes in areas of business law, financial management, and corporate communications is important in the future.

During the project, education on entrepreneurship in Well-Being Services was offered to the students. The project gave students 1 ECTS, where elective studies at Metropolia UAS are usually 3 ECTS credits. The number of elective studies in the curriculum is 10 ECTS credits, so the students have difficulties finding a 1-ECTS-credit study module. The courses organised were well-being entrepreneurship 1 ECTS credits and Hyrrät 10, as an intensive 1-ECTS-credit course. Of these, the most popular was the Hyrrät 10 course, which was carried out on three occasions during the project and later in the spring of 2015 during the implementation stage of the project in entrepreneurial education in various fields.

In addition to teaching, workshops on foresight, networking, ownership transfer and service design were organised during the project, as well as an international workshop. Student participation in these workshops was very low. Descriptions of the courses and other events can be found on the website: http://hyrrat.metropolia.fi.

Developing Teachers' Entrepreneurship Education Competence

Teachers' views on entrepreneurship training provided by the degree programme were consistent with the students' responses in questions assessing entrepreneurship competence. For the promotion of teachers' entrepreneurship education skills, an entrepreneurship development programme was organised during the project, with Outi Hägg from the Aalto University participating and providing her expertise. Twelve teachers from Metropolia UAS and one teacher from Omnia Adult Education Centre participated in the programme.

The aim of the training programme was to model the process by which entrepreneurship skills are developed in the field for Well-Being Services and describe what entrepreneurship education expertise is all about. This process was facilitated by two principal lecturers of the Faculty of Well-Being and Human Functioning who used the methods of collaborative development structure to teach. They also presented the results in the Active Learning Environments in Health Care congress in the summer of 2015 (Mäkinen & Harra, 2015).

The development programme was scheduled for one academic year and consisted of four workshops and independent studying by utilising the Moodle learning platform. The themes of the workshops were the perceptions and experiences of entrepreneurship, entrepreneurial skills, strengthening entrepreneurship skills, and entrepreneurship education. During the training, the Tree-model® of entrepreneurship by Hägg & Peltonen (Peltonen, 2014) was further developed and the basis of entrepreneurship education in the field of Well-Being Services were discussed. Teachers also considered how entrepreneurship could be integrated in their own teaching.

The *"Come for a visit"* entrepreneurship education theme day was held during the project. In addition to entrepreneurship education themes, the

Helsinki Entrepreneurship village, Me and MyCity, was visited during the project. The theme day was attended by teachers of Metropolia UAS and also by teachers from other UASs. During the day, it was agreed to undertake a benchmarking visit to Lahti UAS' co-operative for social and healthcare students. Benchmarking indeed occurred later in the spring. This experience can be utilised in the future for implementing entrepreneurship education in the form of a cooperative in Metropolia UAS.

Three meetings were held with the teachers who participated in the entrepreneurship education in the well-being sector. These meetings covered topics such as the situation of entrepreneurship education and the possibilities for its development in the future. The goal is to continue collaborative, educational planning each semester.

The Development of Entrepreneurs' Competences and Guidance to Business Transfer

Workshops on foresight, networking, and service design were organised for developing the business environment of Well-Being sector companies. Only a few entrepreneurs participated in the workshops, but enthusiasm towards co-operation and development was clear. Through the workshops, we developed our know-how on current themes of supporting entrepreneurship and formed a network for promoting entrepreneurship education. The workshop materials can be found at the HYRRÄT-website.

A Well-Being Entrepreneurship Fair was held in spring 2014 together with actors supporting Well-Being entrepreneurship (social services and healthcare entrepreneurs TESO, Finnish physiotherapy and rehabilitation companies FYSI ry, Finnish Association of Physiotherapists FAP). The fair was also attended by a business angel patron, MP Sari Sarkomaa, and due to the interesting line-up of guest speakers, we had a full auditorium of participants. A fair number of entrepreneurs also took part in the service design workshop and business transfer meeting place.

The workshop was facilitated, experiential, and focused on the feelings in business transfer. Target groups were the students who are interested in the continuation of the business and entrepreneurs considering the business transfer. The purpose was to discuss the fears and sources of power related to ownership change and summarise the relevant issues associated with it. We formed groups with those who were giving up

Promoting Entrepreneurship in Social Services and Healthcare

entrepreneurial activities and those who were continuing the business.

Instruction for participants was: *"We have a five-year birthday party of the company with sparkling wine. Members of the group meet five years after the business transfer has occurred. The transfer has proved to be very successful and now it is necessary to look back at the transitional stage. The group task was: Think about the business transfer period. Tell each other what was scary at that time and what were the sources of the strength? Each group has a news reporter. Plan a news report with her. Debate on key issues and present the brief news (headline)."*

During the business transfer part of the project, organised with the help of additional financing, workshops were held in co-operation with the national business transfer project of the Federation of Finnish Enterprises. Participation of entrepreneurs in these workshops was low. However, through the workshops, the UAS acquired business transfer know-how and networks were created with regional supporters of business transfer. We created a general model for business transfer (Figure 2) where in the UAS context, with the support of business transfer network, well-being enterprises (sellers, transferors) are transferring to the students (buyers, transferees). As a result of the project, supporting business transfers in Well-Being Services entrepreneurship has been integrated into the learner's path curriculum as part of entrepreneurship education courses.

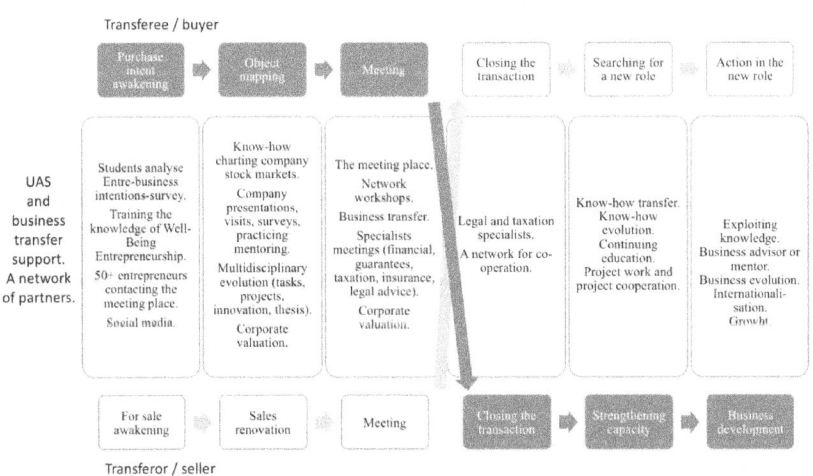

Figure 2: Business transfer process in the Well-Being Services.

We also applied this general business transfer model to bachelor and master-level training by producing their own designs for these implementations.

Section 4: A Foundation for Policy-Driven Structural Changes and Networking

Nowadays, it is recognised that entrepreneurship education should be carried out in close co-operation with businesses and parties promoting entrepreneurship, utilising the most practical and authentic methods. In the Well-Being degree programmes of Metropolia UAS, the practical training would offer a very good opportunity for this. The number of private sector companies among possible providers of practice placements is still disproportionately low. In addition, entrepreneurship could be one way of gaining business experience already during studies. Co-operative enterprises could be good starting points for this.

Entrepreneurship education should not be based on lecture-based teaching and should not be restricted to field-specific curricula. Based on this survey, teachers seem to be ready to apply various creative forms of entrepreneurship education. Students should be provided with education according to their existing knowledge level, and the Entre Intention survey could be used as the basis of group division. The Entre Intention measurement tool is based on Ajzens (1991) theory of planned behaviour model.

Already at the beginning of studies, students could be grouped based on their interest towards entrepreneurship: students showing a strong intention, those showing weak intention, and those who have a negative attitude towards entrepreneurship. Based on this division, educational activities could be planned, for example, as follows: Providing those with a strong intention practical opportunities to build their own businesses as well as to continue and develop their existing businesses; motivating those with a negative intention using various means (e.g., by having those with a strong intention tutoring them); focusing on developing internal entrepreneurship as a working life competence in the students holding a negative attitude. Similar ideas have been presented by the Seinäjoki UAS' research team (Joensuu et al., 2014).

The integration of entrepreneurship, innovation, leadership, and thesis project studies should be developed to build a seamless continuum whereby time is given to entrepreneurial maturation. Innovation Project studies have been carried out as multidisciplinary 10-credit courses in Metropolia UAS for many years. In case of new innovations, it would be really important to support the development of Start-Up- and Spin-Off- entrepreneurship. In addition, growing and internationalising companies could be created in ownership transfer situations with the help of new, innovative products.

The development of entrepreneurship education has not been a development priority in Metropolia UAS. The current vision and strategy do not support or guide these activities. In connection with the project, we were able to be involved in developing the Helsinki entrepreneurship education strategy in a project called HYPPYRI (YES Metropolia, 2014). The strategy supports entrepreneurship education in the capital region. The city of Helsinki is one of our major financiers, so hopefully the entrepreneurship education strategy is also adopted in Metropolia UAS. Strategically controlled operations are resourced and organised with continuity in mind. Leadership and enthusiastic actors from different fields of education are needed for entrepreneurship education in Metropolia UAS. Co-operation between different fields of education is needed so that the teaching resources, RDI activities, and entrepreneurship networks can be strategically developed.

Collaboration between the higher education institutions in the metropolitan area and the development of entrepreneurship education continuum with the vocational and upper secondary schools would be very significant and bring added value, also for the development of entrepreneurship in the welfare sector. The development of these types of projects would enhance co-operation in the education sector and create operational models.

A useful tool for the assessment of entrepreneurship promotion quality in educational institutions has been published in the EU, *A Guiding Framework for Entrepreneurial Universities* (European Commission & OECD, 2012). The introduction of the framework across the university and UAS field in the country would be important. This would provide comparative information on the emphasis placed in different higher education institutions on entrepreneurship education. In the HYRRÄT project, a preliminary translation of the framework was made (Kolehmainen, 2014) and it was sent to Metropolia UAS management and the metropolitan area higher education co-operation partners for fine-tuning.

In the future, the Entre Intention survey, measuring students' entrepreneurial intentions, should be introduced in Metropolia UAS. In addition, the ASTEE measurement tool for the effectiveness of entrepreneurship education published in the summer of 2014 should also be tested in practice (Vestergaard et al., 2014). Teachers' entrepreneurship education competence could be assessed by using the Measurement tool for Enterprise Education (Lappeenrannan Teknillinen Yliopisto, 2012). This is what every teacher in the well-being sector could use for self-evaluation, for example, when preparing for development discussions: How have I developed in the field of entrepreneurship education and what are the areas I want to develop in the future?

Reliable and comparable indicators for assessing entrepreneurship education would provide knowledge on the state of entrepreneurship education in different degree programmes, departments, and the whole of Metropolia UAS. We could compare our operations to other universities of applied sciences in Finland and even abroad. With the help of the evaluation, we could focus our entrepreneurship education activities accurately and estimate their effectiveness.

The response rate to the initial and final inquiry we made was extremely low. In the future, in order to obtain reliable results, the inquiries must be part of work duties so that everybody would be obliged to answer. The information could be gathered from new students as part of orientation studies at the beginning of their studies, and from graduating students together with the Opala-feedback after the maturity test. Teachers could answer the inquiry as part of the annual development discussions. This small survey carried out in the HYRRÄT project shows that there is still a lot to be done in the promotion of entrepreneurship.

This entrepreneurship project in Metropolia UAS has had an effect on various parties in the UAS and has also started the development of entrepreneurship promotion strategies in the Helsinki metropolitan area. The project brought out not only the importance of a control strategy but also the importance of continuous and diverse quality assessment of entrepreneurship education. The school functions should be evaluated, teachers' entrepreneurship activities should be evaluated, and the students' entrepreneurial intentions and entrepreneurial skills should be evaluated as well. The introduction of converging indicators will allow comparisons to be made between various educational institutions nationally as well as internationally. With the help of measurements, entrepreneurship promotion and financing can be better directed to meet the need.

Section 5: Discussion and learning points

HYRRÄT Promoting Entrepreneurship in Well-Being Services project was the first ESF-project on entrepreneurship promotion in Metropolia UAS. The project funding decision came in the middle of the semester, when it was hard to get project workers due to their teaching responsibilities. At the launch of the project, all project workers were working full-time in their own areas of responsibility, so the project start-up was delayed and project only started running properly in the autumn term of 2013. During the project, the project workers also changed, and the project came in under budget. Fortunately, we got an extension to the project and for implementing its results.

At the beginning of the project, knowledge of the Entre Intention survey was lacking, so it was not utilised in measuring students' entrepreneurial attitudes. Questionnaires were compiled on the basis of surveys conducted in several universities of applied sciences (Paajanen, 2001; Annala, 2007; Tanttu et al., 2008; Myntt, 2009; Toiviainen, 2010; Siltanen, 2011; Tuomisalo, 2011; Pulli & Sorvisto, 2013). The number of students and teachers participating in the survey remained very low, despite multiple reminders. At the time of the project, Metropolia UAS was going through a wide-ranging administrative reform and fixed-term teachers were laid off. These factors might have had an influence on the teachers' eagerness to answer the questionnaire. Students in Metropolia UAS generally answer very poorly to various inquiries, so the low response rate did not come as a surprise.

Both teachers and students had experience of working as an employee and also of entrepreneurship. In addition, they had family members and relatives working as entrepreneurs. In the final survey, the number of students who had relatives and acquaintances working as well-being sector entrepreneurs was surprising. Is it possible that such a large number of well-being sector companies are in the students' sphere of influence?

It would be important to get this experience introduced into the entrepreneurship education in universities of applied sciences. In order to gain a comprehensive, reliable picture of the phenomena in question, the inquiry should be carried out linked to a course; for example, in the form of a graded assignment. In the future, it would be very important to identify students with this experience already at the beginning of studies so that entrepreneurship education provision could be focused on their needs. In achieving this, the Entre Intention survey would be an important tool. The ASTEE survey would also serve this purpose well.

It was also surprising how common business transfer within 1–5 years in companies of students' relatives and acquaintances seemed to be according to the answers. After all, only four students participated in the events of the business transfer project. Out of these four, two occupational therapy students participated in arranging the business transfer meeting place at the well-being entrepreneurship fair and two students participated in the first workshop and one of them also made an assignment on the initial status of a company starting the business transfer process. Business transfer processes tend to be long-lasting, so the students intending to continue the business as well as the entrepreneurs giving up their company would both benefit from the guidance. Unfortunately, the survey was anonymous and we did not receive the students' contact information.

Teachers and students expressed moderate interest towards entrepreneurship in both surveys. Teachers stressed the importance of developing entrepreneurship in co-operation with different fields of education. The weakest average score in teachers' responses was for the claim: *"I need training or coaching related to entrepreneurship"*. The students felt that entrepreneurship requires realistic thinking and a positive attitude, and believed that entrepreneurship requires much more work compared to paid work. Least enthusiasm was expressed towards participation in UAS entrepreneurship courses. The differences between the initial and final survey are probably due to the diversity of educational programmes of the students who answered. Only three students who responded to this survey took part in the student events organised by the project.

Teachers' views on entrepreneurship training provided by the degree programme were consistent with the students' responses in questions assessing entrepreneurship readiness. The students felt they had least competence in the areas of business law, financial management, and corporate communications. These subjects are not included in the curricula of the well-being degree programmes. Entrepreneurship in the field of well-being is highly regulated, and knowledge of these subjects would be needed. Increasing co-operation with the business degree programmes in areas of business law, financial management, and corporate communications is important in the future.

From the project participants' perspective, the project has given the resources to address well-being sector entrepreneurship and entrepreneurship education. We as teachers have increased our expertise and formed useful contacts with promoters of entrepreneurship in the metropolitan area and beyond. Teachers involved in entrepreneurship education have strengthened their co-operation. Co-operation with entrepreneurs is considered important and, therefore, creating strong co-operation with local entrepreneurs is linked to the planning of the new Metropolia UAS campus in Myllypuro.

Conclusion

This chapter described how we have promoted entrepreneurship as a project in Metropolia UAS, social services, and healthcare, and reached a better understanding of the ways to practice teaching and learning entrepreneurship in higher education. We carried out the studies by diversifying entrepreneurship education; in particular, the webpages and Hyrrät 10 course as an educational tool were the most useful. We developed teachers' entrepreneurial skills on the entrepreneurship educational studies. Also, we developed entrepreneurs' competences and guidance to business transfer and created a foundation for policy-driven structural changes and collaboration with outsiders supporting entrepreneurship. The development of entrepreneurship education continues in Metropolia UAS. We have obtained funding for business transfer to support the well-being sector and the development of women entrepreneurs' skills and competences.

Chapter 9

About the author

MHS Sirkka-Liisa Kolehmainen is a senior lecturer at Metropolia University of Applied Sciences. She can be contacted at this e-mail: sirkka-liisa.kolehmainen@metropolia.fi

Bibliography

Ahmaniemi, R.; K. Ristimäki; L. Tuomi; M. Tuuliainen; S. Niinistö-Sivuranta; M. Vieltojärvi & R. Rissanen (2015). *Arenen yrittäjyyssuositukset.* 12.3.2015. Arene, Suomen Yrittäjät.

Ajzen, I. (1919). *Attitudes, personality and behavior.* Bristol: J. W. Arrowsmith Limited.

Annala, R. (2007). Yrittäjyys sosiaali- ja terveysalan koulutuksessa – katsaus Satakunnan ammattikorkeakoulun sosiaali- ja terveysalan yrittäjyysosaamiseen opettajille suunnatun kyselyn kautta. *Opinnäytetyö.* Kuntoutusohjauksen ja -suunnittelun koulutusohjelma. Satakunnan ammattikorkeakoulu. Pori.

Arene (2011). *Ammattikorkeakoulujen yrittäjyyden kehittämistä koskevat suunnitelmat.* Arene. Release 16 Mar 2011.

European Commission (2002). *Final Report of the Expert Group on the Transfer of Small and Medium-Sized Enterprises.* Brussels: European Commission.

Euroopan komissio (2003). *Vihreä kirja. Yrittäjyys Euroopassa.* Yritystoiminta julkaisut.

Euroopan komissio (2010). *Komission tiedonanto. Eurooppa 2020. Älykkään, kestävän ja osallistavan kasvun strategia.* Bryssel 3.3.2010. KOM (2010) 2020.

Euroopan yhteisöjen komissio (2008). *Komission tiedonanto neuvostolle, Euroopan parlamentille, Euroopan talous- ja sosiaalikomitealle ja alueiden komitealle. "Pienet ensin" – Eurooppalaisia pk-yrityksiä tukeva aloite" ("Small Business Act")* Bryssel 25.6.2008. KOM (2008) 394 final.

European Commission (2012a). *Facilitating Transfer of Business. Guidebook Series. How to support SME Policy from Structural Funds.* Brussels: European Commission.

European Commission (2012b). *Flash Eurobarometer 354.* Entrepreneurship in the EU and beyond. Conducted by TNS Option & Social at the request of the European Commission, Directorate-General Enterprise and Industry. Survey co-ordinated by the European Commission, Directorate-General for Communication (DG COMM "Research and Speechwriting" Unit).

European Commission & OECD (2012). *A Guiding Framework for Entrepreneurial Universities.*

Heinonen, J. & I. Vento-Vierikko (2002). *Sisäinen yrittäjyys: uskalla, muutu, menesty.* Helsinki: Talentum.

Hytti, U. & C. O'Gorman (2004). What is enterprise education? An analysis of the objectives and methods of enterprise education programmes in four European countries. *Education + Training*, Vol. 46, No. 1, pp. 11–23.

Joensuu, S.; E. Varamäki; A. Viljamaa; T. Heikkilä & M. Katajavirta (2014). *Yrittäjyysaikomukset, yrittäjyysaikomusten muutos ja niihin vaikuttavat tekijät koulutuksen aikana.* Seinäjoen ammattikorkeakoulun julkaisusarja A. Tutkimuksia 16. Seinäjoen ammattikorkeakoulu.

Jussila, E.; J. Hytönen & H. Salminen (2005). *Yrittäjyyskasvatus. Yrittäjyyskasvatus ammattikorkeakoulujen koulutusohjelmien opetussuunnitelmissa -benchmarking-hanke.* Korkeakoulujen arviointineuvoston verkkojulkaisuja 3:2005.

Kainlauri, A. (2007). *Ideasta hyvinvointialan yrittäjäksi.* Juva: WS Bookwell Oy.

Kivelä, P. (2002). *Ammattikorkeakouluopiskelijoiden suhtautuminen yrittäjyyteen. Ammattikorkeakouluissa opiskelevien arvot, asenteet ja intentiot yrittäjyyttä kohtaan sekä perhetaustan vaikutus niihin.* Tampere. Multiprint Oy.

Koiranen, M. (1993). *Ole Yrittäjä. Sisäinen ja ulkoinen yrittäjyys.* Tampere: Tammer-Paino Oy.

Kolehmainen, S-L. (2014). *EU, OECD 2012: A Guiding Framework for Entrepreneurial Universities. An initial translation in Finnish and applied to the needs of Metropolia UAS.*

Kyrö, P. & A. Ripatti (2006). Yrittäjyyden opetuksen uudet tuulet. Teoksessa Kyrö, P. & A. Ripatti (Toim.) *Yrittäjyyskasvatuksen uusia tuulia.* Yrittäjyyskasvatuksen julkaisusarja 4/206, Hämeenlinna: Tampereen yliopiston kauppakorkeakoulu, pp. 10–31.

Laitinen-Väänänen, S.; L. Vanhanen-Nuutinen; R. Ahmaniemi; S. Boman & V-M. Lamppu (2013). *AMK-tutka*, Suomen Yrittäjät, Arene.

Lappeenrannan teknillinen yliopisto (2012). *Yrittäjyyskasvatuksen mittaristo™.* Online Resource: https://developmentcentre.lut.fi/muut/mittaristo/ [Accessed 16 October 2016].

Metropolia (2012). *Metropolia Ammattikorkeakoulun henkilöstöraportti 2012.*

Metropolia (2014). *Opiskelijamäärien tilasto 2014.*

Myntt, A. (2009). Henkilön yrittäjäominaisuudet yrittäjyyden tukena – Turun ammattikorkeakoulun restonomiopiskelijoiden asenteet yrittäjyyteen. *Opinnäytetyö.* Palvelujen tuottamisen ja johtamisen koulutusohjelma. Turun ammattikorkeakoulu. Turku.

Mäkinen, E. & T. Harra (2015). *Hyvinvointialan yrittäjyyskasvatuksen rakentuminen*. Tiivistelmät – Posteriesitykset. Jatkuva osaamisen kehittäminen. Vaikuttavat oppimisympäristöt terveysalalla. Kolmas terveysalan koulutuksen kansallinen konferenssi. 1. – 2.6.2015. Helsinki: Metropolia ammattikorkeakoulu, Terveysala & Turun yliopisto, Hoitotieteen laitos.

Opetusministeriö (2009). *Yrittäjyyskasvatuksen suuntaviivat*. Opetusministeriön julkaisuja 2009: 7. Helsinki: Yliopistopaino.

Oske (2008). *Hyvinvoinnin klusteriohjelma 2007-2013*. Online Resource: http://docplayer.fi/949596-2-0-0-7-2-013-hyvinvoinnin-lusteriohjelma.html [Accessed 16 October 2016].

Paajanen, P. (2001). *Yrittäjyyskasvattaja. Ammattikorkeakoulun hallinnon ja kaupan alan opettajien näkemykset itsestään ja työstään yrittäjyyskasvattajana*. Akateeminen väitöskirja. Jyväskylä Studies in Business and Economics 16. Jyväskylä: Jyväskylän yliopisto.

Paasio, K.; P. Nurmi & J. Heinonen (2005). *Yrittäjyys yliopistojen tehtävänä?* Opetusministeriön työryhmämuistioita ja selvityksiä 2005: 10. Helsinki: Yliopistopaino.

Peltonen, K. (2014). Opettajien yrittäjyyskasvatusvalmiuksien kehittyminen ja siihen vaikuttavat tekijät. *Doctoral Dissertations* 175/2014. Aalto-yliopisto. Kauppakorkeakoulu. Johtamisen laitos. Helsinki: Aalto University publication series.

Pulli, M. & M. Sorvisto (2013). Keski-Pohjanmaan ammattikorkeakoulun opiskelijoiden yrittäjyysaikomukset ja -asenteet 2009 – 2011 Entre Intentio –tutkimustulosten analysointia. *Opinnäytetyö*. Liiketalouden koulutusohjelma. Kokkola: Centria ammattikorkeakoulu.

Rae, D. (2010). Universities and enterprise education: responding to the challenges of the new era. *Journal of Small Business and Enterprise Development*. Vol. 17 No. 4, 2010, pp. 591–606.

Roto, J.; J. Grunfelder & L. Rispling (Eds.) (2014). *State of the Nordic Region 2013*. Nord region report 2014:1. Nordic Centre for Spatial Development. Stockholm. Sweden.

Ruohotie, P. & M. Koiranen (2001). Yrittäjyyskasvatus: analyysejä, synteesejä ja sovelluksia. *Aikuiskasvatus*, Vol. 2, 2001, pp. 102–111. Helsinki: Kansanvalistusseura ja Aikuiskasvatuksen Tutkimusseura.

Siltanen, H. (2011). Opiskelijoiden suhtautuminen yrittäjyyteen hoitotyön, liiketalouden sekä sosiaali- ja kauneudenhoitoalan koulutusohjelmissa. *Opinnäytetyö*. Laurea-ammattikorkeakoulu. Kauneudenhoitoalan koulutusohjelma. Tikkurila, Vantaa: Laurea.

Tanttu, A.; V. Kuhanen & J. Ritsilä (2008). *Askelia yrittäjyyden polulla.* Jyväskylän ammattikorkeakoulun julkaisuja 82. Jyväskylä: Jyväskylän ammattikorkeakoulu.

Tilastokeskus (2014). *Suomen virallinen tilasto. Yritykset 2013.* Yritysrekisterin vuositilasto 2012. Korjattu 30.1.2014.

Toiviainen, J. (2010). *Yrittäjyyspedagogiikka ja opiskelijoiden yrittäjyysvalmiudet-tapaustutkimus TAMK:n Proakatemiasta.* Kehittämishanke. Tampereen ammattikorkeakoulu. Tampere: Ammatillinen opettajakorkeakoulu.

Tuomisalo, T. (2011). Restonomiopiskelijoiden käsityksiä HAAGA-HELIA ammattikorkeakoulun tarjoamista yrittäjyysopinnoista. *Opinnäytetyö.* Hotelli- ja ravintola-alan liikkeenjohdon koulutusohjelma. Helsinki: HAAGA-HELIA ammattikorkeakoulu.

Vestergaard, L.; A. Fayolle; D. Redford; K. K. Sailer; T. Cooney; S. Singer & D. Filip (2014). *How to assess and evaluate the influence of entrepreneurship education. Astee – Assessment tools and indicators for entrepreneurship education.* A report of the ASTEE project with a user guide to the tools.

YES Metropoli (2014). *Hyppyri -Helsingin yrittäjyyskasvatuksen polku -hanke,* Hämeen ELY-keskus. Online Resource: http://metropoli.yes-keskus.fi/ohjelma/ [Accessed 16 October 2016].

Chapter 10

An Integrated Framework for Stimulating Entrepreneurial Behaviour: A South African Example

Tshidi Mohapeloa

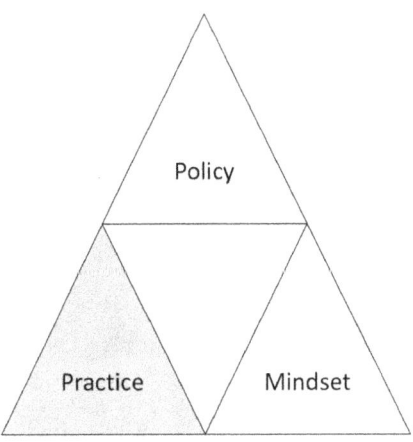

Introduction

My chapter is an important contribution to this section on practice – and to the book *Teaching and Learning Entrepreneurship in Higher Education* – because I describe how Rhodes Business School – a part of Rhodes University in South Africa – has worked with teaching and learning entrepreneurship to stimulate entrepreneurial behaviour of students. I describe how we have used an integrated framework that engages students intellectually, socially, and emotionally. An integrated framework that incorporates community of inquiry (CoI) and action learning (AL) to reach its aim. An integrated framework that also draws on what I call the 4E-Model, which shows how students can be stimulated intellectually, socially, and emotionally when teaching entrepreneurship. I argue that this is best done by focusing on four core themes important for entrepreneurial behaviour: 1) economy; 2) ethics; 3) ecology; and 4) equity (hence the 4E-Model).

In my chapter, I acknowledge that teaching and learning entrepreneurship should cater for the needs and challenges faced by both young graduates with a desire to start their own enterprise and by those without any work or entrepreneurial experience. Thus, targeting young diverse South African students in their 20s with a bachelor degree.

Socially challenged students form a major cohort within the South African context. This includes those who have been economically disadvantaged and/or come from poverty-stricken communities. The poor understanding of these barriers could result in exclusion, marginalisation, and serious infringements for individual student growth and development. This highlights the need for an integrated support at different levels to benefit identified vulnerable students.

Learning occurs through action, community engagement, and conversations with business practitioners to meet global needs that respond to changing global markets. Reading this chapter, you will gain the following three insights:

1. an introduction to the 4E-Model focusing on four core themes important for entrepreneurial behaviour: 1) economy; 2) ethics; 3) ecology; and 4) equity;

2. knowledge of teaching and learning that incorporates community of inquiry (CoI) and action learning (AL) as the framework to engage students intellectually, socially, and emotionally;

3. a case from Rhodes Business School showing the application of an integrated framework (integrating CoI and AL) and discussing its benefits.

My chapter is structured in six main sections. In the first section, I argue for the need to review entrepreneurship education based on the realities faced by entrepreneurs. In section two, I introduce to schools of thought within entrepreneurship education: The Lean-school and the Traditional-school. These schools of thought are my outset for section three, where I present my integrated framework and the 4E-Model we use. In section four, I discuss different approaches to action learning and teaching to show the foundation for applying the integrative framework and the 4E-Model with students. In section five, I present how we then apply the integrative framework and the 4E-Model. Section six presents a discussion of the value of the skills gained by students. Following this I conclude the chapter.

Section 1: Realities Faced by Entrepreneurs

A need to review entrepreneurship teaching and learning has been motivated by the challenges faced by entrepreneurs. At higher education institutions (HEI), learning should engage students intellectually, socially, and emotionally. Thus, the role of academics as change agents requires adaptation to global changing needs in order to accommodate the changing learning spaces.

If the problem is linked to the validity of introducing an integrated approach to effective entrepreneurial teaching at the postgraduate level that integrates entrepreneurship for profit and sustainability into a postgraduate diploma course, then academic platforms and business schools should design an educational programme that addresses these issues, whilst developing entrepreneurs as sustainable managers and leaders. This means academic programmes should not only strive to focus on entrepreneurship teaching and learning but should develop leaders that meet global (and local) market needs, whilst acknowledging students' limitations and abilities.

Leadership Development

The higher education setting is another space where participants can be consciously introduced to sustainability and social justice issues. Entrepreneurs such as business leaders can also participate in this active citizenry to help people live harmoniously within their economy and environment. Sustainable leaders contribute to the development of a sustainable world through diverse roles as managers, consultants, and concerned citizens. For sustainable leaders, the outcome is to create a just and sustainable society. Entrepreneurs' sense of agency and leadership practices gets developed beyond organisational roles (Marshall et al., 2011:2). It is essential to look at an integrating a teaching and learning entrepreneurship approach that encapsulates the development of sustainable leaders in higher education.

Meeting Global Needs

It can be acknowledged that teaching and learning entrepreneurship at higher education institutions should always strive to meet the changing global needs. Thus, it is essential that although entrepreneurship training could be locally or nationally focused the global outlook forms part of such an educational process. Meeting the global needs has been an attractive approach that is explored further through preparation for the changing markets.

Preparations for Changing Markets

Preparing students for changing markets requires an alternative approach to entrepreneurship education. This should integrate both lean start-ups and the traditional business plan methodologies for sustainability outcome. When higher education and post-higher education are faced with complexities that include poor financial literacy and the general lack of business or entrepreneurial understanding among the majority of the population, these tend to contribute towards other socioeconomic implications. These include high rates of unemployment and difficulty in penetrating the employment markets for youths with an undergraduate qualification. This has forced new graduates to consider management qualifications as well as entrepreneurial skills as ways to close the gap of employability in the market. Through this attractive process, graduates see themselves not as employees but as potential employers responding to changing markets.

Challenges Faced by Graduates

Some of the contributing factors of the challenges faced by young graduates on issues around unemployment/employment and enterprise development seem to suggest a less than overwhelming positive outcome. The youth and new graduates are confronted with the unwillingness of the business sector to take on training responsibilities for new graduates, whilst the demand for "work experience" from graduates immediately exacerbates the problems they face. Secondly, universities have failed to respond positively to this situation, as the focus has been mainly on the educational qualification and throughput. However, there are very few postgraduate qualifications aimed at preparing the general graduate for the "world of work" in ways that might fulfil the unreasonable demand for "work experience".

The notions of entrepreneurship are explored together with notions of *enterprise, globalisation, citizenship, sustainability, employability,* and *leadership,* there is a direct relationship especially as these helps justify the need to review entrepreneurship teaching and learning. It is essential to acknowledge that there is a definite link and overlapping relationship between these, as they are realities that influence and effect today's businesses and business leaders. This chapter explores further how these get addressed using an integrated approach to learning and teaching that prepares the postgraduate students to be sustainable, entrepreneurial leaders and future employers.

Section 2: Schools of Thought within Entrepreneurship Education

Entrepreneurial teaching and learning in higher education has been caught between the traditional conventional business plan methodology and the lean start-up for new ventures. It is essential to acknowledge globalisation, innovation, and the role played by technology during start up, forces of disruption, globalisation, regulation buffeting the economies, and the shedding of jobs.

When teaching and learning entrepreneurships, both schools can be incorporated; where lean tends to accelerate entrepreneurs to see opportunities and respond quickly to meet not only local-based businesses with a global outlook, whereas the traditional approach is a trial-and-error process (Blank, 2013). Figure 1 highlights the focus of these different approaches.

It should be emphasised that the core should not be the competing schools of thoughts but gaining a better understanding of the realities faced, whilst ensuring that higher learning academic institutions prepare and respond to these realities.

Elements	Lean	Traditional
Strategy	Business model Hypothesis-driven	Business plan Implementation-driven
Product development process	Customer driven and tested products	Using linear market pre-determined processing to manage production plan
Product engineering	Driven design using iterative and incremental process (prototyping, testing, and redesign)	Specify product and design fully before building it
Attitudes	Failures are embraced, with short time to fix, iteration of idea for rework	Failures are seen as exceptions with severe consequences (fire your executive)
Structure and pace	Rapid, ongoing, with sufficient data to work with	Structured, measured interval (midway or end of operation)

Figure 1: Lean vs. traditional methods (adapted from Blank, 2013).

Section 3: The Integrated Framework

A need for an integrated framework is motivated by the consideration that external and environmental realities influence the beneficiary when teaching and learning entrepreneurship. The ultimate goal is to develop knowledge, skills, and attitudes (abilities), as stated by Rauh-Bieri (in this volume), and thus stimulate students intellectually, socially, and emotionally at their core whilst acknowledging the environment as the external factors. The use of creative and innovative abilities helps entrepreneurs to respond to opportunities and manage an enterprise. Thus, developing an entrepreneurial mindset needs to enhance sustainability and leadership gets developed. In this chapter, entrepreneurial mindset refers to the ability to see opportunities for making money by creatively develop new things saleable from new/existing/recycled resources for market suitability risk-taking, resilience and creativity are the required elements.

Key factors that motivate an entrepreneurial mindset include:

- creating something new or different in order to change and transform value;
- seeing change as the norm and as healthy;
- always searching for change, responding to it, and exploiting it as an opportunity.

Figure 2 helps us to understand how the overarching integrated framework is integrated, as discussed in detail throughout this chapter.

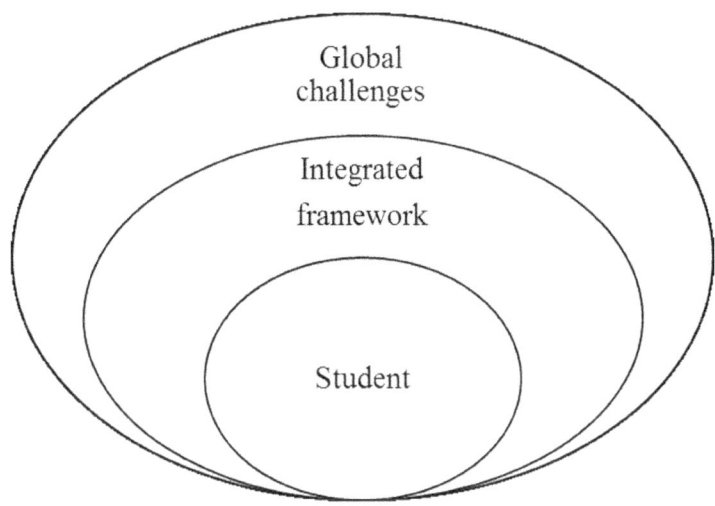

Figure 2: An integrated framework.

According to Otuya *et al.* (2013), there are specific measures towards promoting entrepreneurship education in higher education institutions, including: using innovative methodologies for entrepreneurship-friendly programmes that focus on community integration; challenging the status-quo; being highly participatory (throughout the entrepreneurship cycle); incorporating aspects of role models; encouraging students to embrace change; and ensuring that entrepreneurship research is available to stakeholders (including policymakers). Through addressing some of these aspects that Otuya *et al.* (2013) emphasised, this chapter looks at responding using an integrated approach to achieve a sustainable outcome.

- Sustainable practices should be learned in the classroom through simulation or in business, organisation, or government entities (e.g., innovation hubs/labs);
- Increased awareness on the application, implication, and value added through the focus on sustainability. Combine theoretical learning and action learning that gives context on sustainability (e.g., invite speakers, create opportunities for students to earn academic credit from other faculties, co-teach with environmental issues);
- Support and encourage research development that integrates business, leadership, management, and sustainability (e.g., develop/ strengthen working relation with other cross-cutting fields/ departments);
- Increase institutional capacity by participating in the development of the business school (e.g., improve own knowledge, attend conferences, increase collaboration).

The 4E-Model

The Rhodes Business School's (RBS) strategic emphasis is on a sustainable business model with profound impact, meaning that the importance of an integrated thinking should create connection for shared value to engage economy, ethics, ecology, and equity (4E). This goes to the heart of how the business entrepreneurship students should view the world of business. However, acknowledging the dilemma creates both a challenge and an opportunity for an integrated holistic dimension (Skae, 2014).

The 4E-Model benefits ethical and sustainable entrepreneurial business leaders in different ways. For example, economy and equity require proficiency at core management practices using a customer-centric organisation, people-centred management, and similar practices, whereas economy and ethics require responsible leadership and governance that embrace meaningful stakeholder engagement.

Ethics, when combined with ecology, ushers in the notion that the business and the moral case are not mutually exclusive, and thus the focus is on how the business model works rather than how much money it makes. Lastly, combining ecology and equity show that leaders and managers view the world in a particular way. Opportunities to be sought are a positive sum game, and this requires profound thought leadership and research that articulates how all these components fit together (Skae, 2014). Figure 3 illustrates this further.

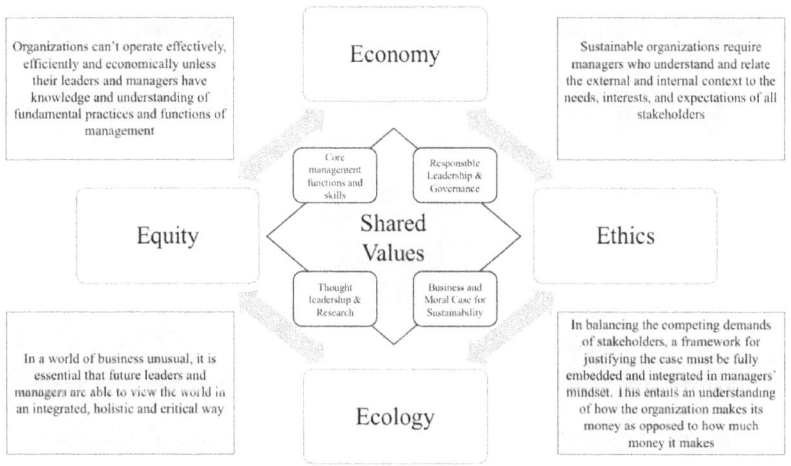

Figure 3: The 4E model (source: Rhodes Business School).

The application of this integrated framework, as used by RBS, is limited to postgraduate students with no entrepreneurial experience or insufficient skills or absence thereof. Through rigorous content, experiential learning a stimulation of an entrepreneurial mindset is strengthen and developed. An elaboration on the application process includes a look at the *what* (content), *who* (target group), and *how*, including its benefits (both intended and unintended).

Engaging Students

How to engage and stimulate students at different levels (intellectually, socially, and emotionally) is the core of this section discussing approaches and methodologies. This acknowledges the role played by higher academic institutions for cognitive stimulation, students as part of the microcosm that depends and relies on social interactions with diverse emotive responses. This guiding theoretical framework and teaching pedagogy is that of adult learning (Knowles, 1984; Merriam et al., 2012), coupled with the CoI model (Garrison et al., 2010) where students' experiences, learning, and teaching incorporate and stimulate their social, emotional, and cognitive needs. In this chapter, adult learning is defined as a range of learning activities (formal, non-formal, and informal) carried out by an adult to acquire new knowledge or skill.

The CLLN-Canadian Literacy and Learning Network (2012) emphasises the following guiding principles for adult learning:

i. Adults must want to learn, meaning strong inner motivation must be present to develop a new skill or acquire a particular type of knowledge;

ii. Learning must use a practical approach for learning that focuses on needs. This should be practical and direct;

iii. Learning for adults should be through active participation, making use of learned skills to be applicable for their relevance;

iv. Learning should focus on realistic problems and then work to find a solution; meaning a process of problem identification that addresses the gaps through practical activities so as to enhance and teach specific skills;

v. Experiential learning can be an asset and a liability depending on whether experience is regarded as negative or positive.

Garrison et al. (2010) use the CoI model to encapsulate three critical elements that are essential for education to be experiential learning: the social presence, the cognitive presence, and the teaching presence. The teaching presence is seen as the teaching and learning building structures or processes. For teaching to stimulate the social presence, a climate or setting should be made where simulated and real-life experiences occur, whereas when the content is stimulating, then cognitive presence occurs. Garrison et al. (2010) further emphasise the importance of a supportive and conducive environment between social and cognitive presence. Through blended learning or learning and teaching commons the CoI frameworks has expanded the community of practice and its validation. However, as the framework's critical review indicated, it has not been directly linked to learning outcomes. The CoI framework, as indicated in Figure 4 below, alludes to social aspect, cognitive stimulation, and teaching process as it is only at their overlapping areas where CoI occurs. This is supported by the underpinning theoretical framework and teaching pedagogy of adult learning, when coupled with the CoI model (Garrison et al., 2010). Meaning students' experiences, learning, and needs in terms of online, social, and cognitive presence should be considered.

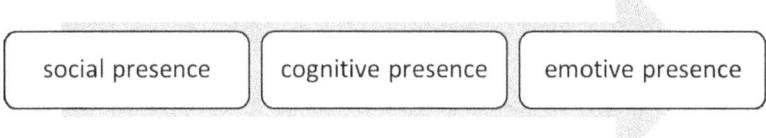

Figure 4: Required stimulation for learning using CoI.

It is imperative to acknowledge that engaging students intellectually requires the ability to incorporate theoretical foundations: experiential, cognitive/affective, and networking approaches (Wing Yan Man, 2005; Otuya et al., 2013). This makes learning a process not only to incorporate skills and knowledge, but also abilities acquired through theoretical foundations. These are developed and acquired during business development exposure and social integrations with significant ethical leaders (Rae & Carswell, 2000; Wing Yan Man, 2005; Otuya et al., 2013). Teaching and learning entrepreneurship has to reflect contemporary research within the field of action learning using different approaches to support and strengthen learning. This leads me to the next aspects that touch on action learning approaches.

In the following sections, I look further at how the teaching and learning of entrepreneurship can be used. Approaches such as community of inquiry (CoI) and different action learning (AL) strategies guide this framework, where students are engaged at different levels.

Section 4: Approaches to Action Learning and Teaching

Action learning implies learning that includes an ability to connect three elements: 1) a decision; 2) an action; and 3) a reflection. This means sustainable practices are not only learned in the classroom through simulation, but also through the use of say a small business development project (what we could call an alpha project) that is used as a learning hub. A project that not only looks at starting a business enterprise but ensuring that an increased awareness of a triple bottom line value gets added through the focus on sustainability. This combination of theoretical learning and action learning provides the context for sustainability.

Action Learning Projects

Through the establishment of an alpha project (a micro enterprise project done by the students as part of their academic training), students are exposed to key elements of a business cycle, from formation, ideation, through to termination. As part of this action learning process, students are granted an opportunity for start-ups and the management thereof. The outcome is for students to start and run an enterprise with a seed funding from the university. These enterprises are guided by academic staff to support leadership development, strengthening governance issues as the enterprise sustainability get developed. A seed loan fund made available is repaid with interest. It is through this alpha project philosophy that the implementation of action learning using a classroom situation, simulation, and outside classroom experience gets integrated to enhance the practical experience.

External Business and Enterprise Experts

External business experts as speakers are invited and share personal experiences as part of a business forum and small class interaction. Through this interaction, students have an opportunity to capture some learning curves as experienced by business leaders in their entrepreneurial development and growth. Participants bring along the diverse knowledge from diverse undergraduate curricula and disciplines and integrate this to create opportunities for students to gain a better understanding of the 4E approach. As part of the teaching and learning process, real case studies are integrated into the learning space with students from other faculties, through co-teaching and group work, as part of exposure to social and environmental issues.

Community Engagements Programmes

Engagements with community projects help support and encourage development that integrates entrepreneurship (including intrapreneurship, social entrepreneurship, and eco-entrepreneurship), business, leadership, management, and sustainability through developing and or strengthening working relations with other cross-cutting fields. Outcome for community projects is to enhance student's critical thinking through engaging creatively with communities so as to gain a better understanding of the world of work. This process incorporates promoting ethical behaviours and taking ownership and responsibility of the future sustainability of projects. This is not only for successes, it is also for failures on projects done with the communities.

For academics, engaging with communities has increased institutional capacity by participating in the development of the business school through ongoing personal improvement of their own knowledge, attending conferences, increased collaboration, etc. This has also gone into the critical thinking at which the teaching on entrepreneurship means constantly realigning on the curriculum content but using blended approaches and learning on these new developments.

As a social value, the advantages of an educational outcome that goes beyond to include sustainability and leadership helps with competitive positioning, giving the graduates entrepreneurial advantages to implement change in a business that is beneficial for both humans and the environment. The major value to students is that they have the ability to use the entrepreneurial skills gained in the course in relation to their global outlooks formed in their undergraduate degrees. Although this has not been tracked by the school for previous students, the current cohort has already initiated enterprises that yield success in terms of ethical leaders with initiatives that integrate sustainability entrepreneurship.

Chapter 10

Strengthening Sustainability in Enterprise Leadership

Entrepreneurs who use sustainable principles help promote social justice (e.g., health), increase productivity, improve the efficiency of resource use, and reduce negative human impacts on the environment. Marshall et al. (2011:3) define sustainability as *"finding ways to live together within the carrying capacity of the planet, with equality and justice for all human communities while allowing vibrant space for other life forms"*. They further identified the following as core elements as drivers for sustainability:

- sense of agency;
- availability of resources;
- consciously created awareness;
- sustainable approach; and
- crafts of practice to take action of some kind in the service of a more environmentally sustainable and socially just world.

Making the triple bottom line to be achieved whilst moral business with the purpose of business making good are achieved by confronting contemporary challenges and opportunities. Principles of sustainability in leadership with outcomes leads to students developing a meaningful and long-term change with lasting or widespread improvement (Hargreaves & Goodson, 2004). Educators as sustainable leaders should aim for learning that engages students intellectually, socially, and emotionally and goes beyond temporary gains in achievement scores towards creating lasting, meaningful improvements in learning (Glickman, 2002; Stoll et al., 2002).

As a product (output) sustainable entrepreneurs gain leadership qualities, skills that facilitate transition, succession, resiliency, improve socio-economic development and creating opportunities that adds value. Student entrepreneurs get opportunities to become leaders that participate in diverse business sectors such as social business, (business and ecology), that focus on energy systems, cultural, and placed-based equity (sustainable behaviour and economics). The developed leadership qualities provide not only the basics of leadership and behaviour change but also on how these relates to environmental stewardship in an organisation, as well as fundamental economic, social, climate, and ecological impacts of sustainability programmes.

Section 5: Application of the Integrated Framework

In this section of my chapter, I show how we apply the integrated framework when we teach entrepreneurship at RBS.

Teaching Entrepreneurship at Postgraduate level

Postgraduate teaching of entrepreneurship at RBS is carried out at two levels. The first is the diploma level, which encompasses an enterprise management programme and as part of the MBA programme. The postgraduate diploma focuses on enterprise management; a one-year full-time qualification that offers enterprise and management qualifications. It is intended to accommodate non-commerce graduates looking at entering an enterprise development or management field. The postgraduate diploma programme is available on both a full-time basis over one year or on a part-time, modular basis over two years. The part-time programme is geared to those who are already employed, whereas the full-time programme is geared to those who have just completed their undergraduate studies.

The philosophy behind the enterprise management is based on enhancing students understanding of developing skills to create sustainable business, which means developing and transforming business enterprises towards a sustainable world through education, making it essential to influence responsible business practice. As an academic institution, RBS incorporates sustainability as part of the curriculum, as this is viewed as a sustainable process. This programme accepts diverse groups of students from different faculties, granting them a platform to develop and strengthen their enterprise and management skills.

The master's programme (e.g., MBA) has a strong emphasis on leadership for sustainability. This means that sustainability is seen, firstly, as an idea of "business continuity" and "organisational longevity", and, secondly, as "sustainable development". The aim is to meet the needs of the present generation without compromising the ability of future generations to meet their needs and aspirations. This is achieved through balancing needs to achieve amongst social responsibility, economic performance, and ecological health to ensure long-term survival and high performance (so-called, "triple bottom line"). A concept achieved through facilitating an adaptive and resilient management perspective for organisations of the future to foster a focus on responsible leadership, engaged business practices and integrated societal accountability (RBS-MBA booklet).

The use of blended learning and virtual space helps with the simulation process that deals with the discourse of physical and cognitive presence, whilst the participation of business experts brings balance to elements of equity, economy, ecology, and ethics which help deal with content. The community engagement processes and the micro enterprise tend to help deal with setting the climate.

Benefits for Stimulation at Three Different Levels

For both diploma and master's level educational experience encapsulate stimulation of social presence. This is achieved when direct community engagement and running an enterprise is done. The running of an enterprise, when combined with expert panel dialogues, tends to stimulate a cognitive presence based on the real-time content selected. Students use difficulties experienced during the enterprise as learning that is not only linked with what literature says but incorporate these with content from experts in the field. The promotion of ethical leaders as core behavioural skills that ensure not only ownership is achieved but responsible leadership for future sustainability. This gets developed and strengthened during the rigorous interrogation and application of sustainability principles in business. This as part of setting climate using content which strengthens teaching presence where sustainability structures and process. This is supported by Neck et al. (2014) when they emphasise the importance of actionable theory through practice. Benefits relevant for teaching and learning at higher education institutions in this chapter's anthology theme can be highlighted in terms of the following three insights:

- The need to have a well-tested and rigorous methodology to prepare students for rapidly changing markets;

- The provision of relevant knowledge and skills for an evolving workforce to become responsible employees, entrepreneurs, leaders, and citizens;
- The promotion of conditions conducive to students' study success.

Well-Tested and Rigorous Methods

Teaching entrepreneurship integrates theory with practice where the ability to plan, forecast, identify customers, raise money whilst defining a business model enhances diverse learning spaces to be explored. Diverse theoretical basis for entrepreneurship such as the theory of creativity (Cougar, 1995; Blanchard, 2010; Swayer, 2012), are fundamental to innovation within the socio-cultural context at which the students are exposed to. Encouraging creativity is thus an essential part of teaching entrepreneurship and should not be undermined. Thus, relevance in terms of learning materials, events, people, or circumstances to form part of the action learning process is required. Swayer (2012) acknowledges the contributions of individual acts, interactional dynamics, and the influence of groups as a collective, whereas Yar Hamidi et al. (2008) highlighted positive linkage in creativity scores when there was prior exposure to entrepreneurial experiences and entrepreneurial intentions.

When a systematic, integrated teaching and learning process is combined with action learning targeting participants with limited or no exposure to entrepreneurial experiences, it stimulates experiential meaningful learning with lasting effects. It further provides students the opportunity to enhance their entrepreneurial intentions through continuous encounters with entrepreneurial activities. Postgraduate students are linked with small businesses for a mutually beneficial learning opportunity that is gained when paired with existing entrepreneurs for joint partnering and being part of a team of an emerging business. The theoretical advantage that students bring is linked with the entrepreneur's practical experience. Thus, partnerships become strengthened where greater understanding occurs and an innovative in and out of classroom teaching using blended approaches is done. However, this tends to blur the student-teacher or mentor-mentee relationship, as roles tend to be swapped one time or another.

Providing an Evolving Workforce

It is essential to acknowledge that institutions of higher learning are confronted with higher levels of advanced technology usage. This means the integration of learning incorporate elements of technology for classroom setting to be accessed virtually. The need for instant learner gratification should be met on varying platforms where constant learning stimulates rigorous debates, reflections, and intellectual stimulation in class. The challenge could be in keeping pace with the vast proliferation of information and its availability, students' social habits, and the way they engage with learning. Incorporating inclusivity (at the classroom level) that accommodates learners with unique needs, provides support to vulnerable learners, with social challenges and hardship.

Relevant Knowledge

Theron & Bitzer (2016) acknowledge the changes in the characteristics and learning needs of students, thus making relevance a pivotal part that requires prominent attention when imparting knowledge to students. They incorporated learning and engagement where students are more engaged if their specific learning meets both social and technological needs. An emphasis on student's engagement means active involvement in their own learning and pursuing a greater understanding that challenges students' work. Engagement can be ambiguous if it does not incorporate cognition, behaviour, emotion, or affect. This complexity needs to be overcome beyond the fragmented domains and context of personal and institutional circumstances.

Engagement at the institutional level incorporates both in-class and out-of-class learning. At an individual level, it is recognised that the demands are becoming increasingly more complex, as society now expects higher learning to deal effectively with complexities such as language, social backgrounds, sensitivity to culture and gender issues, to promote tolerance and social cohesion, and respond effectively to disadvantaged students and students with learning or behavioural problems whilst also using new technologies. The main goal is to keep pace with rapidly developing fields of knowledge while utilising relevant approaches for student assessment, with better responsive approaches that go beyond resourcing but also strengthening the quality of teaching and learning through a multi-faceted approach. If we are to emphasise the value of stimulating cognitive, social, and emotive levels, then I have to allude to the valuable skills gained.

Section 6: The Value of Gained Skills

Entrepreneurship teaching and learning for RBS develops and trains the next generation of entrepreneurs or intrapreneurs (also known as corporate entrepreneurs). The word intraprenuer encapsulates a process in which the development of new business ideas and opportunities occurs within large and established corporations and carried out by an individual or group of individuals. This is, in association with an established enterprise not only to create a new organisation or instigates renewal or innovation within the current organisation. Business schools' entrepreneurial teaching and learning programme should strive to change and challenge existing mindsets for business leaders to develop what Kramer & Porter (2011) call a shared value. Through the application of a shared value, an integrated, sustainable teaching approach should focus on economy, equity, ethics, and ecology (4E).

When exploring teaching and learning for entrepreneurship, it is essential to incorporate entrepreneurial skills. Hayton (2015:11) defines entrepreneurial skills as *"the ability to identify opportunity, look at resources, organise a new venture, and effectively communicate an entrepreneurial vision"*. However, Clifton and Badal (2014) emphasise skilled entrepreneurship, and not innovation, as a critical factor. For this chapter, it is pivotal to acknowledge that innovation is strengthened whenever creativity can be linked to technology making entrepreneurial skills to incorporate these throughout the skills development.

Elements of the entrepreneurial skills have been categorised into four categories: idea identification/creation, capitalising on ideas, traits/behaviours, and management/leadership skills (see Table 1).

Idea Identification / creation	Capitalising on ideas
• Idea generation/envisioning • Opportunity recognition and means-end analysis • Ability to acquire information about a potential opportunity, domain knowledge and associated skills • Recognition of social/market need	• Awareness of environment and factors conducive to opportunity exploitation • Ability to garner the necessary material resources • Ability to convince others of the value of an opportunity • Networking and social embedding
Traits / behaviours	Managerial / leadership skills
• Self-belief, self-awareness, trust in own judgement, etc. • Ability to manage risk and shoulder responsibility • Ability to endure and cope with difficulties. Energy, motivation, persistence, etc.	• Ability to manage others • Ability to overcome institutional and other constraints • Ability to develop an idea as a commercial opportunity • Decision-making capability

Table 1: Categories of entrepreneurship skills (DBIS, 2015:14).

Entrepreneurial skills are a unique set of skills distinct from management and leadership skills (DBIS, 2015:5), from entrepreneurial talent (Clifton & Badal, 2014:39), from entrepreneurial competence (Michelmore & Rowley, 2013:126), or from entrepreneurial behaviour (DBIS, 2015:15). However, for this chapter, it is essential that entrepreneurial skill is defined as proficiency in business performance that may be enhanced by practice and training through multidimensional constructs (Chell, 2013:8). This is achieved through stimulating the *cognitive* (knowledge and what is learnt), the *affective* (emotional expression and what is experienced), *behaviour* (action at strategic, tactical, and personal levels), and *context* (sectoral relevance, occupational, job, and task levels). This means entrepreneurial skills consistently focus on *"opportunity identification/ creation and the qualities required to take advantage of these opportunities as well as to assemble and utilise the resources needed to achieve commercial success on the basis of these opportunities"* (DBIS, 2015:14).

According to Theron & Bitzer (2016), students learning highlights the importance of varied learning engagement and the need to ensure students meet their own learning needs, meaning accommodating diverse needs of the current student body in terms of social and technological needs. This requires an integration of thinking process with integrated sustainable business model outcome (Skae, 2014). Thus, during the application of economy with equity then customer-centric entrepreneurs focusing on people-centred approach to both business and its management. Yet a combination of economy and ethics requires responsible leadership with governance as principles for meaningful stakeholder engagement. Integration of ethics with ecology acknowledges that business can have socially sustainable business models. Lastly, ecology and equity can help entrepreneurs' view of the world. This interconnection becomes not only a shared value but gets cascaded into the teaching and learning approaches used by the school. This alludes to the 4E elements mentioned earlier. This makes it is essential that entrepreneurial learning and teaching should measure sustainability using principles of sustainability. Thus, a look at conducive conditions that promote students' study success and the unintended benefits follows.

Aligning Outcomes with Principles of Sustainability

Preparing students to be future responsible leaders, employees, and entrepreneurs is achieved through incorporating sustainable outcomes. These require a meaningful and long-term change with a lasting or widespread improvement. This is supported by Hargreaves & Goodson's (2004) principles of sustainability. They require sustainable leaders to include both students and educators, making purposive learning to engage students intellectually, socially, and emotionally. Learning and teaching should go beyond temporary gains in achievement scores to create lasting, meaningful improvements in learning (Glickman, 2002; Stoll et al., 2002). For sustainable leadership to matter, it needs to create and preserve sustained resourceful learning that is socially just, over time which promotes diversity and engagement with the environment. Principles of sustainability help guide teaching and learning by ensuring teaching and learning that, following Hargreaves & Fink (2004):

a) *Matters.* It is essential to ensure that teaching and learning needs to create and preserve sustained learning through enhancing experiential learning. This means a learning and teaching approach that integrates action participatory learning and community engagement whilst gaining theory as being essential components. The main outcome is to ensure that students are challenged intellectually, socially, and emotionally on issues that matter to provide entrepreneurial solutions;

b) *Lasts.* The teaching and learning process needs to ensure success over time and eliminate a revolving-door approach. The consistencies and continuation of each module should emphasise and interrogate the ethos and principles at which the higher learning academic institutions embrace whilst ensuring that these are not only sustainable but have prepared the entrepreneur as future global leader;

c) *Spreads.* It is through the diverse leadership interventions and the realities in terms of not only scenarios based on theoretical assumptions but the testing of these assumptions and the development of realistic business enterprise that can develop and expand leaving a sustainable impact with sustainable leadership for others. Thus, through the alpha projects, teams shared decision-making and are held accountable by members, making it a shared responsibility;

d) *Is socially just.* For teaching and learning to be socially just it needs to address issues of social injustices. This should go beyond teaching and learning but should incorporate caring that accept responsibility where schools and students' actions affect the wider environment. Entrepreneurs as leaders are not only interested in maintaining improvement or profits in one's own enterprise but are leaders who care about sustainability. They tend to accept responsibility for their own actions and how it affects the wider environment;

e) *Is resourceful.* To ensure that teaching and learning is resourceful, it needs to develop rather than deplete human and material resources. This can be achieved with systems that provide intrinsic rewards and extrinsic incentives to attract and retain the best. Effective systems provide time and opportunity to network, coach, and mentor whilst key learning and support for successors. Through this, talents are developed while sustainable leadership systems care and encourage leaders to take care of themselves;

f) *Promotes diversity.* Innovation requires diversity at both an environmental level and capacity level for the creation of sustainable, yet different, kinds of excellence in cross-fertilising learning processes (Giles & Hargreaves, in press; Louis & Kruse, 1995; McLaughlin & Talbert, 2001). Recognising diversity whilst cultivating a culture that promotes and provides networks for sharing, yet eliminating, standardisation;

g) *Develops activism.* To ensure that teaching and learning develops activism it needs to undertake activist engagement with the environment, especially when confronted with an unhelpful environment. The activist dimension should be stimulated sufficiently to ensure that it gets used to challenge or change the status quo.

Promote Conditions Conducive to Students' Study Success

The integrated entrepreneurial courses imply that knowledge and expertise is broadened through support from entrepreneurs through field practice and classroom learning either face to face or virtual. The student gets a learning structure that allows teaching on theory and field practice, which is also accessible at the student's own pace (virtual access), thereby improving the possibility of a sustainable approach within the context of inclusive teaching and learning. These are achieved through learning material packaged as online education resources that can also be accessible remotely. It is essential to ensure that learning opportunities go beyond the formal indicators of success (e.g., grades) and for students to internalise and understanding what they learn so as to incorporate it in their lives. The ability to continuously stimulate student's willingness, need, desire, and compulsion to learn while participating could be key to the successful entrepreneurial learning process.

Unintended Benefits for Academics, Business Schools, and Students

Academics as change are continuously forced to adapt to the global changing needs and use academic platforms to intrigue dialogues on sustainability issues. Through seniority roles within academic schools that teach entrepreneurs impart students with management and leadership skills through influencing learning (practice and theory) on sustainable leadership. Further is the constant review of educational programme that address lasting and sustainable learning.

Business School that teaches sustainable entrepreneurship enhance thought leadership they internalise robust ongoing process that address not only business or economic issues but include environment perspective and social injustice issues that directly impede on human. Through academic teaching and learning development programmes, entrepreneurs such as business leaders are encouraged to restore, mitigate, and, when possible, reverse or eliminate the current stressful climate dysfunctional issues by integrating the seven principles with the 4E. Students gain a lifetime learning and the importance of being ethical whilst striving to achieve an equitable distribution of resources, (using poverty, gender, and inequalities lens to balance economies of scale) and to prioritise profit sharing (instead of only profit making), not at the expense of the environment.

Conclusion

In my chapter I acknowledge that entrepreneurs as future leaders have to be ethical, strive for equity, and focus on profit sharing that is not at the expense of the environment. Thus, teaching and learning entrepreneurship should prepare young students for the changing global markets using an integrated framework that develops ethical leaders who are able to build sustainable businesses.

It could be concluded that, through integrated teaching and learning on entrepreneurship, students can be stimulated intellectually, social, and emotionally when teaching exposes students to issues of ecology economy, equity, and ethics. This leads to lifelong learning if done through action learning, community engagement, and the involvement of experts such as business practitioners.

About the Author

Tshidi Mohapeloa is Senior Lecturer and PDEM Coordinator at Rhodes University, South Africa. She can be contacted at this e-mail: t.mohapeloa@ru.ac.za

Bibliography

CLLN-Canadian Literacy and Learning Network (2012). *Principles for adult learning.* Online Resource: http://www.cmec.ca/publications/lists/publications/attachments/283/grale_en.pdf [Accessed 3 October 2016].

Chell, E. (2013). Review of Skill and the Entrepreneurial Process. *International Journal of Entrepreneurial Behaviour and Research.* Vol. 19, No. 1, pp. 6–31.

Clifton, J. & S. B. Badal (2014). *Entrepreneurial Strengths Finder.* New York: Gallup Press.

DBIS-Department of Business Innovation and Skills UK (2015). Entrepreneurship Skills: *Literature and Policy Review.* London

Couger, J. D. (1995). *Creative problem solving and opportunity finding.* Boyd & Fraser Publishing Company.

Garrison, D. R.; T. Anderson, & W. Archer (2010). The first decade of the community of inquiry framework: A retrospective. *The Internet and Higher Education,* Vol. 13, No. 1, pp. 5–9.

Glickman, C. D. (2002). *Leadership for learning: How to help teachers succeed.* ASCD.

Hargreaves, A. & D. Fink (2004). The seven principles of sustainable leadership. *Educational leadership,* Vol. 61, No. 7, pp. 8–13.

Hargreaves, A. & I. Goodson. (2004). *Change over time? A report of educational change over 30 years in eight US and Canadian schools.*

Blank S. (2013). Turn a Great Business Idea into a Great Business. *Harvard Business Review,* May Issue 2013.

Hayton, J. (2015). *Leadership and Management Skills in SMEs: Measuring Associations with Management Practices and Performance.* Department for Business Innovation and Skills, London.

Knowles, M. S. (1984). *Andragogy in action: Applying modern principles of adult education.* New Jersey: Wiley, Jossey-Bass.

Louis, K. S.; S. D. Kruse & Associates. (1995). *Professionalism and community: Perspectives on reforming urban schools.* Thousand Oaks, CA: Corwin Press Inc.

Marshall, J.; G. Coleman & P. Reason (2011). *Leadership for Sustainability: An Action Research Approach*. Greenleaf Publishing Limited.

Merriam, S. B.; R. S. Caffarella & L. M. Baumgartner (2012). *Learning in adulthood: A comprehensive guide*. John Wiley & Sons.

McLaughlin, M. W. & J. E. Talbert (2001). *Professional communities and the work of high school teaching*. University of Chicago Press.

Michelmore, S. & J. Rowley (2013). Entrepreneurial Competencies of Women Entrepreneurs Pursuing Business Growth. *Journal of Small Business and Enterprise Development*, Vol. 20, No. 1, pp. 125–142

Neck, H. M.; P. G. Greene & C. G. Brush (2014). 1. Practice-based entrepreneurship education using actionable theory. *Annals of Entrepreneurship Education and Pedagogy _ 2014*, p. 1.

Otuya, R.; P. Kibas & J. Otuya (2013). A Proposed Approach for Teaching Entrepreneurship Education in Kenya. *Journal of Education and Practice* 14 (8).

Porter M. E. & M. R. Kramer (2011). THE BIG IDEA. Creating Shared Value. How to reinvent capitalism—and unleash a wave of innovation and growth. *Harvard Business Review*.

RBS-Rhodes Business School (2014). *Leadership for Sustainability*: Strategic Intent Document.

Rogers, C. R. (1954). Toward a theory of creativity. *A Review of General Semantics*, Vol. 11, No. 4, pp. 249–260.

Rae, D. & M. Carswell (2000). Using a life-story approach in researching entrepreneurial learning: the development of a conceptual model and its implications in the design of learning experiences, *Education+Training*, Vol. 42, No. 4/5, 220–7.

Sawyer, K. (2012). Extending sociocultural theory to group creativity. *Vocations and Learning*, Vol. 5, No. 1, pp. 59–75.

Skae, O. (2014). The future of management education: Integrated thinking, a 'nobrainer' *The Corporate Report Facilitating Business in South Africa*, Vol. 1. No. 4.

Stoll, L.; D. Fink & L. Earl (2003). It's about learning. London: Routlege Falmer.

Theron. E. & E. Bitzer (2016). Student learning engagement at a private higher education institution. *Tydskrif vir Geesteswetenskappe*. Vol. 56, No. 1, pp. 207–220

Wing Yan Man, T. (2006). Exploring the behavioral patterns of entrepreneurial learning: A competence approach. *Education+Training*, Vol. 5, pp. 309–321.

Yar Hamidi, D.; K. Wennberg & H. Berglund (2008). Creativity in entrepreneurship education. *Journal of Small Business and Enterprise Development*, Vol. 15, No. 2, pp. 304–320.

Chapter 11
The Five Capacities of Entrepreneurship Educators:
from Domain Experts to Supporters of Inherently Evolving, Unpredictable and Individually Founded Learning Processes

Mette Lindahl Thomassen

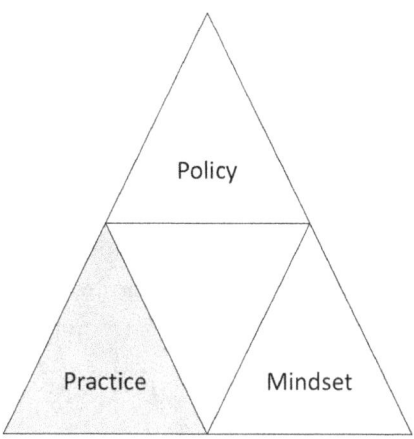

Introduction

My chapter is an important contribution to this section on practice – and to the book *Teaching and Learning Entrepreneurship in Higher Education* – because I suggest that educators in higher education take on a new role when they teach entrepreneurship. I argue that there is a disharmony between: 1) the traditional role of the educator as domain expert educating students *about* entrepreneurship; and 2) the new role of the educator educating students *through* entrepreneurship. In the chapter I therefore distinguish between educating *about* entrepreneurship and educating *through* entrepreneurship. I show how educators practicing within a curriculum designed for educating students *through* entrepreneurship will change their role from domain experts to supporters of inherently evolving, unpredictable and individually founded learning processes. I shall come back to that in more detail in the chapter.

Teaching and learning entrepreneurship is not a new discipline. For the last five decades, entrepreneurship education has moved from the field of business education into the field of STEM (science, technology, engineering, and mathematics) education and further into the field of humanities. This has resulted in a broadening of the scope of entrepreneurship education. It has also affected the pedagogical impetus of the field. As described by Hannon (2006) students are today taught about, for, and through entrepreneurship. Educating *through* entrepreneurship requires educators to escape the narrow role as domain experts and draw on other capacities when forming their role as educators. Hindle (2007) raises and discusses a number of key questions in relation to entrepreneurship education: *where* should entrepreneurship be taught, *what* should be taught, *when* should students be taught entrepreneurship, *who* should teach entrepreneurship, and *how* should entrepreneurship be taught?

My main focus is on two of the key questions proposed by Hindle (2007): 1) *how* should entrepreneurship be taught?; and 2) *who* should teach entrepreneurship? I argue that in modern entrepreneurship education the *how* has to be educating *through* entrepreneurship – a form of experiential learning (Kolb, 1984). And further I argue that this *how* influences the *who*, meaning the role of the educator. In addition, I also discuss what impact this has on the education institutions.

One of the reasons why it is important to discuss the role of educators is because educators are one of the greatest influences in students' learning (Hattie, 2009). Educators are in charge of framing the curriculum by selecting content, choosing learning methods, and carrying it out in practice where dissemination skills and interpersonal relations also influence the learning process (see Parkes & Lamb; Birchley & McCasland; Kolehmainen; Hørsted & Nygaard; and Rauh-Bieri, all in this volume). Educators do not stand alone in influencing the students' learning outcome. Figure 1 shows a number of internal and external factors which influence students' learning outcomes.

The Five Capacities of Entrepreneurship Educators

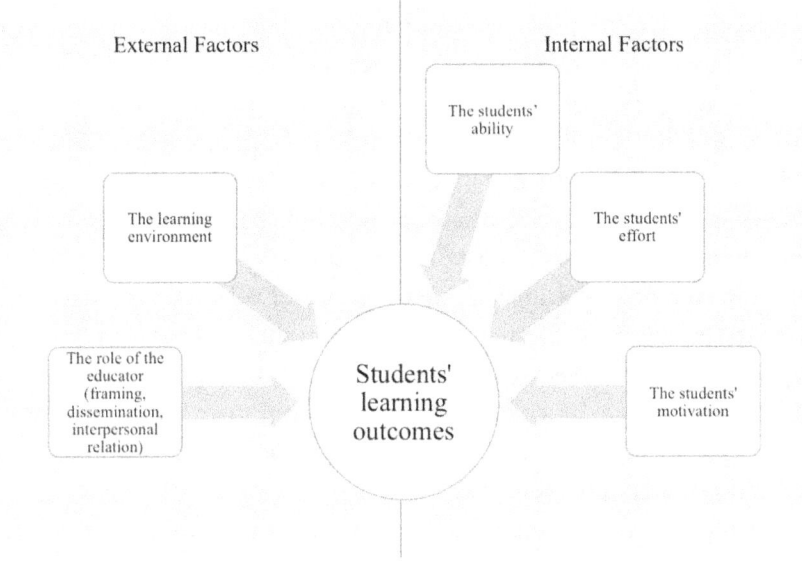

Figure 1: Internal and external factors that influence the students' learning outcome.

Briefly mentioned, other influencing factors include the learning environment, which consists of a physical environment and a socially constructed environment. On a micro level, the learning environment is constituted by the physical class room and the socially constructed learning environment, which is a result of the interaction between actors within the learning design; that is, students, educators, and external agents brought in to contribute in the learning process (Mohapeloa, in this volume). On a macro level, the learning environment is influenced by national culture, legislation, and policy (Pauna & Käle; and Ludewig, both in this volume), regional initiatives (Fadel et al., in this volume), institutional policy (McCormack & Scanlon; and Johnsson et al., both in this volume), and learning culture. The internal factors that influence the students' learning outcome of a learning design are the students' abilities, effort, and motivation to learn (Illeris, 2007). Therefore, the educator is not the only influencer in relation the students' learning outcome, but educators are an important factor, which is why it is important to discuss the educator role in learning and education as well as in relation to entrepreneurship education.

In addition, it is important to ensure that educators are and feel competent in their position, especially with the new requirements of them in modern entrepreneurship education.

Educating *through* entrepreneurship has proven highly effective in relation to positively affecting students' entrepreneurial intention (Moberg, 2013), but the introduction of these learning designs does not come without challenges. I discuss how educating *through* entrepreneurship challenges educators and calls for them to act in different capacities, possibly even necessitating sharing the educator role with other actors in the entrepreneurial ecosystem (Fadel et al., in this volume). Applying this type of curriculum design embodies a paradigm shift from the content-focused education of cognitive constructivism to a holistic view on learning that recognises the importance of social interaction and incentive in knowledge creation.

Entrepreneurship is multidimensional and can be interpreted through innumerable lenses. I define entrepreneurship as: *behaviour related to opportunities which lead to value creation for others*. This definition is inspired by thoughts on entrepreneurship in its simplest form as taking action (i.e., behaviour). Fayolle (2005) suggested a new approach to entrepreneurship education based on a theory of planned behaviour where behavioural predictors and behavioural intent are measured as learning outcome. This affirms the dependence of entrepreneurship on behaviour and addresses the challenges of traditional evaluation methods designed to measure theory-based cognitive learning in relation to entrepreneurship education. Not every form of behaviour is entrepreneurial. Entrepreneurial behaviour is associated with opportunities as, for example, Shane & Venkataraman have addressed in their work at the turn of the millennium (Shane, 2000, 2003; Shane & Venkataraman, 2000).

In addition, at a meta-level, opportunities and taking action are closely intertwined. Poiesz (2014) argues that there are three behavioural determinants: motivation, capacity, and opportunity, but not all behaviour relating to opportunities is entrepreneurial. Eventually, it needs to create value for others. Despite my broad definition of entrepreneurship, I believe my chapter is relevant for entrepreneurship educators who have a narrower scope of venture creation in their learning designs, as long as the applied curriculum is based on an experiential learning design.

I have structured the chapter in six main sections. In section one, I describe the context of entrepreneurship education in higher education and focus on its impact on the position of educators. In section two, I describe the process, purpose, and challenges of educating *through* entrepreneurship. In section three, I discuss in more detail the purpose of educating *through* entrepreneurship. In section four, I discuss the challenges of educating *through* entrepreneurship. In section five, I present five capacities which educators can draw upon while education students *through* entrepreneurship. These are: 1) domain expert; 2) process facilitator; 3) process consultant; 4) coach; and 5) co-creator. Together these capacities form the new role of educators educating *through* entrepreneurship. In the sixth and final section of the chapter, I briefly touch upon some possible implications for Higher Education Institutions when teaching *through* entrepreneurship. The key lesson from my chapter is that modern entrepreneurship education necessitates a broadening of the educators' capacity and requires that the educator moves away from being a domain expert and take on a new role when they teach entrepreneurship.

Section I: The Context of Entrepreneurship Education in Higher Education

The following section describes the context of higher education from a European perspective. The context constitutes the arena in which entrepreneurship education is unfolded. The focus will first be on the purpose and framing of higher education. Then, I show how this influences the traditional educator capacity.

Purpose and Framing of Higher Education

With the second academic revolution, the role of universities expanded from research and knowledge dissemination to also include creating value for society (Etzkowitz, 1990). This influenced the role of educators and researchers at higher education institutes. Educators are employed to develop students' knowledge, skills, and competences within the educator's field of expertise. In Europe, the framing of this development has partially been standardised by the Bologna process (European Commission, 2016). The education structure, the extent of course modules, and the grades are made easily comparable across European borders. However, there are still regional and cultural differences within higher educations. Educators typically develop their own learning designs and choose which didactic methodology to apply. Some educations have governmentally defined learning goals which naturally have a great influence on *what* is taught, but not *how* it is taught. In creating a learning design, educators either use predefined standards for learning goals and curriculum or define the learning goals and the curriculum and plan exercises and lesson content. In the end, the observed learning outcome is evaluated. A number of externally given factors affect the learning design, such as the time allocated (ECTS), the number of students taught, the physical learning environment, the allocated resources, and the learning culture (influenced by national culture and the culture at the education institution). These factors also affect which didactic methodology is applicable in conjunction with educators' pedagogical orientation. At a sociological level, Bourdieu (1977) argues that education is an institution of cultural reproduction which leads to social reproduction through educators reinvesting their cultural capital in their students, leading to mimicry. However, in modern education, reproduction is educating for the past. Today, mimicry is insufficient if students are to solve the challenges of tomorrow; moreover, increasing internationalisation, rapid evolution in technology, and cross disciplinary requirements of the labour market place new demands on graduates, which are just some of the reasons why the educator's capacity must also evolve from the traditional capacity described in the following.

The Traditional Educator Capacity

Since educators are employed to teach within a specific field of expertise, many educators act in the capacity of domain expert; in other words, someone who selects and guides students through a specific knowledge field by dosing knowledge or reinvesting cultural capital, as Bourdieu (1977) describes it. Learning at a cognitive level is in focus – as in Piaget's school of thought – and the learning designs become curriculum-centred. This leads to learners having very limited degrees of freedom in the learning process in relation to what is learned. Students are primarily schooled in reproduction and utilisation of existing theory.

At higher education institutions, domain experts are often limited in their choice of applicable didactics given the large number of students, the limited resources allocated, requirements of evaluation, and the physical learning environments that solely supports knowledge distribution through monologues in auditoriums – the artefact of universities.

Domain experts have a larger cultural capital than have learners as Bourdieu (1977) describes it. It means that students are subordinate to educators, and the power relation is tipped in favour of educators. In the capacity of domain experts, educators become synonymous with "the right answer", which entails obligations as well as empowerment. It entails obligations in the sense that educators need to stay updated within their field of expertise, and they are expected to be able to answer questions relating to this field. It entails empowerment in the sense that, in the capacity of domain experts, educators are able to pass judgement on the level of students' knowledge, skills, and competences within the applicable field of expertise. Hence, the capacity as domain experts gives educators clout and positions educators above learners in terms of power balance. One of the most important tasks as domain experts is to maintain the power position through continuous knowledge acquisition, thus bringing integrity to the position, which contributes to the shaping of the domain experts' professional identity.

As previously mentioned, the traditional educator capacity is under pressure and needs to evolve beyond reproduction. Also, in relation to entrepreneurship education, the traditional educator capacity as domain expert becomes challenged to a high degree when applying didactics that educate students *through* entrepreneurship. In these next sections, it is explained why.

Section 2: The Process of Educating *Through* Entrepreneurship

To understand how the traditional educator capacity is challenged in contemporary entrepreneurship education it is important to understand the process of educating *through* entrepreneurship. The following sections explain the basics of experiential learning and entrepreneurship in an educational context.

Chapter 11

Experiential Learning and Entrepreneurship Education

Educating *through* entrepreneurship is a form of experiential learning. Experiential learning theory is inspired by what Kolb (2015) calls the foundational scholars: William James, John Dewey, Kurt Lewin, Jean Piaget, Lev Vygotsky, Carl Jung, Paulo Freire, and Mary Parker Follett. In this theory, learning is defined as: *"The process whereby knowledge is created through the transformation of experience. Knowledge results from the combination of grasping and transforming experience"* (Kolb, 1984:41).

In experiential learning, the experience is the epicentre from which knowledge is derived, a process made conscious in education through reflexivity (Boud *et al.*, 1985). It is equivalent to what Illeris (2007) describes as the individual's interaction with his or her environment. At the foundation of experiential learning are five assumptions identified by Boud *et al.* (1993):

- experience is the foundation of and the stimulus for learning;
- learners actively construct their own experience;
- learning is a holistic process;
- learning is socially and culturally constructed; and
- learning is influenced by the socio-emotional context in which it occurs.

These assumptions have a large impact on the educator because they expand the borders of learning beyond the classroom and make it explicit that there are numerous factors influencing students' learning which are all beyond the control of the educators. Moreover, students are obligated and empowered in the learning process, and their motivation becomes a key factor in their learning. Illeris (2007) stresses the importance of learners being motivated to learn (i.e., having a learning incentive). It can be hard to accommodate a large number of students in a narrow learning design advocating giving students choice in education. However, this also puts the domain expert under pressure if students choose to move away from the educators' area of expertise.

In the case of entrepreneurship education, the experience is within the entrepreneurial process. When working with learning designs in entrepreneurship education, it is important to be aware of the fact that entrepreneurial processes are inherently evolving and unpredictable by nature. It is a process based on a series of action-reaction sequences with multiple variables and multiple possible outcomes. Kolb (1984) describes the sequence in his experiential learning circle in four phases:

1) concrete experience;

2) reflective observation;

3) abstract conceptualisation; and

4) active experimentation.

In educating *through* entrepreneurship, the educators can only try to facilitate students as they move through these four phases of the experiential learning circle. Each student is the main driver in creating his/her own learning process from concrete experience to active experimentation. This obligates and empowers students while it reduces the educators' control over the process.

Derived from Shane's (2003) theory on the nexus of opportunity, one can argue that the cohesion of entrepreneurship with opportunities also makes the process highly dependent on the individual, since individuals do not have equal opportunities. Moreover, according to Sarasvathy (2011), entrepreneurship is arguably individually founded according to the bird-in-hand principle (Read, 2001; Sarasvathy, 2011). The unpredictability and individual dependence of entrepreneurship make each process unique. In an educational context, this means that it is difficult to plan and anticipate the course of events. The result is that educators can neither foresee every event when planning their learning design nor draw solely on prior experiences in the execution of entrepreneurship education, because they are likely to face unforeseen events every semester. In conclusion, educating through entrepreneurship necessitates a *process* focus rather than a traditional *content* focus.

The Entrepreneurial Process in a Learning Context

The entrepreneurial process is iterative but can be divided into three phases: proof of idea, proof of concept, and proof of business. *Where* in the process the learning design starts and ends depends on the limitations and the scope chosen by educators. Context limitations at higher education institutes can include timeframe, resources available (including labs/test facilities, access to domain experts, materials, etc.), and evaluation requirements. These factors affect the learning environment in which educators need to navigate and place their learning design in.

In an educational context, the stage of proof of business is rarely achieved, but a pre-phase of preparation and opportunity recognition is often added.

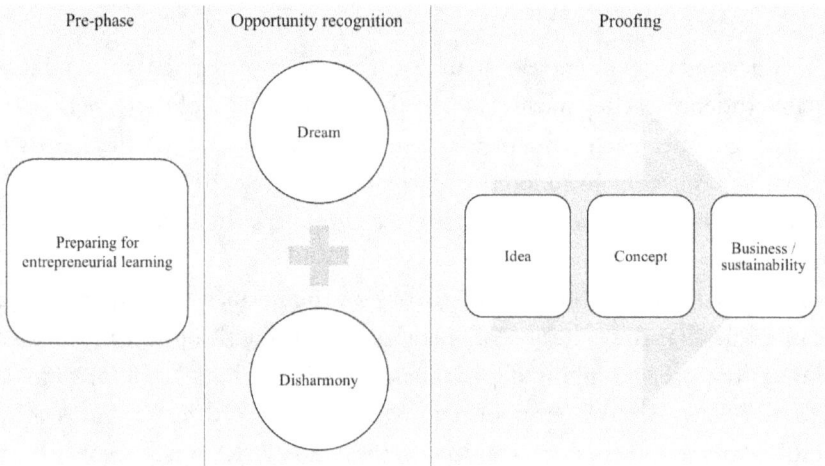

Figure 2: The entrepreneurial process in a learning context.

Some of the education *about* and *for* entrepreneurship can take place during the pre-phase. This may include a multitude of things – from theoretical studies of entrepreneurship to exercises where learners discover their own bird-in-hand as the Model for Entrepreneurial Education (ME2) framework suggests (Entrepreneurship.au.dk, 2015), inspired by the work of Bager *et al.* (2011).

Opportunity recognition is the foundation of idea generation. There are many methodologies concerning idea generation. The ME2 model derives ideas from the disclosure of disharmonies, inspired by the work of Spinosa *et al.* (1997). Another way to generate ideas is through dreams, as suggested in the dream board or vision board methodology promoted by, among others, Allis (2013). The opportunity recognition process is ongoing and is continuously qualified throughout the entire entrepreneurial process. At some point, learners are able to express their ideas. This may be done in a business model canvas, which is essentially the proof of the idea phase.

In the proof of concept phase, prototyping is used extensively. The lean start-up method (Ries, 2011) utilises early prototyping and emphasises the involvement of end users and other stakeholders in the experimentation and feedback loops. When the concept has been fine-tuned or proven, the next hurdle is to realise the value. Proof of business is achieved by making the first sale or by delivering value as intended. Here, it is important to remember that in entrepreneurship there is no final phase. Even though proof of business has been achieved, fine-tuning and further development will inspire new learning loops. For this reason, there will never be a final result of an entrepreneurial process, and in a learning context this means there is no final right answer to a problem, leaving educators unable to objectively evaluate the result of a learning process through entrepreneurship.

A number of frameworks have been developed to support educators who are facilitating through entrepreneurship. The aforementioned ME2 model is one of them. Blenker *et al.* (2016) have further refined their six-step main model of entrepreneurship education though the PACE project developed at Aarhus BSS Department of Management, Aarhus University, Denmark. Design thinking with Stanford's D-School as frontrunner has been widely adapted in entrepreneurship education. Even when educating through the entrepreneurial experience, sequences of educating about and for entrepreneurship can be included to bring knowledge into play and train skills applicable in the entrepreneurial process (Ramsgaard & Christensen, 2016). Furthermore, a specific pedagogy for learners in the pre-idea phase is described in Robinson *et al.* (2016) article about student centred learning in entrepreneurship education. There are various degrees of freedom in learning designs of entrepreneurship education. Educators may limit students by defining an arena in which disharmonies are to be found or defining what dreams should be about. Moreover, educators may define a concrete problem which learners need to solve or a target group of problem holders. This may have a positive effect because it delimits the number of opportunities learners need to consider, but it can have a negative effect on learners' motivation, a cornerstone in learning (Illeris, 2007; Poiesz, 2014) if the arena or problem is not within their sphere of interest. Motivation is essential because learners need to actively construct their own experience as Boud et al. (1993) describe it. In relation to the educator role, the process methodology may or may not be defined and facilitated by educators.

Finally, in an educational context an evaluation of the observed learning outcome is mandatory (European Commission, 2016). This appears to be challenging in relation to entrepreneurship education where *through* didactics are applied. This is vividly discussed in journals and at conferences, and there seems to be a division between having an outcome focus or a process focus in terms of evaluation. This means that evaluations either focus on achievements/values of ideas or on process reflections. Either way, the educator is put in a position where it is difficult to objectively access the observed learning outcome and the feedback will affect the students' future behaviour (Boud et al., 1985). Knowledge about and skills for entrepreneurship may also be assessed; these are easier for the educator to access using traditional assessment methods.

To sum up, education through entrepreneurship is founded on learners' own entrepreneurial experience. The experience requires learners to take action and interact with their environment (Boud et al., 1993; Kolb, 2015). Furthermore, the process is unpredictable and highly individual. The experience can be more or less organised by educators, adding various degrees of freedom to the learning design. The processing of the experience can to some extent be facilitated, but what Kolb referred to as the gasping and transformation into knowledge is an individual process at a cognitive level.

It is challenging to execute these types of learning designs so one might think *why bother?* In the following, the purpose of education *through* entrepreneurship is reviewed.

Section 3: The Purpose of Educating *Through* Entrepreneurship

If all entrepreneurship educators were asked about the purpose of entrepreneurship education, the answers would no doubt be as ambiguous as the definitions of entrepreneurship. In their article, Robinson & Blenker (2014) looked at entrepreneurship courses and their aims. They discovered that the courses can be placed in a matrix, where the horizontal axis represents the framing of the learning activity – from extracurricular activities to curricular activities – and the vertical axis describes the scope or understanding of entrepreneurship upon which the activity is based. The scopes of entrepreneurship education range from the traditional, new venture creation to entrepreneurship as a mindset used in everyday practices. Depending on the paradigmatic position on which educators base the learning design, entrepreneurship education can have different scopes, ranging from venture creation to student emancipation, but they all evolve around value creation and opportunities.

Looking specifically at entrepreneurship education where *through* didactics are applied, the general purpose is to familiarise learners with an engagement in entrepreneurial behaviour and through a learning-by-doing process to equip them to navigate in entrepreneurial processes. Advocating for the application of *through* didactics, Moberg (2013) found that it was the most effective didactic method to positively influence learners' entrepreneurial intent. This study and much other research in relation to entrepreneurship education are founded on or inspired by Bandura's research on self-efficacy, in which actors' belief in their own ability to complete a task is a predictor of the likelihood of the actors taking action. This means that one purpose of entrepreneurship education is the strengthening of learners' self-efficacy.

In broad terms, the purpose of educating *through* entrepreneurship is to strengthen learners' ability to create opportunities, enhance their ability to act upon them, and as enablers build the courage to do so. By educating learners through entrepreneurial processes, the purpose of entrepreneurship education is to strengthen learners' ability to act entrepreneurially and ideally to increase their entrepreneurial intent and thus the likelihood of learners behaving entrepreneurially in the future. From this point of view, using Poiesz's (2014) behavioural predictors, entrepreneurship education must motivate students to act as entrepreneurs, build students' capacities to act entrepreneurially, and provide students with frames that allow them to find or create opportunities. As Honey (2014) would frame it, students need to be willing, able, and allowed to learn how to act entrepreneurially.

From learners' perspective, entrepreneurship education can become emancipating. It enables learners to take charge of their own future – to be the pilot on the plane, as Sarasvathy (2009) describes it. Moberg (2014) further argues that educating through entrepreneurship increases school engagement.

From a societal point of view, the purpose is in the effect of entrepreneurship education. This can include economic growth (Kuratko, 2005), job creation (Hindle, 2007), and learners' increased ability to address societal challenges (Rae, 2010), making them engaged value creators for the benefit of society at large. However, the application of *through* didactics is not business as usual at most higher education institutions. In the next section, the challenges in relation to the application of this type of didactics and its implications on the role of educators are addressed.

Section 4: The Challenges of Educating *Through* Entrepreneurship

As presented in the section above, there are many good reasons for educating *through* entrepreneurship. But implementing this type of didactics in the frames of higher education causes some challenges which affect the educators. This is described in the section below.

Challenges and Their Effect on Educators' Capacity

There are many challenges in relation to educating students through entrepreneurship. It is possible to reduce the challenges by limiting the degrees of freedom which learners have in the learning design. A limitation of the degrees of freedom may preserve educators' locus of control in relation to the learning process, but it may be at the cost of learners' motivation and engagement – key dimensions in learning according to Illeris (2007) – which might have a negative impact on the learning outcome. Furthermore, it arguably contradicts some of the basic assumptions (Boud et al., 1993) of experiential learning.

In entrepreneurship education, the experience upon which learning is based needs to happen during the course. In conjunction with Boud et al.'s (1993) second assumption which obligates and empowers learners, educators face the challenge of creating learning designs that provide opportunities for learners to act and gain experiences. For the educators, this means that the majority of what student learning is based on is out of the educators' control. Moreover, the fourth assumption underlines that learning is socially constructed. This means that learning is dependent on interaction with others, and in an entrepreneurial learning design this interaction is not restricted to participants in the learning design but includes all stakeholders relevant to the idea/project which learners are learning through (the ideology behind the lean start-up). For this type of learning design to be successful, it requires students to be motivated, proactive, and engaged. Furthermore, it challenges the position of educators as domain experts, because the educators lose control over the course of the learning experience, multiple stakeholders are involved in the learning design (see Figure 1), and learners are given control. Aside from this, within one course, learners may move into various domains in their quest for realising their ideas. If we translate this into Kolb's learning cycle (Kolb, 1984) and look at the implications for educators in learning designs without limitations, this means that educators' primary function is to create opportunity for students to have concrete experiences, facilitate a reflective observation, and maybe contribute with scaffolding methodologies to aid the abstract conceptualisation. Educators can also guide in relation to the planning of the active experimentation, but – unlike traditional learning designs where the lectures are the concrete experience – the concrete experience here happens between learners and stakeholders in relation to the project/ideas they are learning through. So, the *who* of entrepreneurship education becomes a *we*, and this dissolves the educators' exclusive privilege as a domain expert and sole influencer in the learning process. This entails a necessity for educators to become process-oriented and leave the content primarily to learners, a paradigmatic shift in education at higher education institutions.

These learning designs do not just challenge educators, they also challenge students. The way students are schooled throughout the entire education system is flipped around, so this way of learning is unfamiliar to them. Moreover, the way of reasoning in entrepreneurial processes is – as described by Sarasvathy (2009) – through effectuation, not through causation which is the mother of modern science, recognised and practiced throughout the entire education system. Some students thrive in the new learning situation whereas others find it anxiety-provoking that both the content and the process of learning are unfamiliar. This means that applying this type of didactics might move some students into their nearest zone of development while it pushes other students into a panic zone where the opportunity to learn is blocked by anxiety. Anxiety-ridden students pose as yet another challenge for educators. Domain experts at higher learning institutions typically deal with students having troubles with *what* they learn, not the *way* they learn. Dealing with learners who are frustrated with the way they learn calls for educators to act in a different capacity than content-centred domain experts. It can be time-consuming and sometimes impossible to find time to deal with all learners' frustrations, especially if the number of students enrolled in the course is high. The pre-phase of the entrepreneurial learning process is designed to circumvent some of the *how*-related frustrations, but this leads to the next challenge for educators (i.e., the time limitation). Since entrepreneurial processes are impossible to plan and predict, it is challenging to create a time-restricted learning design that ensures that the process is equidistant for all students, especially if students are free to choose which ideas they wish to work with. Getting to proof of concept within research-heavy technological innovations can take much longer than getting to proof of concept within event or consultancy services. If educators choose not to limit learners, educators must also realise that the comparison of learners' results is pointless and that evaluations based on process results are inadequate. A good end result is desirable, but it might not be equivalent to a good learning process which advocates for evaluations based on process reflections. It is a dilemma *which* evaluation method to apply, and naturally it depends on the scope and derived from this the learning goals of the course. Maybe the ideal evaluation method for entrepreneurial education with few limitations is a synthesis between result-oriented and process-oriented methods, but no matter what, evaluating the observed learning outcome is a challenge for educators. Entrepreneurship with its unpredictability and individual dependence makes judgements of right or wrong irrelevant in relation to education through entrepreneurship, again challenging educators in the capacity of domain experts.

The above section lists a number of circumstances relating to educating learners through entrepreneurship that challenge the capacity of educators as domain experts. The empowerment of students and the process focus in the open-ended entrepreneurial learning designs call for different qualities in educators. The content-focused disseminator of knowledge needs to evolve.

In conclusion, it is impossible to be a domain expert in all the areas which an entrepreneurial learning process can cover. So, either educators limit the degrees of freedom in the learning design or accept it and draw on other capacities that allow and enable the *who* of entrepreneurship education to become a *we*. We being an expression of including other actors from the entrepreneurial ecosystem (Fadel *et al.*, in this volume) as resources in the learning design.

For the purpose of sensitising educators to their own role in learning design and inspiring them to evolve, five capacities in which educators can act are presented in the following section.

Section 5: The Five Capacities of Educators in Experience-Based Entrepreneurship Learning Designs

In this section I discuss the five capacities of educators when they take upon themselves new roles to teach *through* entrepreneurship.

Parameters Relating to Educators' Capacity

There are a number of parameters which can be used to describe and distinguish between different educator capacities. In the following, context, power relation, scope of learning design, application of educators' professional background, and teaching approach are used as parameters to describe the capacities:

- The context parameter solely focuses on whether the activities are curricular or extracurricular, the reason being that for curricular activities there are some restrictive time limitations and evaluation requirements which affect the capacities options;

- The power relation parameter describes not just what Bourdieu would call the difference in capital, but also how it is used to impact the relation between learners and educators (i.e., *who* has the power over *what*);

- The scope of learning design parameter describes – on a meta-level – the purpose of the learning design. Ideally, the scope of the learning activity influences the design of the learning activity which determines the capacity options. However, it may also have the opposite effect (i.e., that the preferred capacity of educators dictates options in the learning design and thus affects the learning outcome for students, limiting students' learning options);

- The parameter regarding application of educators' professional background refers to the requirements to educators' professional background that will allow them to act in the given capacity and how their background is utilised in the learning design;

- The last parameter, the teaching approach, describes the dominating method for inspiring learning.

The Five Capacities

Using the parameters from the section above, the five identified educator capacities are:

1) *domain experts;*

2) *process facilitators;*

3) *process consultants;*

4) *coaches; and*

5) *co-creators.*

The domain expert is described in the section about educators' capacity at higher education institutions as content-oriented. The domain expert possesses knowledge within a specific knowledge field (e.g., thermodynamics), and for this capacity to be applicable in the learning design, the knowledge domain needs to be relevant to the learners' project/ideas.

In facilitation theory, there are different levels of consciousness in facilitation and dimensions of facilitation. In this context, the process facilitator is what Giddens (1984) refers to as "Discursive Consciousness" which is an explicit awareness and ability to account for motives behind actions.

The process facilitator intentionally facilitates the learning process, giving it some structure – as described by Brockbank & McGill (1998). This can be done through various assignments or formulated requirements that provide a frame for the learning. In an educational context, one could argue that it is a necessity to frame entrepreneurial learning processes in order to achieve the learning goals and assess the observed learning outcome within the given time frame.

Unlike a facilitator, a *process consultant* does not have a predefined learning frame. The learners are in control and are only influenced by the process consultant to the degree they wish to be. The process consultant can help learners navigate in the entrepreneurial process (e.g., by asking learners to identify their next best step) and in this way help drive the process forward without dictating the direction.

The capacity of a *coach* originates from sports, but it is now applied within the fields of personal development and business development. This spread into different fields makes coaching multidimensional, but in general, the coach focuses on helping people release their full potential, as John Whitmore (2009) describes it. Just like the process consultant, a coach has an inquisitive approach and induces motivation and growth by setting goals and reaching achievements (i.e., the coach works with learners' bird-in-hand and their motivation).

The last capacity described in this chapter is the *co-creator*. At education institutions, an example of a co-creator can be a researcher who creates a spin-off. It is rarely seen in entrepreneurship education that educators contribute to the value creation process on equal terms with learners, but in theory this would imply a total eradication of the power imbalance between educators and learners and recognition of the learners' contributions in the value creation process.

The following Table 1 presents the identified capacities described according to the parameters of context, power relation, scope of learning design, educators' professional background, and teaching approach.

	Educators' capacity	Context	Power Relation	Focus of Education	Educators' professional background	Teaching Approach
Educating *about* entrepreneurship	Domain expert	Curricular	The educator has the power over learners	→ Focus on content. Educating learners to understand and navigate in a specific knowledge field.	Required in order to be relevant in relation to the project which students are learning through.	Dosing theory
Educating *for* entrepreneurship	Process facilitator	Curricular and extra-curricular	The educator as facilitator controls the process. Learners control what is created.	→ Focus on process. Educating through a pre-planned learning frame with open ends in order to drive a process forward.	Facilitation competences are required.	Structuring the process and asking questions
Educating *through* entrepreneurship	Process consultant	Extra-curricular	The educator as consultant guides the process. Leaners are in charge of process, content and value creation.	→ Focus on process. Supporting learners to navigate in an open-ended learning process.	Activation of network and ability to find structure in an entrepreneurial process take precedence over formal education.	Asking questions
	Coach	Extra-curricular	The educator as coach enables learners to develop on a meta-level.	→ Focus on the development process. Personal development of learners.	Coaching competences are required.	Asking questions
	Co-creator	Extra-curricular	The educator and the learner plays equal roles.	→ Engaging in process. Collective value creation.	Becomes relevant in contributing to the value creation.	Participation

Table 1: The five capacities of entrepreneurship educators ranked according to emphasis (About, For, Through) and described according to the parameters of context, power relation, scope of learning design, educators' professional background, and teaching approach.

The capacities from the top down evolve from being teacher-led to not only being student-centred but also student-driven. There is no one right answer with respect to the capacity which fits entrepreneurship education. Throughout a specific learning design, educators can act in multiple capacities. As an example, in their case study, Ramsgaard & Christensen (2016) advocate for a mix of explanation-based learning and experience-based learning in entrepreneurship education, which necessitate an application of multiple educator capacities.

It is educators' awareness of the capacity they can and do apply in a given situation, what Bourdieu (2004) would refer to as reflexivity, where educators must take themselves as their object. This may help circumvent some of the challenges regarding entrepreneurship education in relation to *through* didactics.

Section 6: Implications for Higher Education Institutions

In order to enable and maybe even convince educators to escape the narrow capacity of domain experts and to assume other capacities than their preferred ones, competence development may be called for. The objectives of such competence development should be making the value and applicability of each capacity explicit and making educators confident of assuming various roles. An expansion of applicable capacities is not only beneficial for educators who educate through entrepreneurship. The awareness and utilisation of multiple capacities can also diversify education in other fields and maybe help to bridge the rift between traditional subject-centred education and progressive student-centred education, also addressed by Lackéus et al. (2016).

Moreover, there is an issue in connection with responsibility within the learning design when the *who* of entrepreneurship education becomes a *we*. It is important for education institutes to be aware of this and assess the institute's readiness for this in relation to defining the job of the employed educators.

Furthermore, a revision of curricular frames may be called for in order to examine what the curriculum could and should include. Also, if any of the extracurricular elements were to be incorporated into curricular learning designs, how may the learning designs be reframed to accommodate for this and how are the new elements to be evaluated? Finally, management might consider diversification of educator profiles and direct attention to which parts of the education should be reproduced and which should be innovated.

Conclusion

In conclusion, educating *through* entrepreneurship is a form of experiential learning. In entrepreneurship education, the learning designs may have varying degrees of freedom which may potentially affect learners' anxiety level and motivation. Due to the unpredictability and individual dependency of entrepreneurship, it is difficult for educators to solely rely on prior experiences, thus making it difficult to plan and predict the course. Moreover, educators are challenged in relation to the evaluation of the observed learning outcome since there is no definitive right or wrong in an entrepreneurial process and no measure of the value of students' achievements. This calls for an expansion of educators' roles at higher education institutions. Depending on the framing and scope of the learning design, educators' professional background, and the project through which learners are gaining experience, educators can act in the capacity of:

- *domain experts;*
- *process facilitators;*
- *process consultants;*
- *coaches;* and
- *co-creators.*

Drawing on different capacities gives educators the opportunity to escape the narrow capacity of a domain expert and include other resources from the entrepreneurial ecosystem. This better enables a match between the educators' function and the didactic methodology of the learning design. Finally, it ensures that educators can be comfortable in the position of educating students *through* entrepreneurship by making the distinction between the different capacities conscious and explicit.

About the Author

Mette Lindahl Thomassen, MSc Marketing, is employed as Associate Professor of Entrepreneurship at VIA Engineering, VIA University College. She currently serves as coordinator of VIA Student Incubator and carries out research within the field of entrepreneurship education. She can be contacted at this e-mail: melt@via.dk

Bibliography

Allis, R. (2013). *The Startup guide – creating a better world through entrepreneurship.* Online Ressource: http://startupguide.com/life/dreams/ [Accessed 3 October 2016].

Bager, L. T.; P. Blenker; P. Rasmussen & C. Thrane (2011). *Entreprenørskabsundervisning- Proces, refleksion og handling.* Aarhus: Aarhus Universitet.

Boud, D.; R. Cohen & D. Walker (1993). *Using Experience for Learning.* Buckingham: SRHE and Open University Press.

Boud, D.; R. Keogh & D. Walker (1985). *Reflection. Turning experience into learning.* London: Routledge.

Bourdieu, P. (1977). Cultural reproduction and social reproduction. In J. Karabel & A. Halsey (Eds.), *Power and ideology in education.* Oxford: Oxford University Press, pp. 56–69.

Bourdieu, P. (2004). *Science of Science and Reflexivity.* Chicago: University of Chicago Press.

Brockbank, A. & I. McGill (1998). *Facilitating reflective learning in higher education.* Buckingham: SHRE and Open University Press.

European Commission (2016). *The Bologna Process and the European Higher Education Area.* Online Ressource: http://ec.europe.eu/education/policy/higher-education/bologna-process_en.htm [Accessed 3 October 2016].

Entrepreneurship.au.dk (2015). *ME2 – Model for entrepreneurial education.* Online Ressource: http://eship.au.dk/en/undervisning/me2-model-for-entrepreneurial-education/ [Accessed 3 October 2016].

Etzkowitz, H. (1990). The second academic revolution: The role of research in economic development. In S. E. Cozzens, P. Healey, A. Rip & J. Ziman (Eds.), *The research system in transition.* Dordrecht: Kluwer Academic Publishers, pp. 109–124.

Fayolle, A. (2005). Evaluation of entrepreneurship education: behaviour permorming or intention increasing? *International Journal of Entrepreneruship and Small Business*, Vol. 2, No. 1, pp. 89–98.

Giddens, A. (1984). *The constitution of society: Outline of the theory of structuration.* Cambridge: Polity.

Hannon, P. D. (2006). Teaching Pigeons to dance: sense and meaning in entrepreneurship education. *Education + Training,* Vol. 48, No. 5, pp. 296–308.

Hattie, J. (2009). *Visible learning- A synthesis of over 800 meta-analyses relating to achievement.* Oxon and New York: Routledge.

Hindle, K. (2007). Teaching entrepreneurship at university: from the wrong building to the right philosophy. *Handbook of research in entrepreneurship education,* pp. 104–126.

Honey, P. (2014). *Managers – Help your staff to be successful.* Online Ressource: https://www.talentlens.co.uk/blog/learning-styles/help-staff-to-be-successful [Accessed 3 October 2016].

Illeris, K. (2007). *How we learn. Learning and non-learning in school and beyond.* New York: Routledge.

Kolb, D. A. (1984). *Experiential Learning.* Englewood Cliffs NJ: Prentice-Hall.

Kolb, D. A. (2015). *Experiential Learning. Experience as the source of learning and development.* New Jersey: Pearson.

Kolb, D. A.; R. E Boyatzis & C. Mainemelis (2001). Experiential learning theory: Previous Research and new directions. In R. Sternberg & L. Zhang (Eds.), *Perspectives on Thinking, Learning and Cognitive Styles.* New York: Routledge, pp. 228–248.

Kuratko, D. (2005). The Emergence of entrepreneurship education: DEvelopment, Trends and Challenges. *Entrepreneurship Theory and Practice,* Vol. 29, No. 5, pp. 577–597.

Lackéus, M.; M. Lundqvist & K. W. Middleton (2016). Bridging the traditional-progressive education rift through entrepreneurship. *International Journal of Entrepreneurial Behavior and Research,* Vol. 22, No. 6, pp. 777–803.

Moberg, K. (2013). *Effektmåling af entreprenørskabsundervisning i Danmark.* Odense: Young Enterprise Denmark.

Moberg, K. (2014). Two approaches to entrepreneurship education: The different effects of education for and through entrepreneurship at lower secondary level. *International journal of management education,* Vol. 5, No. 3, pp. 512–528.

Poiesz, T. (2014). *REdesigning Psychology – In Search og the DNA of Behaviour.* Haag: Eleven international publisher, Pavilion.

Rae, D. (2010). Universities and enterprise education: responding to the challenge of the new era. *Journal of Small Business and Enterprise Development,*Vol. 17, No. 4, pp. 591–606.

Ramsgaard, M. B. & M. E. Christensen (2016). Interplay of entrepreneurial learning forms: a case study of experiential learning settings. *Innovation in Education and training international.*

Read, S.; S. D. Sarasvathy; N. Dew; R. Wiltbank & A-V. Ohlsson (2011). *Effectual Entrepreneurship.* London and New York: Routledge, pp. 72–83.

Ries, E. (2011). *The Lean Startup – How Today's Entrepreneurs Use Continuous Innovation to Create Radically Successful Businesses.* New York: Crown Business.

Robinson, S. & P. Blenker (2014). Tensions between rhetoric and practice in entrepreneurship education; an ethnography from Danish higher education. *European journal of higher education,* Vol. 5, No. 3, pp. 1–14.

Robinson, S.; H. Neergaard; L. Tangaard & N. Krueger (2016). New horizons in entrepreneurship: from teacher-led to student-centered learning. *Education + Training,* Vol. 58, No. 7/8, pp. 661–683.

Sarasvathy, S. (2009). *Effectuation: Elements of Entrepreneurial Expertise.* Cheltenham: Edward Elgar Publishing Limited.

Shane, S. (2000). Prior Knowledge and the Discovery of Entrepreneurial Opportunities. *Organization Science,* Vol. 11, No. 4, pp. 448–469.

Shane, S. (2003). *A general theory of entrepreneurship: the individual-opportunity nexus.* Cheltenham: Edward Elgar Publishing Limited.

Shane, S. & Venkataraman (2000). The Promise of entrepreneurship as a field of research. *The academy of management review,* Vol. 25, No. 3, pp. 217–226.

Spinosa, C.; F. Flores & H. L. Dreyfus (1997). Disclosing New Worlds: Entrepreneurship, Democratic Action, and the Cultivation of Solidarity. *Concepts and Transformation,* Vol. 2, No. 3, pp. 279–286.

Aarhus BSS Department of Management Aarhus University (2016). *PACE – Promoting a culture of entrepreneurship.* Online Ressource: http://mgmt.au.dk/research/innovation-entrepreneurship-and-information-systems/pace/ [Accessed 3 October 2016].

Section 3: Mindset

Chapter 12
Guiding Students Towards an Entrepreneurial Mindset by Using the Berkeley Method of Entrepreneurship

Charlotta Johnsson, Ikhlaq Sidhu, Mari Suoranta & Ken Singer

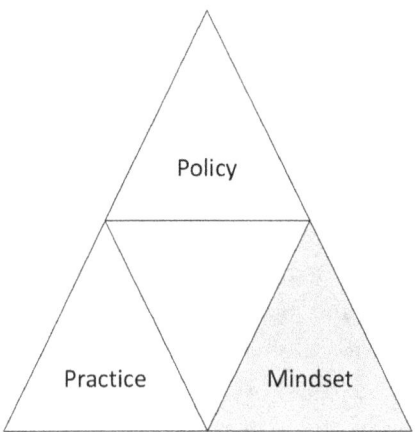

Introduction

Our chapter is an important contribution to this section on mindset – and to the book *Teaching and Learning Entrepreneurship in Higher Education* – because we present a novel teaching and learning approach called the Berkeley Method of Entrepreneurship (BMoE), which, in addition to the traditional elements of theory and practice, stresses the importance of including elements related to entrepreneurial mindset in an entrepreneurship curriculum. The method uses behavioural games and debriefing sessions as tools, and it results in students with an entrepreneurial mindset who, therefore, create more start-ups, ultimately leading to economic growth. Reading the chapter, you will gain the following three insights:

1. mindset is of great importance for entrepreneurs and should therefore be included in entrepreneurship education;

2. the mindset of successful entrepreneurs can largely be captured by a set of identified behavioural patterns;

3. games and debriefing sessions are suitable tools for teaching and learning mindset. They provide the students with a means for exploring their own mindset and behaviours and give them a starting point for a possible change.

Entrepreneurship matters (Sidhu *et al.*, 2015a). In modern open economies, it is more important for economic growth than it has ever been. Hence, citizens should be trained to start companies. One opportunity to create new companies is in areas of innovation and new inventions. In most countries, universities generate lots of new innovations. Thus, the universities that not only innovate (through research) but also train entrepreneurs will be at the forefront of growing their countries' economies (Bramwell & Wolfe, 2008). Today, many universities have extended their traditional missions (education, research, and outreach) to also include innovation and entrepreneurship. The newer goal is often expressed as: education, research, and outreach-and-innovations. Hence, entrepreneurship and innovation are being included in curricula at adaptive universities (Sidhu *et al.*, 2015a); two examples are presented in the chapters by McCormack and Scanlon as well as Ludewig, in this volume. The general role for universities in relation to entrepreneurship is discussed in the chapters by Mohapeloa (in this volume), Fadel *et al.* (in this volume) and Pauna & Käle (in this volume).

As entrepreneurship is included in curricula in higher education, it is important that the corresponding courses are filled with relevant material; and hence it is important to understand *"what makes a good entrepreneur"* and *"what creates a vibrant entrepreneurial culture"*. Entrepreneurship is a community with its own strong culture; that is, there is an unformulated understanding of what it means to *"become an entrepreneur and belong in the entrepreneurial community"* (Johnsson *et al.*, 2016a). Our understanding of entrepreneurship originates from the innovative culture in and around Silicon Valley, CA, USA.

Traditional pedagogical approaches in teaching and learning are centred on theory and practice, whereas the mindset part, the *"become and belong*" aspect (how to be and act), is often left out. Our belief is that a successful entrepreneurship course should, in addition to the traditional elements of theory and practice, include elements related to entrepreneurial mindset. Furthermore, it is our belief that an action-reflection approach is suitable for the mindset related part. For the action part, we propose games as a suitable vehicle, and for reflection we propose debriefing sessions as a suitable tool to use. We believe that using behavioural games and debriefing sessions will help the students to adapt their mindset to that of a successful entrepreneur; ultimately, leading to more entrepreneurs, more start-ups, and economic growth.

We have structured our chapter in four sections. In section one, we present the basic concept of BMoE; in other words, what it is, why it has been developed, where it has been used, and how the pedagogy is built up. In section two, we explain the concepts of behaviour and games, and we give examples of entrepreneurial behaviours and corresponding BMoE games. Then, in section three, we provide you with a suggestion of how you can proceed in case you would like to use BMoE and start guiding your students towards a more entrepreneurial mindset. In section four, we present research on which BMoE is based and ideas for future relevant research related to BMoE.

Setion I: What is BMoE?

BMoE – a new method for teaching and learning entrepreneurship – is under development (Sidhu *et al.*, 2014; Global Venture Lab Report, 2013) at the Sutardja Center for Entrepreneurship and Technology, UC Berkeley, USA.

Teaching and Learning BMoE

Entrepreneurship is an applied discipline, yet we are teaching and researching as if it were part of the natural sciences (Simon, 1996). Entrepreneurship cannot be taught in the same way as other traditional science subjects; we cannot teach it prescriptively as we teach, for example, maths or physics. These subjects are taught in a manner where something is proven to be always true and where students can practice these formulas which are always true. In entrepreneurship, we are teaching students to do things that have never been done before and in an environment, that has not existed until this time. Therefore, we cannot rely on teaching "recipes" for things that have worked in the past. Neither can entrepreneurship be tested in the same way as other subjects; in other words, by repeating what has been read in a textbook. Just because a student understands the ideas and theories presented in a textbook, it does not mean that the student can do the things that are required for entrepreneurship and innovation. Instead, the students would benefit from extending their theoretical and practical understanding of entrepreneurship with an understanding of the entrepreneurial mindset (Bootcamp, 2015). Generally, the mindset is a way of thinking that influences the way someone sees and acts in a situation; the mindset is reflected in the person's behavioural patterns. BMoE stresses the importance of explicitly including mindset in entrepreneurship education. Other alternatives of teaching and learning entrepreneurship are given in, for example, Lamb and Parkes' chapter in this volume stressing the importance of having the entrepreneurship education reflecting what entrepreneurs do (practice) in addition to the literature knowledge (theory), and in the chapter by Rauh-Bieri, also in this volume, the need for developing the student-practitioner is discussed.

For Whom Is BMoE Intended?

Entrepreneurship is often thought of as the act of commercialising an innovation. Entrepreneurship is also about the capability of translating science, technology, engineering, and mathematics (STEM) understanding into useful innovations. The economic engine has, over time, been technology (Today's Engineer, 2007). Clearly, a good understanding of STEM subjects is a useful prerequisite for innovations and entrepreneurship. However, the opposite also holds, and an understanding of fundamental ideas and mindsets from entrepreneurship can be useful for STEM learning in general (Duval-Couetil *et al.*, 2011). Entrepreneurs are more willing to be outside their comfort zones, and real learning occurs when a person is challenged and is outside of this zone (Sidhu, 2014). The relationship between STEM learning and entrepreneurship is therefore bi-directional. STEM is a useful pre-requisite for innovations and entrepreneurship, and understanding and applying the entrepreneurship mindset is advancing STEM learning. Therefore, entrepreneurship education is not only to be the engine of economic growth and wellbeing through the creation of jobs and new ventures, it is also to develop individuals who understand entrepreneurial processes and have entrepreneurial skills and ways of thinking (Täks et al., 2015). For both the students who select entrepreneurship as their career path, as well as for the students who do not, the mindset part of the education is important and creates value. This also applies outside of the STEM area, such as social services and healthcare (discussed in the chapter by Kolehmainen, in this volume), or to people in general and job-seeking people in particular (as discussed by Hørsted and Nygaard, in this volume).

Where Has BMoE Been Used?

BMoE has already been used in practice on different occasions; boot camps, courses for undergraduate and graduate students, networks and conferences for academia, and industry. The occasions serve different purposes that complement each other.

- The BMoE bootcamp is only one-week long and facilitates immersive learning for new venture creation. The material is presented at a high speed with the goal of giving undergraduate students a glimpse of, and an appetite for, a complete venture creation journey. The BMoE bootcamp attracts about 100+ undergraduate students per occasion and is offered twice a year at the Sutardja Center for Entrepreneurship and Technology at UC Berkeley. Concepts from BMoE are also included at the EIA boot camp, organised by the European Innovation Academy (EIA). The EIA boot camp is three weeks long and attracts 300+ international students every year;

- The courses are semester-long and provide interested undergraduate and/or graduate students with a deeper understanding of the theoretical material, more time to digest the material, and also more time on learning about the mindset of successful entrepreneurs. Concepts from BMoE have also been incorporated in entrepreneurship courses around the globe (e.g., Sweden, Finland, Chile);

- The network (called Global Venture Lab at UC Berkeley) is an international alliance of academic institutions sharing common research and educational programmes. The goal of the network is to share and discuss best practices between academic institutes and to foster innovation and entrepreneurship in a university environment with the intent to help create new companies and industries.

BMoE Pedagogy

BMoE is focused around learning rather than teaching, and the students are pushed to proactively develop their own understanding rather than wait for someone to teach them what they need to know. The students are trained to frame problems and find ways to solve them, and then reflect on what they have learned from the process. The pedagogy of BMoE is based on the following five principles, see also Figure 1:

- Students are learning by doing (Kolb, 1984);
- Instructors host the environment for students to interact directly with the problem. Students make their own decisions and learn inductively (Prince & Felder, 2006);
- Behaviour training for students is done through games and exercises (Verzat et al., 2009);
- Learning outcomes prosper when focusing on goals and processes instead of grades;
- Learning leverages on mimicking real-world entrepreneurial situations (Prince, 2004).

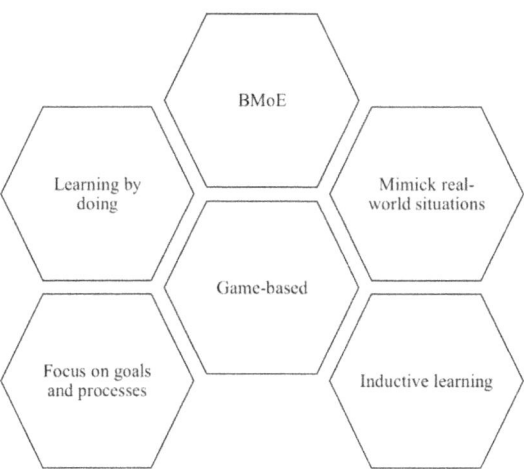

Figure 1: The five principles of BMoE.

In addition to mindset, BMoE also stresses the aspects of networks and frameworks. The network aspect includes assuring infrastructure and a supporting, safe, and effective environment (e.g., diverse networks, ability to connect, facilities, services, clarity of rules of engagement, ecosystems, and mentors). The framework aspect includes, for example, opportunity recognition, MVP, raising funds, business models, case studies, sales process, and other tools and processes associated with entrepreneurship.

Section 2: Mindset and Games

BMoE is based on a two-folded hypothesis:

1. the mindset of an entrepreneur can be described as a set of behavioural patterns;

2. an inductive game-based teaching approach is a successful vehicle for introducing and re-enforcing behavioural patterns to students.

BMoE Mindset

The mindset of successful entrepreneurs has been studied and a proposal describing their most dominant characteristics is given through 10 behavioural patterns. The proposal is based on extensive interaction with entrepreneurs in the Silicon Valley area and on a literature review (e.g., Hwang and Horowitt (2012)). The set of behavioural patterns is listed in Table 1. A more thorough description of the behaviours is found in Sidhu et al. (2015b). It is important to note that this is ongoing research, which implies that the 10 behavioural patterns should be interpreted as best current status. It cannot be excluded that more patterns will be added or current patterns modified/removed. The 10 behavioural patterns describe the typical mindset of successful entrepreneurs. If everyone in a community acts like this, there will be a vibrant entrepreneurial culture.

No	Behaviour
1	*Pay It Forward* "Agree that you will get help from others, and pay it forward."
2	*Storytelling* "Realize something new by induction, and then learn to communicate the story with a new language."
3	*Friend or Foe* "If you can't tell: Learn to trust others without expecting anything in return."
4	*Seek Fairness* "Make deals that seek fairness (in positive sum transactions), not advantage (in zero sum transactions."
5	*Plan to Fail* "It is necessary to be Wrong sometimes. Plan to Experiment. Plan to Fail. (Fail Fast) Analyze, Adapt and repeat. The smarter you think you are, the harder this is going to be."
6	*Diversify* "Diversify your networks. Connect to people you would not normally, then go and listen. Open Up. And connect them to others."
7	*Role Model* "Be a role model for other entrepreneurs and innovators."
8	*Believe* "Believe that you can change the world."
9	*Good Enough* "Perfection is no good but good enough is perfect."
10	*Collaboration* Individual vs team, and competitors vs partners

Table 1: Ten behavioural patterns characterising an entrepreneur.

BMoE Games

BMoE includes behavioural training as well as reflections on mindset. For this, an inductive game-based teaching approach is used together with debriefing sessions. Various games, referred to as BMoE games, have been developed. A game can be defined as a structured playing, usually undertaken for enjoyment and sometimes used as an educational tool. Or a game may be described as an "artificial situation" in which players engage in an artificial conflict against one another or all together against other forces. Games are regulated by rules, which may take the form of procedures, controls, obstacles, or penalties (Verzat et al., 2009).

The key components when describing BMoE games are captured by eight aspects:

Keywords: *important keywords*; Time needed: *time needed to run the games*; Material needed: *material needed to run the game.*

1. Behavioural pattern: *link to the BMoE behaviour(s) in Table 1;*
2. Learning purpose: *present the analogy with entrepreneurship;*
3. Setting up the game: *include the instructions and rules;*
4. Playing the game: *describe the action;*
5. Winning the game: *how is the game evaluated;*
6. Alternatives: *variants of the game;*
7. Instructor experience: *examples of common challenges that may occur;*
8. Reflection topics: *what to discuss in the debriefing sessions.*

The idea is to let the games invoke a certain behaviour or mindset of the student (e.g., Storytelling (behaviour 2) or Collaboration (behaviour 10)). After the game, the student should reflect on his/her own behaviour and compare it with that of successful entrepreneurs. The result of the reflection can be either an ignition for the student (confirming that he/she wants to become an entrepreneur), an extinguisher (confirming that the student does not want to be an entrepreneur), or a wake-up call (the student realising that he/she needs to learn more about this mindset).

Example: Storytelling Game

Our first example relates to BMoE behaviour 2, "Storytelling", and has been used on different occasions (Johnsson et al., 2016c). In the storytelling game, the students will be exposed to a game in which their communication and storytelling attitudes will come into play. After the game, it is important to allow for reflections in debriefing sessions, in which the outcome of the game can be discussed and lessons learnt.

In the storytelling game, the students are paired in groups of two. They are asked to sit with their backs to each other (i.e., with their heads facing in two opposite directions). Person A will thereby be able to see a figure shown on the screen, whereas Person B will not be able to see the figure. Person B is given paper and pencils. The instructor allows the students approximately five minutes to work, during this time the figure that Person A sees on the screen should be transferred to the paper that Person B has. Person B is not allowed to turn his/her head around (i.e., the only way to transfer the figure is by communication between the two students).

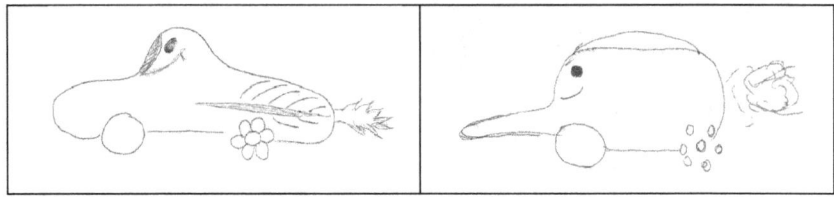

Figure 2: The car on the right was used as the instruction-figure. The car on the left is the outcome from one of the groups participating in the storytelling game.

After the game is over, the students are asked to look at the figure that has been drawn and to discuss it. It is imperative that the instructor also lets the student reflect on and speak about the entrepreneurship analogy of the game. An entrepreneur (represented by Person A) often has an idea in his/her head, the role of the entrepreneur is to make sure that the idea is understood by the other team members or to potential customers (represented by Person B). Making sure that two persons understand an idea in the same way is not easy and requires effort from both parties. The entrepreneur (Person A) should explain the idea, but it is equally important that he/she listens to the questions that are asked. By listening to the questions, the entrepreneur (Person A) can get an understanding of where misunderstandings are. The team member (Person B) should listen but also ask questions and state confirmation phrases. The act of transferring a figure/idea from one person to another is an act of teamwork. Very often, the act of listening to questions or stating confirmation phrases are not considered, so when the game is executed there is often an active speaker (Person A) and a passive listener (Person B). After the debriefing sessions, the students state that they have a better understanding of the importance of storytelling.

A more complete description of the Storytelling Game is included in Appendix A. Appendix A uses the template mentioned above and developed specifically for the BMoE games when presenting the information relevant for the game. Additional BMoE games have been developed (Johnsson et al., 2016c); some examples of these and their corresponding behaviours, are:

- Puzzle Game (Behaviour 2: Friend or Foe (i.e., Trust));
- Rejection Therapy Game (Behaviour 5: Plan to Fail (i.e., Resilience));
- Music Video Game (Behaviour 6: Diversify);
- Trade-Up Game (Behaviour 2, 5, and 8: Storytelling, Plan to Fail, and Believe);
- Scavenger Game (Behaviour 2, 6, 9, and 10: Storytelling, Diversify, Good Enough and Collaboration).

Section 3: Implementing the BMoE

BMoE is novel in its approach since it is mindset-focused and uses inductive game-based teaching. If you are interested in using BMoE for guiding your students towards a more entrepreneurial mindset, we would recommend the following iterative six-step implementation approach:

- STEP 1: Review your course. Look through your course material and determine how much of the current material is related to theory and practice, and how much is related to mindset? This will give you a good overview of the current focus of your course;
- STEP 2: Extend your course. Include a general lecture about mindset. The aim of this lecture is to have the students understand that mindset is an important aspect of entrepreneurship, equally important as theory and practice;
- STEP 3: Identify your BMoE game(s):
  - Step 3a: Look though the 10 behaviours (Table 1), and estimate the importance of understanding this behaviour for your students. Give each behaviour a rating (e.g., high, medium, low, or similar);
  - Step 3b: Select the BMoE game that best matches with the identified behaviour (i.e., the behaviour that you rated the highest);
- STEP 4 and 5: Expand your course. Include the identified BMoE game(s) in your course. The full description of the BMoE game is found, for example, in Appendix A or elsewhere;
- STEP 5: Include a debriefing session in your course. Make sure the students have time for sharing their reflections and that the analogy between the game and the entrepreneurial mindset is discussed;
- STEP 6: Evaluate if you would like to include another entrepreneurial mindset in your course. If so, go back to STEP 3.

The six-step iterative approach for implementing BMoE in your class is also visualised in Figure 3:

Step 1: Review your course. What does it include that ...
... relates to explicitly training the mindset of the student?
... relates to practice and providing the students with skills?
... relates to theory and providing the students with knowledge?

Step 2: Expand your course. Give the student the context...
... by including a general introductory lecture about entrepreneurial mindset, explain common behavior of successful entrepreneurs.

Step 3: Choose your BMoE-Game ...

BMoE-Behavior	Your preference:	
1. Pay it Forward	Low	...by giving each behavior a ranking based on your view of the importance of understanding the behavior.
2. Story Telling	High	
...	...	... by selecting the BMoE-game that best matches with the highest ranked behavior.
...	...	
...	...	
10. Collaboration	Medium	

Step 4 & 5: Expand your course ...
...by running the identified BMoE-Game
... by chairing the corresponding debriefing session.

Step 6: If you want more - go back to Step-3.

Figure 3: The six-step approach for implementing BMoE in your course.

BMoE uses games and debriefing sessions as vehicles for action and reflection. We believe that by implementing and applying BMoE in your course, the outcome will be more students with an entrepreneurial mindset who, therefore, create more start-ups, ultimately leading to economic growth.

Section 4: Research Related to BMoE

Research has been conducted in various fields and served as an input when developing BMoE. In addition, research can be performed based on BMoE and the outcome of its implementations.

Research on Which BMoE Is Based

BMoE is related to research performed and theories developed in other areas such as pedagogy, sociology, and psychology:

Chapter 12

- theory of planned behaviour (Ajzen, 2011);
- fixed and growth mindset (Dweck, 2006);
- community of practice (Wenger, 2006);
- metacognition (McCormick, 1997) and learning journals (Ballantyne et al., 1995);
- MIND-methodology (Johnsson et al., 2016a).

BMoE is related to the MIND-methodology, a generic pedagogical model that highlights important aspects in teaching and learning, see Figure 2. The methodology has been used in entrepreneurship and leadership education for more than 10 years, but it is not until lately that it has been explicitly formulated; in fact, this work has largely been done in parallel with the development of BMoE. MIND-methodology includes four building blocks. The first building block, Theory, stresses the learning of theory and thereby acquiring knowledge; the second building block, Practice, highlights the importance of practicing and thereby getting skills; and the third building block, Mindset, underlines the importance of changing or confirming an individual's mindset and thereby experiencing personal growth. The fourth building block, Engagement and Networking, is supporting the other three and is a means for improving the students' self-efficacy and self-awareness; in addition, it enables scalability of a curricula/programme (Johnsson et al., 2016a).

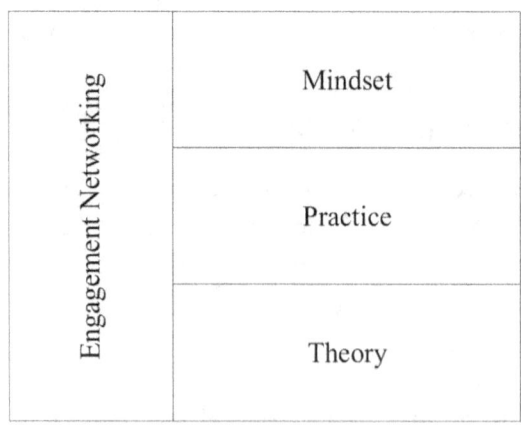

Figure 4: *The building blocks of the MIND-methodology.*

In the context of entrepreneurship, and according to the theory of planned behaviour (Ajzen 2011), most individuals will only be motivated to start their own company if a) they think doing so is a good thing to do (the attitude), b) at least someone in their personal network supports the idea (the subjective norm), and c) the individual thinks he/she has the time, resources, etc. to do so (the perceived behavioural control). Starting the company is not just the act of incorporation – entrepreneurship is more complex than that. On the behavioural level, starting a company is the end result of dozens of previous steps and actions (Johnsson et al., 2016a). Each behaviour in turn comes with its own combination of attitude, subjective norm, and perceived behavioural control. Previous education has taught some students to ideate and create but not to sell or commercialise their products. In fact, on the level of subjective norms, traditional classroom settings have fostered a culture of risk aversion (see BMoE behaviour 5, "Plan to Fail"). Through mechanisms such as multiple-choice testing, it has produced excellent students by rewarding rote learning and compliance but often penalising experimentation or risk-taking – behaviours that are crucial for entrepreneurship and innovation. This is one of the reasons that make it crucial to explicitly include mindset training in entrepreneurship education; the students should understand, through inductive reasoning, that risk-taking can be a positive thing (Johnsson et al., 2016a).

In addition to the theory of planned behaviour, the mindset of a person is critical to understanding the behaviour the individual will engage in. Mindset constitutes a certain set of attitudes and beliefs and is therefore central to behaviour. A common distinction in mindset has been made between fixed and growth mindset (Dweck, 2006). Accordingly, people with a fixed mindset believe that skills and ability reflect inherent traits that are stable. They build their identities around their level of ability. Research has shown, however, that this way of thinking exerts constraints on performance in the long-term. This is due to the fear these individuals experience when faced with challenges as they frame these situations are threatening. Due to their fear of failing or of losing, they avoid taking on new challenges or entering situations where others can question their credibility. On the other hand, people with a growth mindset believe in the malleability of skills and ability. Moreover, they believe that success is the reflection of effort. For persons with a growth mindset, the reward comes from overcoming challenges and impossible situations. They feel internally rewarded for the process rather than the result. As they continuously take on new challenges, they continue to grow and expand their skills and abilities. It is therefore of the greatest importance that the atmosphere in which entrepreneurship is taught is based on the growth mindset.

In addition to the academic atmosphere in which entrepreneurship is taught, networking plays an important role. Theories from social sciences state that knowing and learning are acts of participation in complex social learning systems; in other words, to form and acquire knowledge, it takes one or several brains in living bodies, but it also takes a complex social, cultural, and historical system that has accumulated learning over time (Wenger, 2000a). A community of practice is an example of such a learning system, and belonging to such a community is essential to our learning. There are different ways to belong to a community of practice; one of them is engagement (i.e., the possibility to do things together with peers in the community), another one is networking (i.e., to meet and spend time together with peers in the community). The way we engage and network in a community profoundly shapes our experience of who we are (Wenger, 2000a). For teaching and learning entrepreneurship, this means that it is vital to introduce and include students in various entrepreneurship networks, organisations, or clusters, and to encourage their engagement in those (see behaviour 10, "Collaborations").

Academic learning and engagement in various communities of practice can, with advantage, be combined with individual reflections. The importance of reflection in individual and organisational learning has been pointed out by several practitioners and scholars (Kolb & Fry, 1975; Ballantyne & Packer, 1995; Thorpe, 2004). A tool that can be used for serving this purpose is the so-called learning journal (Johnsson et al., 2013). A learning journal is similar to a diary; however, the material covered is professional and/or personal, but not private. The individual journals are to be written frequently (e.g., daily or several times per week). In a learning journal, students should be allowed to express themselves freely when reflecting on their own experiences, thoughts, doubts, etc. The learning journal also allows them to get a helicopter view of their own learning progress and to see how their initial body of knowledge expands over time, which is referred to as metacognition (McCormick,

1997). The positive effects of metacognition and learning journals justify the inclusion of debriefing sessions in BMoE. It is important to keep in mind that the new knowledge they are exposed to cannot be too distanced from their current body of knowledge (Vygotzky, 1978).

Based on the above-mentioned research fields, the MIND-methodology has been developed as a means of demonstrating the underlying pedagogy behind BMoE and similar approaches in leadership education. The results from applying it in a leadership curricula in Sweden show promising results for the main stakeholders; students and future employees (Johnsson et al., 2016b). Students' feedback years after graduation reveals that explicit mindset activities are highly valued. In addition, salaries and salary increases provided by their eventual employers are higher than average, which indicates that the students possess qualities sought after in today's labour market. We believe that similar results hold when applying the MIND-methodology in entrepreneurship curriculum, and that the mindset training (i.e., BMoE games and debriefing sessions) improves the possibility for the students to become successful entrepreneurs.

Possible Future Research Related to BMoE

There are several areas related to BMoE that would be suitable for future research. The development of additional games complementing those already developed is one area of importance. It would also be of interest to follow the development of the entrepreneurial mindset of the students attending the courses and participating in the games in a longitudinal study. The aim would be to capture their development over time and study what effects the games have. In addition to studying this development, it would be interesting to measure it. Ongoing parallel research performed at the Sutardja Center for Entrepreneurship and Technology addresses this issue, and a first version of the Berkeley Innovation Index (BII), a tool for measuring the innovation capability in individuals and organisations, has been developed (Sidhu et al., 2016). Since BMoE is developed under the assumption that innovation capability and entrepreneurial mindset can be learnt, the BII index could be used in a longitudinal study to measure its progress over time. Yet another research area that would be of high interest is to perform a study between various cultures, examining the effects that national and geographical culture have on the identified entrepreneurial behaviours. The result could be used to highlight what mindsets and behaviours are most and least developed in a certain geographical area, and hence give a hint of what mindsets and games are most needed in that area. The result could also reveal new, undiscovered entrepreneurial mindsets and behaviours that are successful in areas outside of Silicon Valley.

Other, more generic aspects of research are, for example, the role of the educator's mindset (Thomassen, in this volume) and the governmental policies on entrepreneurship (Birchley and McCasland, in this volume).

Conclusion

This chapter presents a novel approach in teaching entrepreneurship referred to as Berkeley Method of Entrepreneurship (BMoE). The method stresses the importance of including the mindset aspects in entrepreneurship curriculum, and it uses games as the vehicle for practicing the mindset. The mindset aspect is often not included in traditional entrepreneurship teaching and learning curriculum, in which the main focus is on theory and practice alone. By using inductive games and debriefing sessions, the students get a tool for exploring their own mindset and behaviours and can compare it with that of successful entrepreneurs. Ten behaviours have been identified, and games are under development covering single or multiple behaviours. The games are combined with reflection and debriefing sessions. The result of the reflection can be either an ignition for the student (confirming that he/she wants to become an entrepreneur), an extinguisher (confirming that the student does not want to be an entrepreneur), or a wake-up call (the student realising that he/she needs to learn more about this mindset). BMoE is related to research; theories developed in other areas such as pedagogy, sociology, and psychology; theory of planned behaviour; fixed and growth mindset; community of practice; reflective learning; and MIND-methodology. Teaching and learning entrepreneurship is important since it is the engine of economic growth and wellbeing through the creation of jobs and new ventures. BMoE has been developed by an international group led by the Sutardja Center for Entrepreneurship and Technology at UC Berkeley, and it has been used for both week-long boot camps, semester-long courses, as well as conferences.

About the Authors

Charlotta Johnsson is Associate Professor at Lund University, Sweden, and was a visiting scholar at the Sutardja Center for Entrepreneurship and Technology at UC Berkeley in 2013/2014. She can be contacted at this e-mail: charlotta.johnsson@control.lth.se

Ikhlaq Sidhu, Professor, is the founding Director of the Sutardja Center for Entrepreneurship and Technology at UC Berkeley, USA. He can be contacted at this e-mail: sidhu@berkeley.edu

Mari Suoranta is Associate Professor at Jyvaskylää University, Finland, and was a visiting scholar at the Sutardja Center for Entrepreneurship and Technology at UC Berkeley in 2008 and 2013. She can be contacted at this e-mail: mari.suoranta@jyu.fi

Ken Singer is a serial entrepreneur and Managing Director at the Sutardja Center for Entrepreneurship and Technology at UC Berkeley, USA. He can be contacted at this e-mail: ken.singer@berkeley.edu

Chapter 12

APPENDIX A: BMoE Game

Name of Game: Storytelling Game

- **Keywords:** Storytelling, empathy, perspective-taking, common language, communication;
- **Time needed:** approx. 10 mins;
- **Material needed:** paper and pen; beamer for image or large poster with an image.

1. Behavioural Pattern

(Present the behaviour(s) in focus in this game)

Perhaps one of the most important abilities of an entrepreneur is the skill of effective storytelling. As entrepreneurs innovate and create new products, they are faced with the challenge that they move into novel space that has not been described before; in other words, not only the development of new products but moreover the development of a "language" or "story" that can explain the innovation, which is crucial for successful entrepreneurs. They need to learn to describe their innovation to others and communicate their idea. This is easier said than done. We often forget the most obvious: what may seem obvious to us is not at all obvious to the person we are communicating with. Understanding and practicing strategies to overcome this bias are therefore important for aspiring entrepreneurs.

2. Learning Purpose

(Present the analogy with entrepreneurship)

The aim of the game is to underline the importance of storytelling for successful entrepreneurship and teach students effective strategies for communication. Students develop a shared language with their partner that both can understand and relate to. This requires an understanding of the other's previous knowledge, associations, empathy, and mutual perspective-taking. Also, they need to listen to cues that are being given by their partner and others around them. The ability to ask the right questions (understanding which information is missing and asking for it) and providing it are crucial for success in this game and storytelling as an entrepreneur.

3. Setting up the Game

(Includes the instructions and rules)

Students should pair up. Person 1 should sit or stand so that he/she faces the screen. Person 2 should sit back-to-back with Person 1, so that he/she cannot see the screen. Person 2 needs a pen and paper.

Person 1 (facing screen) can only use language to communicate what is on the screen, and Person 2 (back to screen) must capture it on paper.

Goal: Capture the image as accurately as possible in the shortest amount of time.

4. Playing the Game

(Describe the action taking place when running the game)

Person 1 (facing screen) begins to describe what he/she sees to his/her partner, who has to draw the image without seeing it but only hearing the instructions from his/her partner. Ideally, the communication between the pair is facilitated through the development of a shared "language" (i.e., common understanding has to be established by asking and responding to each other's questions). For example, common points of reference (e.g., looks like an apple) or positions (e.g., top left) are useful for effective communication. Through the communication, both partners learn to put themselves in the perspective of the other.

5. Winning the Game

(Describe the evaluation criteria of the game)

The purpose of the game is that the images drawn are as accurate as possible; accuracy includes aspects such as all objects being drawn, the order of objects being correct, objects are in the correct positions, details in objects are available.

6. Alternatives

(Explain variants of the game)

Pairs can be put together by gender, age, discipline, nationality, language, etc. – differences in pairs will make the communication harder but also more rewarding, as participants are more likely to experience, for example, that their own assumptions are not shared by others. Rules can be changed so that only person 1 can describe the image while Person 2 cannot ask questions back. This option requires a higher level of empathy and perspective-taking in the describer and can be played as a follow-up to the original version, ideally after the reflection.

7. Instructor Experience/Examples/Challenges That May Occur

(Examples of common challenges that may occur)

Interestingly, pairs who communicate in a language that is not their mother tongue are sometimes more accurate, as they have to come up with words to substitute for words they can't remember, and they therefore make more precise descriptions.

8. Reflection Topics

(What to discuss in the debriefing session)

The importance of perspective-taking and empathy in communication; development of shared common understanding; biases in thinking (things are not as clear as we think they are); assumptions we make but do not communicate may lead to misunderstanding/lack of information sharing.

Bibliography

Ajzen, I. (2011). The theory of planned behavior: Reactions and reflections. *Journal of Psychology and Health*, Vol. 9, pp. 1113–1127, August 2011.

Ballantyne, R. & J. Packer (1995). Making Connections: Using Student Journals as a Teaching/Learning Aid, HERDSA ACT.

Bootcamp of BMoE (2015). An introductory lecture to BMoE given by Prof. I. Sidhu. August 2015.

Bramwell, A. & D. A. Wolfe (2008). Universities and regional economic development: The entrepreneurial University of Waterloo. *Research Policy*, Vol. 37, No. 8, pp. 1175–1187.

Duval-Coueril, N.; T. Reed-Rhoads & S. Haghighi (2011). Investigating the impact of Entrepreneurial Education on Engineering Students. *Open Catalyzing Innovation*, Washington USA, March 2011.

Dweck, C. (2006). *Mindset: the new psychology of success*. New York: Random House.

Global Venture Lab (2013).

Hwang, V. & G. Horowitt (2012). *The Rainforest: The Secret to Building the Next Silicon Valley*. Los Altos Hills: Regenwald.

Johnsson, C.; C-H. Nilsson; G. Erlingsdottir; F. Nilsson & G. Ahlsen (2013). Metacognition and Learning Journals in Higher Education. *International Journal of Economics and Management Engineering*, Vol. 3, No. 4, pp. 152–159, 2013.

Johnsson, C.; R. Loeffler; I. Sidhu & C-H. Nilsson (2016a). A Student-Centered Approach and Mindset-Focused Pedagogical Approach for Entrepreneurship and Leadership. *Applied Innovation Review*, Issue 2, pp. 57–63, June 2016.

Johnsson, C.; C-H. Nilsson & S. Kleppestö (2016b). Learning Leadership – on including leadership training in higher education. *ASEE International Forum*, June 2016.

Johnsson, C.; M. Suoranta; I. Sidhu & K. Singer (2016c). On Using Games for Practicing Entrepreneurial Mindset. *In 11th European Conference on Innovation and Entrepreneurship (ECIE)*, Jyväskulä, Finland, September 2016.

Kolb, D. A. & R. Fry (1975). Toward an applied theory of experiential learning. In C. Cooper (ed.) *Theories of Group Process*, London: John Wiley.

Kolb, D. (1984). *Experiential learning: experience as the source of learning and development*. Prentice Hall, Englewood Cliffs, NJ.

McCormick, C.B. & M. Pressley (1997). *Educational Psychology: Learning, Instruction, Assessment*. New York, Addison Wesley Longman.

Prince, M. (2004). Does active learning work? A review of research. *Journal of Engineering Education*, Vol. 93, No. 3, pp. 223–231.

Prince, M. & R. Felder (2006). Inductive teaching and learning methods: Definitions, comparisons and research bases. *Journal of Engineering Education*, Vol. 95, No. 2 pp. 123–138.

Sidhu, I. (2014). Seminal Entrepreneurship and Innovation Skills can in fact be learned. Online Resource: http://www.engineeringleadership.net [Accessed on 22 April 2014].

Sidhu, I.; K. Singer; M. Suoranta & C. Johnsson (2014). Introducing Berkeley Method of Entrepreneurship. Internal report nr 20140326, Center for Entrepreneurship and Technology, University of California, Berkeley, CA.

Sidhu, I.; K. Singer; C. Johnsson & M. Suoranta (2015a). Introducing the Berkeley Method of Entrepreneurship – a Game-Based Teaching Approach. *American Society for Engineering Education (ASEE) Annual Conference 2015*, Seattle, WA, USA, June 14–17, 2015

Sidhu, I.; C. Johnsson; K. Singer & M. Suoranta (2015b). A Game-based Method for Teaching Entrepreneurship. *Applied Innovation Review*, Issue 1 pp. 51–65, June 2015.

Sidhu I.; J-E. Goubet & Y. Xia (2016). Measurement of Innovation Mindset. 22nd IEEE International Technology Management Conference, Trondheim Norway, June 13–15, 2016.

Simon, H. A. (1996). *The Sciences of the Artificial*. Cambridge, MA: MIT Press.

Thorpe, K. (2004). Reflective learning journals: From concept to practice. *Journal Reflective Practice*, Vol 5. Issue 3, pp. 237–243, 2004.

Today's Engineer (2007). Teaching Today's Engineering Students To Be Tomorrow's Entrepreneurs. Published by IEEE-USA Today's Engineer. Online resource: http://www.todaysengineer.org/2007/jul/entrepreneurship.asp [Accessed July 2014].

Verzat, C.; J. Byrne & A. Fayolle (2009). Tangling with spaghetti: Pedagogical lessons from games. *Academy of Management Learning & Education*, 8(3): 356–369.

Vygotsky, L.S. (1978). *Mind in Society: Development of Higher Psychological Processes*. Harvard University Press.

Wenger, E. (2006). Communities of practice a brief introduction. Online resource: http://wenger-trayner.com/wp-content/uploads/2013/10/06-Brief-introduction-to-communities-of-practice.pdf [Accessed in 2015].

Wenger, E. (2000a). Communities of Practice and Social Learning Systems. Published by SAGE. Online resource: http://org.sagepub.com/cgi/content/abstract/7/2/225 [Accessed in 2015].

Wenger, E. & W. Snyder (2000b). Communities of practice: the organizational frontier. Online resource: http://content.ebscohost.com/pdf25_26/pdf/2000/HBR/01Jan00/2628915.pdf [Accessed in 2015].

Chapter 13
Teaching Unemployed University Graduates to Think Like Entrepreneurs

Anne Hørsted & Claus Nygaard

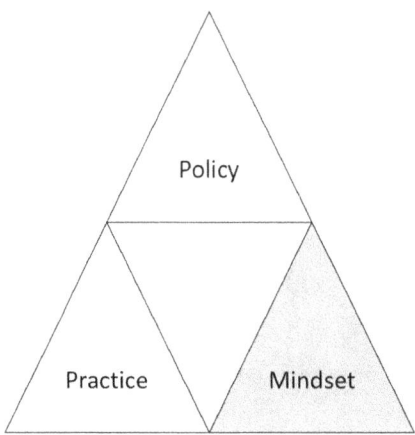

Introduction

Our chapter is an important contribution to this section on mindset – and to the book *Teaching and Learning Entrepreneurship in Higher Education* – because we showcase an intensive course (Camp Future) that helps unemployed university graduates with a university degree to find a job in a tough job market. We argue that this is best done by helping unemployed university graduates to change their mindset – in relation to their own situation and how to land their next job. In short, we teach to transform the mindset of unemployed university graduates to think like entrepreneurs. For us designing a course with this aim is natural. The cost of unemployment to society is rising. This is nothing new. With the recent economic crisis, our public sectors have been hit hard by increased unemployment rates. This counts for nation states all over the world. Even Denmark, the internationally acclaimed model of a welfare state

283

built on social democratic values, is experiencing a difficult time. As the number of young people completing university education is rising, so too is the unemployment rate. In Copenhagen, with 680,000 inhabitants, the unemployment rate is currently 5.1%, and out of that there are a little more than 5,000 unemployed graduates with an academic university degree, costing the city more than 1 billion Danish kroner each year (Danmarks Statistik, 2016). In order to make a difference, we have developed a six-week intensive course named Camp Future, which helps unemployed university graduates to think like entrepreneurs. We have repeated the course 16 times over the past three years. More than 250 people have participated. On average, 64% of the participants find a job following their participation in Camp Future. Reading this chapter, you should gain at least three insights:

1. the differences between two approaches to curriculum: content stream and process stream, and their roles for teaching an entrepreneurial mindset;
2. ideas about how curricula can be designed for teaching an entrepreneurial mindset;
3. insight into ways in which participants may work during a course to develop an entrepreneurial mindset.

The chapter has three sections. In section one, we introduce Camp Future as a concept and curriculum. In section two, we discuss how Camp Future is linked to the academic field of entrepreneurship education. In section three, we give examples of the entrepreneurial work and following jobs of participants.

Section 1: Camp Future as a Concept and Curriculum

In 2012, Claus Nygaard developed the concept of Camp Future. He was of the opinion that an education targeting unemployed university graduates could make a difference and help create jobs if the education was centred around an entrepreneurial mindset. He developed a case-based curriculum (Branch *et al.*, 2015), where each participant in Camp Future was to solve a real-life challenge given by a company. In the first eight repetitions of the course, participants worked in groups for six weeks to solve the company challenge, after which the course ended. Following that, the course was extended to 10 weeks and changed so that now each participant is linked directly to a company for six weeks and has the obligation to solve the company challenge him or herself, and furthermore continue as an "employee" in the company during a four-week internship. Let us take a more detailed look at Camp Future today. Camp Future is a 10-week course divided into two parts. Six weeks of intensive education and a four-week internship. The course is developed within what Nygaard & Bramming (2008) called the process stream of curriculum theory. Based on a desk study of curriculum theory, they formulated two broad streams of curriculum theory: 1) a content stream, and 2) a process stream.

	Content stream	Process stream
Curriculum	Syllabus/Guide for teaching.	Learning-centred action plan.
Agency	Teacher-driven activities.	Student-driven activities.
Learning	De-contextual learning.	Contextual learning.
Orientation	Input orientation.	Output orientation.
Evaluation method	Summative.	Formative/developmental.
Main focus points	Curriculum design, syllabus planning, teaching, exams, and evaluation.	Learning design, process facilitation, supervision, and self/peer assessment.

Figure 2: Two broad streams within curriculum theory (based on Nygaard & Bramming, 2008).

Curriculum as a Learning-Centred Action Plan

The curriculum is designed as a learning-centred action plan (Bolhuis, 2003; Nygaard & Bramming, 2008). On the very first day of the course, each participant meets with the owner or manager of the case company, who then presents the challenge to be solved over the coming six weeks. Challenges can be: "Create an export market strategy for introduction of a new product on the German market"; "Make an implementation plan for a new product management system in the organisation"; "Create a social media strategy for our company"; "Develop a brand strategy for our company"; "Develop a CSR strategy for our company"; "Create a concept for employee training through gamification"; "Create an app for customer relation management".

Agency to Student-Driven Activities

Participants need to take individual action from the very first day of the course. They are given full agency in their learning process. They learn through trial and error processes as they engage in a personal learning process as reflective practitioners (Schön, 1983, 1987) in solving the challenge given by the company. By "reflection" Schön (1987) means knowing-in-action. *"When the practitioner reflects-in-action in a case he perceives as unique, paying attention to phenomena and surfacing his intuitive understanding of them, his experimenting is at once exploratory, move testing, and hypothesis testing. The three functions are fulfilled by the very same actions"* (Schön, 1983:147). Student-driven activities span exploration (e.g., what goes on inside and outside the company). Student-driven activities are more testing (i.e., constantly trying out different problem definitions, methods, and solutions). Also, student-driven activities are hypothesis testing (i.e., coming to terms with possible links between problems and solutions). Camp Future is developed with the view of participants as a heterogeneous group of people who all engage differently in the course. In our view, participants have different experiences and different personal aims for participating in the course. Therefore, we have to centre students' action plan for learning rather than the syllabus itself. It appears that Camp Future has succeeded in developing a culture of deep learners (Marton & Säljö, 1976; Ramsden, 1988), where participants aim to make a qualitative and positive difference for the companies they work for during their studies.

Contextual Learning

Our view of learning follows the process stream, as it focuses on contextual learning (Nygaard & Andersen, 2005; Nygaard & Holtham, 2008; Nygaard & Bramming, 2008; Nygaard, 2015). We can reach an operational definition of learning by referring to Nygaard & Holtham (2008:13–14), who write that learning is:

1. *"never a simple repetition of previous learning. People learn based on their experiences and expectations."*

2. *"both an individual and social process."*

3. *"a contextual process tied to particular situations."*

4. *"a process affected by the identity of the learner."*

5. *"a process affected by the social position of the learner… and by the learners' embeddedness in social collectivities."*

Nygaard (2015) further defines learning with the following eight statements:

6. *"learning is the construction and maintenance of meaning."*

7. *"learning is based on experiences whereby learning is different to people."*

8. *"learning involves acquiring new personal knowledge, skills and competencies that can be used to resolve forthcoming challenges in life."*

9. *"learning is the ability to doubt and to question one's own assumptions."*

10. *"learning is both an individual and a social process."*

11. *"learning is a contextual process tied to an order of behaviour that changes over time."*

12. *"learning is a process affected by (and a process that affects) the identity of the learner."*

13. *"learning is a process affected by (and a process that affects) the social position of the learner, and the learners' embeddedness in ongoing social relations."*

Following the sentiments of these sentences that all help define learning, Camp Future aims to embed participants in business contexts where they have to make sense of the challenge they face. Participants learn individually and socially at the same time. And their contextually embedded learning process affects their identity as they change from unemployed academic to a worthy "employee" and intern who can make a qualitative difference for the case company. As such, there is a close link between the learning-centred curriculum and student identity creation (Nygaard & Serrano, 2010).

Evaluation Methods

The success of the process-based curriculum is usually evaluated by focusing on aspects like student participation, student reflection, and student learning. At Camp Future, participants are evaluated based on the solution they offer the company. If a company asks for someone to "create an export market strategy for introduction of a new product on the German market", the participant is evaluated on the content and presentation of the market strategy plan. This may include an analysis of market conditions, competitor analysis, customer segmentation, logistics analysis, and an implementation plan calling for action. All participants present their work/solution in front of the entire class and representatives for the case company. This is a formative evaluation focusing on the quality of the solution and advice given to the company.

Main Focus Points

To sum up, the process stream is a non-linear process aiming to develop the curriculum as a designed programme of learning. It starts from the urge to establish a range of activities and methods that will lead to an improvement in student learning. Students learn from their personal experiences and personal reflections in relation to the situation they face; hence, the learning process of each student is different. The teacher does not know beforehand what, when, how, and where each student learns. Developing a curriculum based on the process stream is therefore very different from formulating a syllabus. Curriculum development becomes an iterative process of coordination and facilitation, unfolding as students engage in the course and give feedback about their personal learning and progress with solving the company challenge. Also, to ignite a process of reflection within the student, an adequate and sufficiently challenging base of theoretical literature and tools are taught. Working closely with students' learning outcomes, the main roles of the curriculum designer and teacher subscribing to the process stream are facilitation, coordination, supervision, and evaluation. Following students' learning processes and learning outcomes requires that their personal development and the transfer between different themes of the course are closely monitored by a small group of facilitators. Overall, the process is iterative, in which the main functions of the responsible teachers become facilitation, coordination, supervision, and evaluation. We would argue that this flexible way of working enhances competence development and the improvement of students' learning outcomes.

Section 2: The Philosophy of Camp Future as Entrepreneurship Education

University graduates face requirements for continuous learning. *Learning for the future* is a tag of the knowledge society (Tinkler *et al.*, 1996). *Flexible societies* (Blackler *et al.*, 2007), *flexible markets* (De Geus, 1998), *flexible networks* (Christensen & Kreiner, 1991), and *flexible jobs* (Handy, 1990) characterise the business community. Flexibility is the very key to the knowledge society. Flexibility, innovation, and creativity are in high demand to secure the competitive advantage of firms (Florida, 2005), hence the employability of university graduates. Several studies argue that educating graduates with entrepreneurial mindsets is a prerequisite in flexible societies. Secundo *et al.* (2016) pinpoint that higher education institutions face challenges in teaching graduates to develop an entrepreneurial mindset. They reach this conclusion based on a cross-case analysis of 22 postgraduate programmes at European universities. Colette (2013), on the other hand, suggests that expectations of outcomes from entrepreneurial education in higher education may have spiralled beyond what is both realistic and possible. Based on a study in the UK HE sector, he argues for a more realistic and measurable perspective of the expectations of entrepreneurship and enterprise education. Solesvik *et al.* (2013) argue that even though many studies of entrepreneurship education have been conducted, in general they have failed to highlight whether entrepreneurship studies have promoted students to develop an entrepreneurial mindset. To support their argument, they further point to studies by Souitaris *et al.* (2007) and Oosterbeek *et al.* (2010). A literature search on entrepreneurial education and entrepreneurial mindset shows a large body of academic articles and books on the subject, and the argument that runs through many of these is that developing entrepreneurial mindsets is valuable for society. However, there are many approaches to the educational endeavour, and there are different explanations of what makes an entrepreneur. Some talk of entrepreneurial mindsets (Davis et al., 2016; Solesvik et al., 2013; Haynie et al., 2010; Ireland et al., 2003; McGrath & MacMillan, 2000). Others talk of entrepreneurial traits (Kolb & Wagner, 2015; Rauch & Frese, 2000). Yet others about entrepreneurial skills, abilities, and capabilities (Brandenburg et al., 2016; Kucel et al., 2016). To further reflect on our curriculum and the intentions and outcomes of Camp Future, we chose to use the term mindset. Ireland et al. (2003:989) defined entrepreneurial mindset as *"the ability to rapidly sense, act, and mobilize, even under uncertain conditions"*.

With Camp Future, we aim to help unemployed university graduates develop a new mindset – a new self-understanding – guided by the ability to rapidly sense, act, and mobilise under uncertain conditions. Although Camp Future is not an entrepreneurship education per se, we aim to have participants seek new opportunities in new areas – untying themselves from the path dependencies of past walks of life. It requires that they free themselves from traditional thoughts about the job market where job makers offer jobs to job takers. It requires that they no longer see themselves as unemployed university graduates in search and competition for the next vacant job in their usual trade. It requires that they see themselves as a resource that can generate positive an outcome (money, network, knowledge, innovation, methods, etc.), that is valuable in the marketplace. When unemployed university graduates apply for their dream job, there are several hundred applicants all competing for the job. We wish to teach unemployed university graduates that alternatives exist, and fruitful alternatives we will argue, as we have succeeded in helping in average of 64% of our participants at Camp Future back on the job market.

We use the philosophy of the red chair, as we continuously preach to our participants that as unemployed university graduates they have to change their focus from competing for the red chair (the vacant job) to focusing on what value they can add to a company. In a way, this is a play on the red ocean-blue ocean strategy. In the red ocean, unemployed university graduates try to impress employers with references to their own past merits (documented in CVs). Thus, they reduce themselves to a possible but passive asset on the job market. In the blue ocean, unemployed university graduates try to impress employers by showing what future value they can add to the company, and they present an implementation plan for how they will work if they get a job. And in their implementation plan, they also focus on the difference between the value they create and the cost they will be to the company; thus, making it clear what value the employer gets, and thereby reducing the risk for the employer in a situation of asymmetrical information. Asymmetrical in the sense that the employer cannot know in much detail what the unemployed academic can really achieve in a potential job. So, the more clearly the unemployed academic can show what value will potentially be added and what methods and networks will be used to do so, and also present a strategic implementation plan for the forthcoming work, the higher the chances are of getting a job.

The entrepreneurial mindset with the ability to rapidly sense, act, and mobilise under uncertain conditions is built into Camp Future right from the start. The unemployed university graduates answer a web survey before they start on the course, where they rank themselves and their perceived competencies in relation to the company challenges contained in the course. For each course, new companies sign up, and some return with new challenges. Based on the participants own self-evaluation and ranking of company challenges, we make a match between participant and company. As mentioned before, on the very first day of the course, participants meet their case company. Here, the roles are changed so that it is the unemployed academic who interviews the case company representative for one and a half hours about the challenges they are facing. As the case company is often from an industrial sector or service sector not familiar to the participant, this is a situation under uncertain conditions. Often, the participants feel that they are on thin ice, having started a new course at 9am and having to interview a manager about their industry and business at 1pm. We wish to train their ability to rapidly sense the challenges companies are facing and be able to act and mobilise resources on the fly to persuade the manager that they can solve the challenge in six weeks.

Having conducted the interview, we then teach participants the 15 academic tools to analyse company challenges, formulate solutions to the challenges, and develop a strategic implementation plan. During this process, the participants will be taught during eight full days. They will receive three one-on-one supervision sessions where they are coached about their work for the company. They will receive one full day of training in positive psychology and how to use your strengths to your advantage when working under uncertainty. They will be taught about self-presence and how to present yourself to get your message across. All together, we have developed a curriculum that is an ongoing action plan for learning and self-development of aspects of an entrepreneurial mindset.

Section 3: Camp Future and the Entrepreneurial Work and Following Jobs of Participants

Over the past four years, we have taught more than 250 participants. Most of them have got full-time jobs using their entrepreneurial mindset when "selling themselves" to employers, showing the value they add to companies and demonstrating how they will work in practice. A minority of the participants have started their own business – becoming entrepreneurs in that sense of the word where they start a company to produce or sell a product. However, some have positioned themselves as free agents, working as professionals in the knowledge and service economy. This is probably due to the fact that they are all university graduates with a long university education, strong on methods and processes of knowledge creation.

In this third section, we will briefly look at some of the work done by two participants and discuss their following career.

The first participant is Anne (the first author of this chapter). In 2014, she graduated from university with a master degree in pedagogy and learning. During her time on Camp Future in early 2015, she worked to solve a challenge for a Danish consultancy company that uses gamification as their pedagogical method. She had to help develop a platform for a new game that could help the company increase their education and consultancy in both the private and public sector. As other participants, Anne engaged in her work and used the different tools to analyse the company challenge. After her participation on Camp Future, she started her internship in the Danish business consultancy firm cph:learning, owned by Claus (the second author of this chapter). There she became responsible for designing continuous education modules for professional clients. This kind of work was unlike anything she had studied for at university. During her internship there, she was continuously trained to create blue ocean strategies for clients, using her entrepreneurial mindset to rapidly sense, act, and mobilise resources under uncertain conditions. After one year of continuous training on large projects with clients, she now works as a self-employed free agent in the consultancy sector.

The second participant is Niels. In 2012, he graduated from university with a master degree in industrial design. He participated on the very first Camp Future course, where he worked on a challenge to implement e-learning at a Danish production school. The school had decided to use iPads as a teaching and learning tool, but no overall strategy had been developed. It was his job to help the school come to an understanding of the potentials and pitfalls of the use of e-learning. Niels engaged in solving the challenge, and together with his group he made an impressive catalogue of learning tools (not only e-learning tools) that the school could use in their curriculum development. After his participation on Camp Future, he also started his internship in cph:learning, where he focused on the use of augmented reality for strategy communication and implementation. For Niels, this kind of work was also unlike anything he had studied for at university. During his internship, he was forced to use an entrepreneurial mindset to rapidly sense, act, and mobilise resources under uncertain conditions. He entered a business sector that he basically knew very little about. He began working with technological development aimed at large corporate clients where he had to plan and participate in business meetings at the strategic level. After almost two years of continuous work to launch a very complex technological product, including work on a technological project aimed at having dairy cows use technology to call the vet if they become ill, Niels had to seize work on those projects. Our judgement is that the market was not mature enough for his project ideas – in a sense, his mindset was too entrepreneurial. He now works as a self-employed free agent in the consultancy sector.

Conclusion

In this brief chapter, we have aimed to show how a change in perception of curriculum from content stream to process stream has helped us perceive teaching and learning differently. We have described how our Camp Future course for unemployed university graduates has been designed to develop an entrepreneurial mindset with participants, teaching them to rapidly sense, act, and mobilise resources under uncertain conditions.

Camp Future is not a revolution. Its pedagogical model is teaching and learning through cases where companies present participants with real-life challenges. As such, case teaching and case learning is nothing new. However, the cherishing of unemployed university graduates to develop an entrepreneurial mindset – at one of the most vulnerable times in their professional life, where they have been made redundant at work or struggle to find a job – is new. To us, Anne (a former participant at Camp Future) and Claus (the professor behind Camp Future), there is no doubt that the success of Camp Future in getting unemployed university graduates into the job market comes from continuously addressing the need for adding value in the marketplace. If graduate programmes at universities could stop teaching students for a position in the red chair and start developing entrepreneurial mindsets, we would not only reduce unemployment but also add more value to society.

About the Authors

Anne Hørsted is adjunct professor at the University of Southern Denmark, senior consultant at cph:learning in Denmark, and adjunct professor at the Institute for Learning in Higher Education. She can be contacted at this e-mail: anne@lihe.info

Claus Nygaard, professor, PhD, is executive director at the Institute for Learning in Higher Education and executive director at cph:learning in Denmark. He can be contacted at this e-mail: info@lihe.info

Bibliography

Blackler, F.; M. Reed & A. Whitaker (2007). Editorial introduction: Knowledge workers and contemporary organizations. *Journal of Management Studies*, Vol. 30, No. 6, pp. 851–862.

Bolhuis, S. (2003). Towards process-oriented teaching for self-directed lifelong learning: a multidimensional perspective. *Learning and Instruction*, Vol. 13, No. 3, pp. 327–47.

Branch, J.; P. Bartholomew & C. Nygaard (2015). *Case-Based Learning in Higher Education*. Oxfordshire, UK: Libri Publishing Ltd.

Brandenburg, S.; T. Roosen & M. Veenstra & B. Mettina (2016). Toward an adapted business modeling method to improve entrepreneurial skills among art students. *Artivate: A Journal of Entrepreneurship in the Arts*, Vol. 5, No. 1, pp. 25–33.

Christensen, S. & K. Kreiner (1991). *Projektledelse i løst koblede systemer – ledelse og læring i en fuldkommen verden*. Copenhagen: DJØF.

Colette, H. (2013). Entrepreneurship education in HE: are policy makers expecting too much? *Education + Training*, Vol. 55, No. 8/9, pp. 836–848.

Danmarks Statistik (2016). *Bruttoledigheden er stort set uændret*. Danmarks Statistik.

Davis, M. H.; J. A. Hall & P. S. Mayer (2016). Developing a new measure of entrepreneurial mindset: reliability, validity, and implications for practitioners. *Consulting Psychology Journal: Practice and Research*, Vol. 68, No. 1, pp. 21–48.

De Geus, A. (1998). Planning as learning. *Harvard Business Review*, Vol. 66, No. 2, pp. 70–74.

Florida, R. (2005). *Cities and the Creative Class*. Routledge.

Handy, C. (1990). *Understanding Organizations*. Penguin Books.

Haynie, J. M.; D. Shepherd; E. Mosakowski & P. C. Earley (2010). A situated metacognitive model of the entrepreneurial mindset. *Journal of Business Venturing*, Vol. 25, No. 2, pp. 217–229.

Ireland, R. D.; M. A. Hitt & D. G. Sirmon (2003). A model of strategic entrepreneurship: the construct and its dimensions. *Journal of Management*, Vol. 29, pp. 963–990.

Kolb, C. & M. Wagner (2015). Crowding in or Crowding Out: The Link between Academic Entrepreneurship and Entrepreneurial Traits. *Journal of Technology Transfer*, Vol. 40, No. 3, pp. 387–408.

Kucel, A.; P. Róbert; M. Buil; N. Masferrer (2016). Entrepreneurial skills and education-job matching of higher education graduates. *European Journal of Education*, Vol. 51, No. 1, pp. 73–89.

Marton, F. & R. Säljö (1976) On qualitative differences in Learning – Outcome and process. *British journal of Educational Psychology*, Vol. 46, No. 1, pp. 4–11.

McGrath, R. G. & I. MacMillan (2000). *The Entrepreneurial Mindset: Strategies for Continuously Creating Opportunity in an Age of Uncertainty*. Harvard Business School Press.

Nygaard, C. (2015). Rudiments of a Strategy for Technology Enhanced University Learning. In C. Nygaard; J. Branch & P. Bartholomew (Eds.), *Technology Enhanced Learning in Higher Education*. Libri Publishing Ltd., Oxfordshire, UK.

Nygaard, C. & I. Andersen (2005). Contextual Learning in Higher Education. In R. G. Milter; V. S. Perotti & M. S. R. Segers (Eds.), *Educational*

Innovation in Economics and Business IX. Breaking Boundaries for Global Learning. Springer Verlag.

Nygaard, C. & P. Bramming (2008). Learning-centred Public Management Education. *International Journal of Public Sector Management*, Vol. 21, No. 4, pp. 400–416.

Nygaard, C. & C. Holtham (2008). The Need for Learning-Centred Higher Education. In C. Nygaard & C. Holtham (Eds.), *Understanding Learning Centred Higher Education*. Frederiksberg, CBS Press, pp. 11-29.

Nygaard, C. & M. Serrano (2010). Students' Identity Construction and Learning. Reasons for developing a learning-centred curriculum in higher education. In L. E. Kattington (Ed.), *Handbook of Curriculum Development*, Nova Publishers.

Oosterbeek, H.; M. van Praag & A. Ijsselstein (2010). The impact of entrepreneurship education on entrepreneurial skills and motivation. *European Economic Review*, Vol. 54, No. 3, pp. 442–454.

Ramsden, P. (1988). *Improving Learning: new perspectives*. Kogan Page.

Rauch, A. & M. Frese (2000). Psychological approaches to entrepreneurial success: A general model and an overview of findings. In C. L. Cooper & I. T. Robertson (Eds.), *International review of industrial and organizational psychology*. New York, N.Y.: Wiley & Sons, pp. 101–141.

Schön, D. A. (1983). *The Reflective Practitioner*. New York: Basic Books.

Schön, D. A. (1987). *Educating the Reflective Practitioner*. San Francisco: Jossey-Bass.

Secundo, G.; V. Ndou & P. Del Vecchio (2016). Challenges for Instilling Entrepreneurial Mindset in Scientists and Engineers: What Works in European Universities? *International Journal of Innovation & Technology Management*. Vol. 13, No. 5, pp. 334–351.

Solesvik, M. Z.; P. Westhead; H. Matlay & V. N. Parsyak (2013). Entrepreneurial assets and mindsets. *Education + Training*, Vol. 55, No. 8/9, pp. 748–762.

Souitaris, V.; S. Zerbinati & Al-Laham, A. (2007). Do entrepreneurship programmes raise entrepreneurial intention of science and engineering students? The effect of learning, inspiration and resources. *Journal of Business Venturing*, Vol. 22, No. 4, pp. 566–591.

Tinkler, D., B. Lepani & J. Mitchell (1996). *Education and Technology Convergence. A Survey of Technological Infrastructure in Education and the Professional Development and Support of Educators and Trainers in Information and Communication Technologies*. Commissioned Report No. 43, National Board of Employment Education and Training. Canberra: Employment and Skills Council, Australian Government Publishing Service.

www.ingramcontent.com/pod-product-compliance
Lightning Source LLC
Chambersburg PA
CBHW071221080526
44587CB00013BA/1453